Ch'unhyang, heroine of Korea's Love Story

Korea guide

**A Glimpse of Korea's Cultural Legacy
Revised Fourth Edition**

Text and Photos
by
Edward B. Adams

Seoul International Tourist Publishing Company
33-16 Nonhyon-dong, Kangnam-ku, Seoul, Korea Tel. 542-9308

First published: October, 1976
Second Printing: April, 1977
Third Revised Printing: Jan, 1980
Fourth Revised Printing: March, 1983

Library of Congress Catalog Card Number 77-670017

Published by Seoul International Tourist Publishing Company, 33-16 Nonhyon-dong, Kangnam-ku, Seoul, Korea. Registration Number, 14-9. Copyright©1983 by Seoul International Tourist Publishing Company.

Printed and bound by Samwha Printing Co., Seoul, Korea

Price: ₩12,000

INTRODUCTION

Korea Guide is a tourist handbook which can be used for readily obtaining useful information about the Republic of Korea. The sixty-seven diverse chapters were carefully chosen to present a wide range of subjects known to be of high interest to foreigners wishing to learn more about this country. Yet for the tourist who may stay in Korea for only a few days *Korea Guide* has much to offer in making his travel in a picturesque nation much more enjoyable.

Over 265 color photographs, many in full page spreads, present their own pictorial essay of cultural and historic impressions. Many of the photographs depict aspects of Korean culture that are rapidly disappearing from the modern Korean scene. The Tourist Directory with ads will help the newly-arrived visitor to know quickly what is available and how to contact agencies for travel planning.

Recently there has been an upsurge of pride demonstrated by the government in promoting the heritage of the folk culture tradition. Modern hotels at the more famous tourist sites are being rapidly built, along with museums, amusement parks and tourist centers. Korea is now proud of its rich cultural legacy which is often uniquely Korean. In the past, the West has thought of Korea as only a cultural bridge between China and Japan, yet now it is known that in many cases the origin of the culture was in Korea.

For the average tourist or foreign resident the cultural heritage is often what he wishes to learn about and see. With many color photographs an attempt is made to follow a loose pictorial thread of visual beauty of nature and traditional customs which will illustrate to the foreigner the marvelous heritage inherited by the Koreans. The photographs will portray their own theme of picturesque impressions of Korea with its tradition and customs amid a rapidly developing nation. Often what has remained from bygone years is religious in nature, with shamanism and Buddhism being the oldest active religions in the country.

A few pictures are used depicting Korea's current economic development, such as the recent highway network, metropolitan centers or the miraculous progress of her industries. The modernization theme is often adequately emphasized through the many government publications.

For a brief moment through the blue eyes of one foreigner a glimpse can be taken from the "rice paper windows" of Korea's cultural and historic legacy which is still relatively unknown to the Western world. The overwhelming beauty of Korea can be seen in its people . . . . faces of all ages . . . . for without its people the Korean landscape is without purpose.

Photographs of the industrial shipping port of Inchon, pleasure haunts of Cheju Island or shopping centers of Seoul have not been given primary pictorial importance . . . . while an attempt is made to move close to the people . . . . to visit the rural farming villages during harvest and spring planting . . . . to stand in awe before the radiant colors of a festival . . . . or witness the shadows of royalty still faintly blending with a modern society. These are often the subjects that excite foreign visitors in present day Korea. The photographs alone should provide an impression in color of Korea's cultural legacy.

Buddhist and Confucian tradition blended with shaman cults is a dominant thread running through the lives of all Koreans. For this reason many of the photographs portray this theme. Ceremonial activities are still important and evident in today's society. Buddhist culture though primarily adhered to by older women actually influences the lives of all Koreans. The historic footprints of Buddhist tradition have been pressed indelibly into the landscape, as seen from many broken stone remains throughout the countryside. The Koreans have many reasons to be justly proud of their heritage, and possibly in some small way this series of photographs will enlighten the foreigner to a marvelous culture.

In the first portion of *Korea Guide* general information is presented concerning the people, history, geography, education, government and miraculous economic development during the last fifteen years. The second portion describes what can be seen and done within the capital and its vicinity. The palaces, Kanghwa Island, Panmunjom, Folk Village with museums and the world of shopping take primary importance. *Korea Guide* then recommends six scenic tourist areas further from Seoul. Also Korea's five major cities beyond the capital are described.

In the fourth portion of *Korea Guide* the Buddhist legacy is developed through visits to important temples located throughout the peninsula. The intriguing legend of the world famous Emillie Bell in Kyongju with its pathos and mystery is a tale worth telling.

The fifth portion of *Korea Guide* is a conglomerate collection of fascinating subjects dealing with various aspects of Korean life, culture and tradition. Holidays, religions, sports, inventions, silk and food are just a few. The Korean dress, traditional dances and arts of Korea as introduced by the recent *5000 Years of Korean Arts* exhibit in the US are captivating subjects. The mysterious institution of the Korean *kisaeng* always provokes inquisitive questions from the foreign newcomer. Also, a look is taken at the feminine tradition in an attempt to understand the role of women in modern Korea. Have you wondered about the characteristics of your zodiac year, or that ginseng is this country's oldest export? A chapter on the Korean-American centennial year of 1982 is included in this 4th Edition. Finally, the ancient wisdom of acupuncture and mask dance drama tradition are explored.

The last portion of *Korea Guide* is the Tourist Directory which gives the "ins" and "outs" of what to do and where to go in Seoul with useful information on agencies helpful to tourists.

To render Korean names and sounds into the Roman alphabet a modified form of the McCune-Reischauer system of romanization is used without the diacritical marks. Some deviation was made from this system because of personal preference and the belief that the change would further aid the foreign reader in more accurately pronouncing Korean words.

One should be aware that there was also a very different system of romanization that was developed by the Ministry of Education (MOE), which will almost certainly cause missounding of Korean names by English-speaking people. For example the southern province of Cholla-pukto becomes Jeonra-bugdo, while the personal names of Kim and Pak (Park) become Gim and Bag. To avoid the many problems inherent in the different romanization systems the newcomer should try to learn the Korean phonetic *han'gul* alphabet which is one of the easiest in the world. In December 1982 the Ministry of Education agreed to scrap the MOE system in favor of the M-R system.

Some of the materials used in *Korea Guide* have already appeared in articles published by the *Korea Herald* or *Korea Times*. In the publication of any book there are many who assist and often greatly contribute to the result. Probably my greatest indebtedness is to Chung Pyung-jo, Secretary to the President of Dongguk University, who though a young scholar by Korean standards has already a great depth of understanding in the field of Buddhism.

Others who advised me on portions of *Korea Guide* were Hwang Su-young, President of Dongguk University and former Director of the National Museum; Rhi Ki-yong, Professor and Dean of Dongguk University; Alan C. Heyman, foremost Korean music and dance scholar; Lee Do-hyun, Professor of Seoul National University and Korean dance drama specialist; Yi Ku, son of the last crown prince and head of the Yi Dynasty family; Rii Chong-ha, a close friend who introduced me to many members of the royal family through the Yi Dynasty Association and Lee Hyo-chai, Professor of Sociology at Ewha Womans University.

Many others who helped me through their contacts and publications were Zo Za-yong, founder and Director of the Emileh Museum, Kim Che-won, former Director of the National Museum for 25 years; Park Chin-whan, President of Seoul Agricultural College and former Presidential Assistant for Economic Affairs; Hahm Pyung-choon, Professor of Law at Yonsei University, former US Ambassador and now Presidential First Secretary; and finally but not least Park Chan-il, former First Secretary to President Rhee, friend and advisor.

My appreciation goes to Lee Kyoo-hyun, former Minister of Culture and Information and presently Ambassador to Canada; Kim Yong-kwon, former Director of Korea Overseas Information Service (KOIS).

I am also deeply grateful for the promotional assistance received from Hong Song-chul, former Minister of Health and past President of the International Cultural Society of Korea (ICSK); Kim Kyu-taik, President of ICSK and many staff members of ICSK.

The promotional aid given to me by Kim Hyung-shik, Director of Business Affairs at Seoul International School, should be acknowledged and appreciation given. Also in the publishing field my appreciation goes to Choi Dong-ho of the Seoul International Tourist Publishing Co.; members of the Samhwa Printing staff and James Wade and who served as proofreader in the final stages.

My final appreciation goes to the entire staff of Seoul International Tourist Publishing Company and my wife, who worked many long hours in preparation of this fourth edition.

E. B. Adams

Table of Contents

VI. TOURIST DIRECTORY

Korea
guide

A GLIMPSE OF KOREA'S CULTURAL LEGACY
By Edward B. Adams
Seoul Int'l Tourist Publishing Co.

photo by Kang. Woon-gu

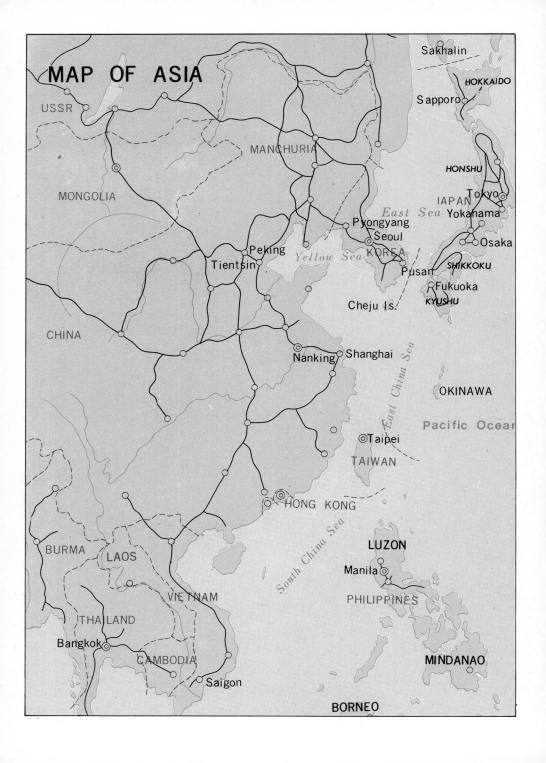

MAP OF ASIA

USSR

MONGOLIA

MANCHURIA

CHINA

Peking

Tientsin

Nanking

Shanghai

Yellow Sea

East Sea

Pyongyang

Seoul

KOREA

Pusan

Cheju Is.

JAPAN

HONSHU

Tokyo

Yokahama

Osaka

SHIKKOKU

Fukuoka

KYUSHU

Sakhalin

HOKKAIDO

Sapporo

East China Sea

OKINAWA

Pacific Ocean

Taipei

TAIWAN

HONG KONG

South China Sea

BURMA

LAOS

VIETNAM

THAILAND

Bangkok

CAMBODIA

Saigon

LUZON

Manila

PHILIPPINES

MINDANAO

BORNEO

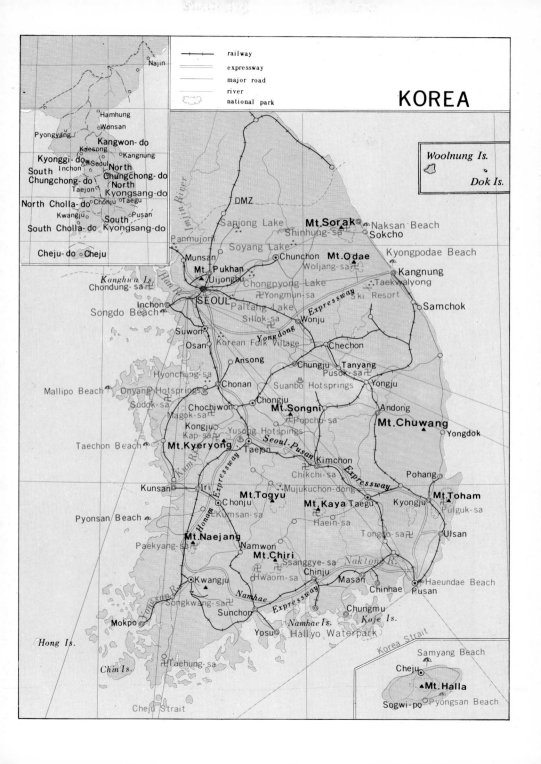

KOREA

| railway |
| expressway |
| major road |
| river |
| national park |

Woolnung Is.

Dok Is.

Najin

Hamhung
Wonsan
Pyongyang
Kangwon-do
Kaesong
Kyonggi-do   Kangnung
South   Inchon Seoul North
Chungchong-do   Chungchong-do
Taejon   North
Kyongsang-do
North Cholla-do   Chonju Taegu
Kwangju   Pusan
South
South Cholla-do   Kyongsang-do

Cheju-do Cheju

DMZ
Sanjong Lake   Mt.Sorak   Naksan Beach
Shinhung-sa   Sokcho
Panmunjom   Soyang Lake   Kyongpodae Beach
Munsan   Chunchon   Mt.Odae
Mt.Pukhan   Woljang-sa   Kangnung
Uijongbu   Chongpyong Lake   Taekwalyong
Kanghwa Is.   Yongmun-sa   Ski Resort   Samchok
Chondung-sa   SEOUL   Paltang Lake
Inchon   Sillok-sa   Wonju
Songdo Beach   Yongdong
Suwon   Expressway
Osan   Korean Folk Village   Chechon
Ansong   Chungju Tanyang
Hyonchung-sa   Pusok-sa
Mallipo Beach   Onyang Hotsprings   Suanbo Hotsprings   Yongju
Sudok-sa   Chonan   Chongju
Taechon Beach   Chochiwon   Mt.Songni   Andong
Magok-sa   Popchu-sa   Mt.Chuwang
Kongju   Yusong Hotsprings   Yongdok
Kap-sa   Mt.Kyeryong   Taejon   Seoul-Pusan   Expressway
Kunsan   Iri   Kimchon   Pohang
Chikchi-sa
Chonju   Mt.Togyu   Mujukuchon-dong   Mt.Toham
Pyonsan Beach   Kumsan-sa   Mt.Kaya Taegu   Kyongju   Pulguk-sa
Haein-sa   Tongdo-sa   Ulsan
Mt.Naejang   Namwon   Tongdo-sa
Paekyang-sa   Mt.Chiri   Naktong R.
Ssanggye-sa   Chinju
Hwaom-sa   Masan   Haeundae Beach
Songkwang-sa   Kwangju   Chinhae Pusan
Namhae   Expressway   Chungmu
Sunchon   Koje Is.
Mokpo   Yosu   Namhae Is.   Hallyo Waterpark
Hong Is.   Korea Strait
Taehung-sa   Samyang Beach
Chin Is.   Cheju
Mt.Halla
Sogwi-po   Pyongsan Beach
Cheju Strait

Imjin River
Han R.
Kum R.
Hanam
Yongsan R.

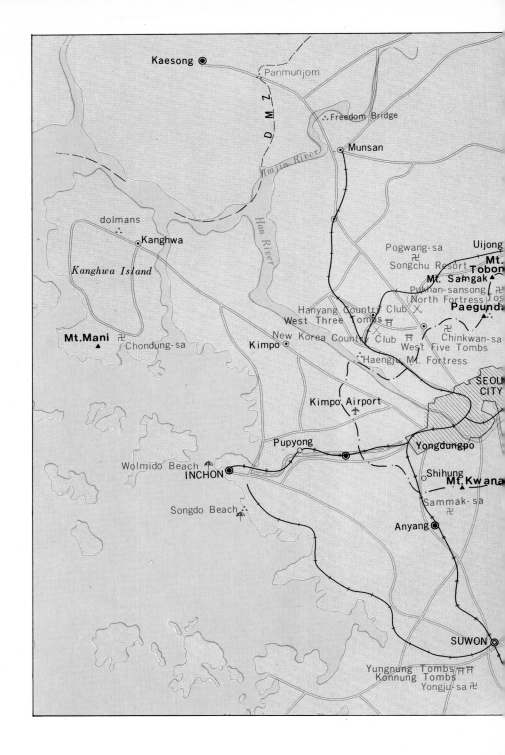

Kaesong ◉

Panmunjom

D M Z

∴ Freedom Bridge

Imjin River

Munsan ◉

Han River

dolmans ∴
◉ Kanghwa

Kanghwa Island

Pogwang-sa 卍
Songchu Resort
Uijong
Mt. Tobon ▲
Mt. Samgak ▲
Pukhan-sansong 卍
(North Fortress) ✕
Paegunda ▲

Mt.Mani 卍
▲ Chondung-sa

Hanyang Country Club ✕
West Three Tombs 卅
New Korea Country Club ✕ 卅
Kimpo ◉
Chinkwan-sa 卍
West Five Tombs
∴ Haengju Mt. Fortress

SEOUL CITY

Kimpo Airport ✈

Wolmido Beach ☂
Pupyong ○
◉
Yongdungpo

INCHON ◎

Shihung
Mt.Kwana ▲
Sammak-sa 卍

Songdo Beach ☂

Anyang ◉

SUWON ◎

Yungnung Tombs 卅卅
Konnung Tombs
Yongju-sa 卍

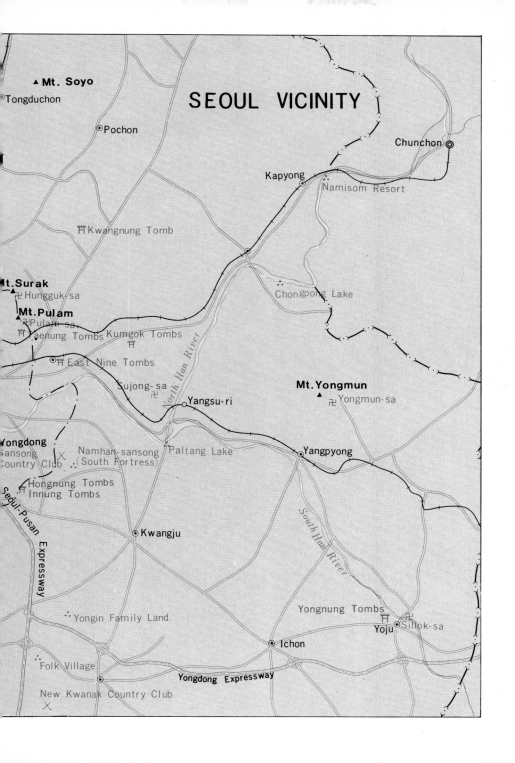

SEOUL VICINITY

▲ **Mt. Soyo**
Tongduchon

Pochon

Chunchon ◎

Kapyong

Namisom Resort

Kwangnung Tomb

Mt.Surak
Hungguk-sa

Chongpong Lake

Mt.Pulam
Pulam-sa
aenung Tombs Kumgok Tombs

East Nine Tombs

Mt.Yongmun
Yongmun-sa

Sujong-sa
Yangsu-ri

North Han River

Yongdong
ansong
Country Club
Namhan-sansong
(South Fortress) Paltang Lake

Yangpyong

Hongnung Tombs
Innung Tombs

Kwangju

Seoul-Pusan Expressway

South Han River

Yongin Family Land

Yongnung Tombs
Yoju Sillok-sa

Ichon

Folk Village

Yongdong Expressway

New Kwanak Country Club

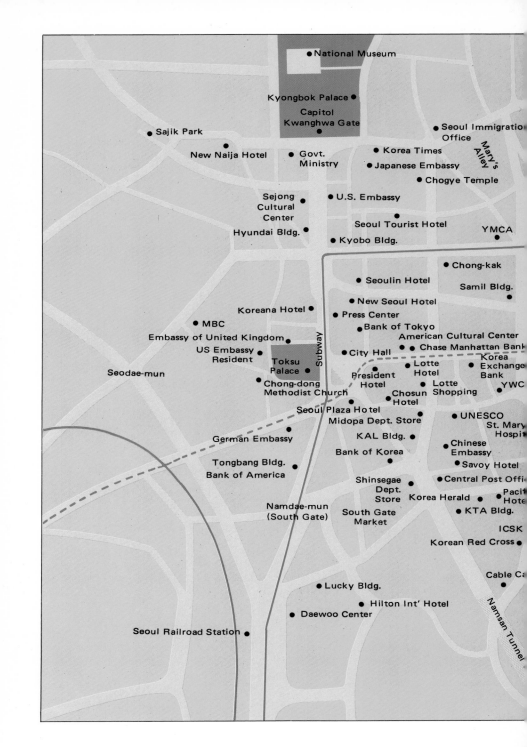

- National Museum
- Kyongbok Palace
- Capitol
- Kwanghwa Gate
- Sajik Park
- Seoul Immigration Office
- New Naija Hotel
- Govt. Ministry
- Korea Times
- Mary's Alley
- Japanese Embassy
- Chogye Temple
- Sejong Cultural Center
- U.S. Embassy
- Hyundai Bldg.
- Seoul Tourist Hotel
- YMCA
- Kyobo Bldg.
- Chong-kak
- Seoulin Hotel
- Samil Bldg.
- Koreana Hotel
- New Seoul Hotel
- MBC
- Press Center
- Embassy of United Kingdom
- Bank of Tokyo
- American Cultural Center
- US Embassy Resident
- Subway
- City Hall
- Chase Manhattan Bank
- Seodae-mun
- Toksu Palace
- Lotte Hotel
- Korea Exchange Bank
- President Hotel
- Lotte Shopping
- YWC
- Chong-dong Methodist Church
- Chosun Hotel
- Seoul Plaza Hotel
- Midopa Dept. Store
- UNESCO
- St. Mary Hospit
- German Embassy
- KAL Bldg.
- Chinese Embassy
- Bank of Korea
- Savoy Hotel
- Tongbang Bldg.
- Bank of America
- Central Post Offi
- Shinsegae Dept. Store
- Pacif Hote
- Namdae-mun (South Gate)
- Korea Herald
- South Gate Market
- KTA Bldg.
- ICSK
- Korean Red Cross
- Cable Ca
- Lucky Bldg.
- Hilton Int' Hotel
- Daewoo Center
- Namsan Tunnel
- Seoul Railroad Station

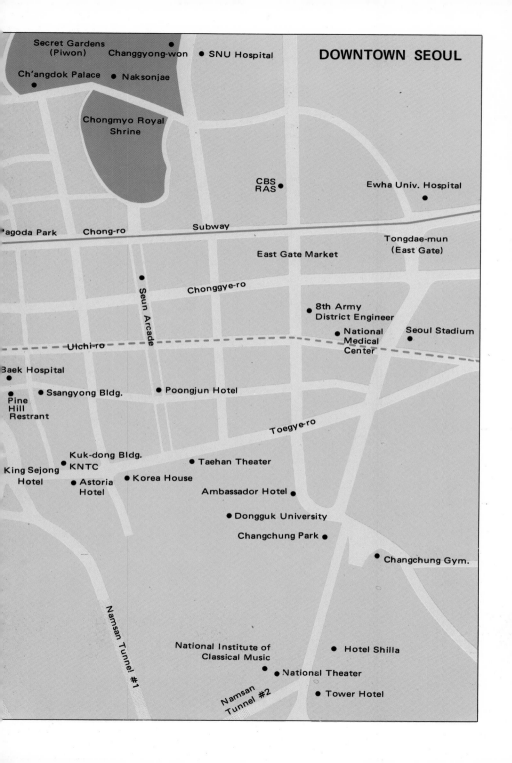

DOWNTOWN SEOUL

Secret Gardens (Piwon)
Changgyong-won
SNU Hospital
Ch'angdok Palace
Naksonjae
Chongmyo Royal Shrine
CBS RAS
Ewha Univ. Hospital
Pagoda Park
Chong-ro
Subway
East Gate Market
Tongdae-mun (East Gate)
Seun Arcade
Chonggye-ro
8th Army District Engineer
National Medical Center
Seoul Stadium
Utchi-ro
Baek Hospital
Pine Hill Restrant
Ssangyong Bldg.
Poongjun Hotel
Toegye-ro
Kuk-dong Bldg.
KNTC
Taehan Theater
King Sejong Hotel
Astoria Hotel
Korea House
Ambassador Hotel
Dongguk University
Changchung Park
Changchung Gym.
Namsan Tunnel #1
National Institute of Classical Music
Hotel Shilla
National Theater
Namsan Tunnel #2
Tower Hotel

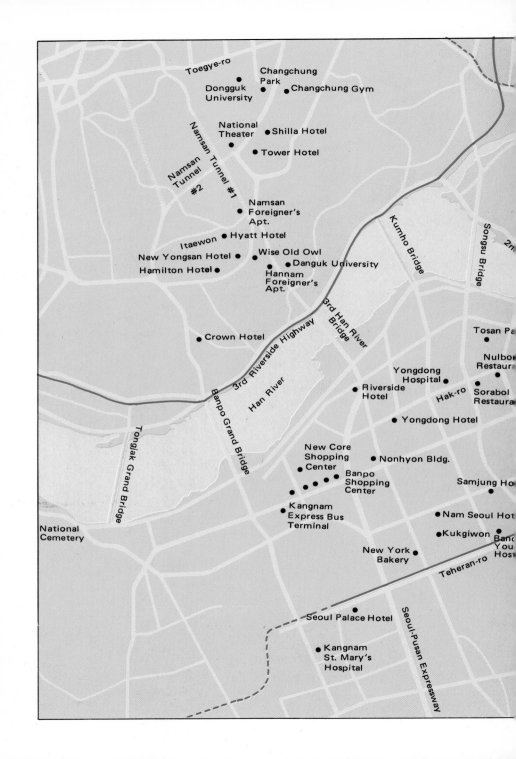

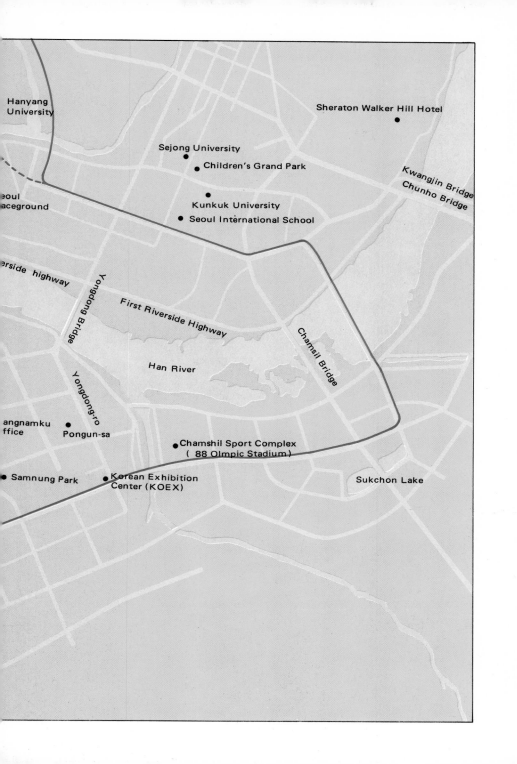

Hanyang
University

Sheraton Walker Hill Hotel

Sejong University

Children's Grand Park

Kwangjin Bridge
Chunho Bridge

eoul
aceground

Kunkuk University

Seoul International School

erside highway

Yongdong Bridge

First Riverside Highway

Chamsil Bridge

Han River

Yongdong-ro

angnamku
ffice

Pongun-sa

Chamshil Sport Complex
(88 Olmpic Stadium)

Samnung Park

Korean Exhibition
Center (KOEX)

Sukchon Lake

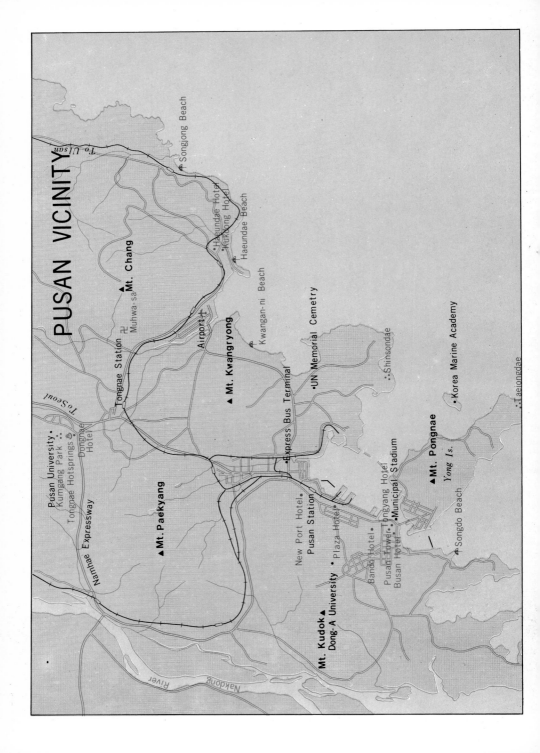

PUSAN VICINITY

To Ulsan

Songjong Beach

Haeundae Hotel
Kukkong Hotel
Haeundae Beach

▲Mt. Chang
Muhwa-sa

Kwangan-ni Beach

Tongnae Station 卍

Airport ✈

▲ Mt. Kwangryong

•UN Memorial Cemetry

•∴Shinsondae

Express Bus Terminal

•Korea Marine Academy

∴Taeiongdae

To Seoul

Pusan University•
Kumgang Park ∴
Tongnae Hotsprings ∵ 卍
Dongnae
Hotel

▲Mt. Paekyang

Namhae Expressway

New Port Hotel•
Pusan Station •
Plaza Hotel•

Bando Hotel•
Pusad Towel•
Busan Hotel• •Municipal Stadium
Tongyang Hotel•

▲Mt. Pongnae
Yong Is.

•Songdo Beach

Mt. Kudok▲
Dong-A University

Nakdong
River

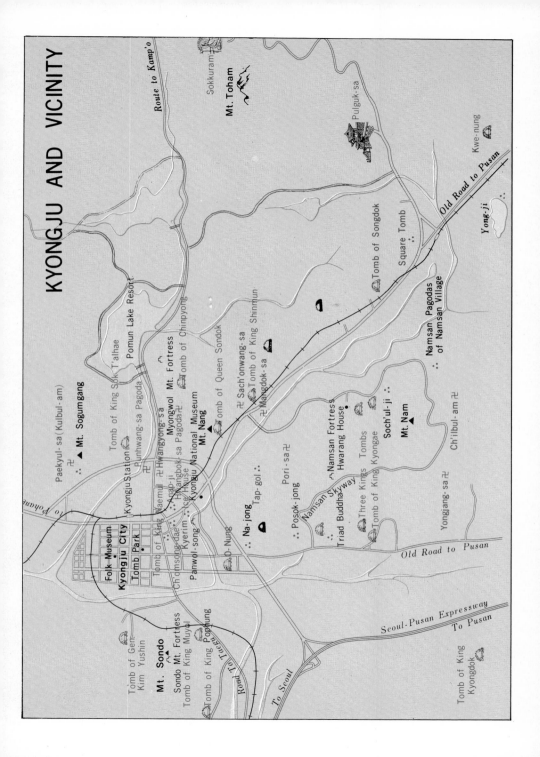

KYONGJU AND VICINITY

Chapter I.
Introducing Korea

Songkwang Temple, South Cholla

Historical Sketch

Choson, the earliest name given to the Korean kingdom established by a legendary founder, Tan'gun, about four thousand years ago, denotes "morning freshness and calm." However, Korean history is a story of survival of a people constantly beset by larger nations bent on domination; yet the resilient Koreans emerge to retain their own distinctive character, culture, and ultimately their hard-won independence.

Ancient countries often trace their origins to a legend and this is the case with Korea. The foundation legend of Korea based on the mythology of Tan'gun is deeply embedded in Korean culture. Early records present Ung, a god who visited earth in the regions of the Ever White Mountain along the Yalu River and who transformed a bear into a woman and later married her. Their offspring was Tan'gun who assumed leadership of the primitive clans and established his capital at Pyongyang in 2333 BC.

Tan'gun built an altar for worship on Mani Mountain, the highest peak on Kanghwa Island near Seoul. The site of this altar is still seen and honored on Foundation Day (Tan'gun Day), a National Holiday. Archeological evidence shows that the Korean peninsula has been inhabited from the early paleolithic era, primarily along the coastal regions.

The Three Kingdoms Period (57BC-668 AD):

In response to Chinese encroachment, political unity began to appear in Korea, patterned roughly along Chinese order but still retaining many Korean characteristics. Three monarchial states were in existence on the peninsula by the first century AD. Their traditional founding dates are 57 BC for Silla, 37 BC for Koguryo and 18 BC for Paekche.

Located closer to China, Koguryo was the first to be influenced by Chinese culture including the introduction of Buddhism. Koguryo emerged initially as the most powerful, largest and most advanced of the three states. Its territory extended from south of the Han River to far beyond the present northern boundaries on the east bank of the Liao River on the Liaotung peninsula. Known as excellent horsemen and brave warriors, these people eventually established their capital in Pyongyang (now northern Korea's capital).

The Paekche Kingdom occupied the southern corner of the peninsula of Korea. The people were northern tribes who kept moving south to avoid Koguryo and Chinese domination. Paekche established its first capital south of the Han River near present day Seoul but later moved to Kongju and finally to Puyo.

Silla was the last to develop and was the farthest removed from Chinese influence. Its society was markedly aristocratic and less warlike. At first the monarchy rotated among the Pak, Sok and Kim clans. The legendary origin of the first son of these three clans was from an egg; thus the kingdom was often referred to as the "chicken people." In the mid-fourth century the monarchy became permanently hereditary in the Kim clan. The capital was established and remained at Kyongju.

The rise of the Three Kingdoms in Korea coincided with the decline of the Han Dynasty in China, which finally fell in 220 AD. During the next four

◁ *Koryo pagoda near at Namsan-ri, Tamyang-up, South Cholla (Treasure No. 56)*

hundred years of Chinese domestic confusion the Three Kingdoms were left free to develop without outside political interference. On the other hand, conflicts among the Three Kingdoms continued to grow with varying alliances as Silla continually grew stronger. This uneasy balance of power among the Three Kingdoms persisted until well into the seventh century and might have continued indefinitely had not events in China intervened.

In 618 the T'ang Dynasty replaced the Sui and the new rulers were to preside over one of the most brilliant eras in Chinese history, which also reached a peak of influence over neighboring countries. T'ang rulers, also wishing to dominate the Korean peninsula, decided to take advantage of the hostilities between the Three Kingdoms and play one off against the other. Accordingly a treaty was made with Silla to help her conquer the other two kingdoms.

The first attack was on Paekche and the kingdom fell in 660. Silla troops were led by the famed General Kim Yu-shin, a remarkable military leader whose exploits are still celebrated in Korea today. Now it was Koguryo's turn, but defeating the fierce and proud Asian warriors of the north was no easy matter. It was only in 668 when dissension in the Koguryo court gave an advantage to the Silla and T'ang armies that the defeat of Koguryo was possible.

T'ang rulers who had long coveted Korea and now claimed the territories of Paekche and Koguryo also fully intended to occupy Silla as well. Revolts within the two conquered territories, which were supported by Silla troops, rather than suppressed, caused grave concern for China. When a T'ang force was dispatched, the Silla armies defeated it in a very conclusive manner. After much bickering and face-saving, a treaty was reached under which China recognized Silla as an independent state ruling all of the area south of the Taedong River near Pyongyang. Thus the Korean peninsula achieved unification under Silla rule.

The Unified Silla Period (668-936):

Silla reached a peak of prosperity and power about the middle of the eighth century while the capital city in the Kyongju valley region reached a population of over one million people, ten times the size of the present city of Kyongju. Buddhism continued to spread and prosper throughout the kingdom and today some of Korea's outstanding treasured relics come from the creative genius and religious fervor of artisans of this period. Broken images, carved reliefs and pagoda fragments are now scattered in great number about the vicinity of the ancient capital. Korea's most remarkable temple, Pulguk-sa, situated a few miles from Kyongju City, was recently renovated by the government. In the stone cave behind this historic temple is the Sokkuram grotto, created during the reign of King Kyongdok and now estimated by world scholars as the most unique and classically beautiful piece of Buddhist sculpture in the Far East.

After the eighth century Silla began a gradual decline stemming in part from the contradictions involved in applying the Chinese Confucian system to an aristocratic society. The battle for power between many factional parties was one principal reason for Silla's decline. Weak and immoral rulers further caused rebellions to persist. Finally in 927 the capital was sacked and the king who was reveling unconcernedly at Posokjong was killed. A few years later his successor abdicated and General Wanggon established the kingdom of Koryo. Thus the great dynasty which lasted almost a full millennium came to an end.

The Koryo Dynasty Period (936-1392):

While Silla still held sway in the south a rebellion emerged in the north led by a man called Kungye, a Silla aristocrat who had been banished from the Silla court. He gained territory north of the Han River but was soon overthrown by one of his lieutenants, a man named

Wanggon who was to call his small kingdom Koryo, a shortened form of the old Koguryo and the name from which the modern word "Korea" is derived. General Wanggon became King T'aejo, the first monarch of the Koryo Dynasty, and established his capital at Songdo, his birthplace (now called Kaesong), just west of the modern Panmunjom area. He was unusually benevolent toward the former royalty of Silla and gave them prominent positions in the government, even taking a princess of the royal Silla Kim clan in marriage.

King T'aejo was strongly influenced by Buddhism and that religion was to see its palmiest days in Korea during the Koryo period. The religion received special court protection with regrettable results due to the excessive influence of Buddhist priests who were behind the scenes in politics. This unwholesome power of the clergy was to eventually contribute to the fall of Koryo.

Meanwhile Confucianism, which had entered Korea during the Silla period and had been greatly enhanced by Sol Ch'ong, the recognized father of Korean literature and inventor of the *idu* system, and Ch'oe Ch'i-won whose prolific writings had placed him well ahead of his time, now began to gain influence. A National University was established with many provincial schools. Any aspirant for government appointment had to pass a national examination on the Confucian classics.

During this period the *Samguk Sagi* was compiled by an official named Kim Pu-shik and is now one of the oldest records of this nation's history. Shortly after, an unoffical history was written by Priest Ilyon entitled the *Samguk Yusa*. Though devoted largely to legends it also contains considerable historical material. One of this record's chief virtues is that Priest Ilyon wrote about traditions as he found them rather than trying to fit history into a Confucian political framework.

Koryo had been faced with incessant harassment from northern tribes such as the Tartars and Mongols. In the 13th century Mongol hordes invaded Korea.

During this period the Koryo courts were completely dominated by the family of General Ch'oe Chung-hon and his descendants while the rulers were mere figureheads. In 1270 a peace treaty was imposed fifty years after the first Mongol invasion. Meanwhile the king and court had taken refuge on Kanghwa Island.

Also during the 13th century one of Korea's greatest cultural achievements was undertaken. While in exile on Kanghwa Island, King Kojong had the *Tripitaka* carved on wood blocks, a project which had earlier been undertaken but destroyed. This was to be done as a pious gesture to secure divine favor against the Mongol invaders. These 81,258 wood blocks which took sixteen years to complete can still be viewed at Haein Temple near Taegu. Declared one of Korea's most important National Treasures, they remain the world's oldest and most comprehensively complete collection of Buddhist scriptures.

In ceramics the Koryo potters achieved an excellence which has never been equalled in developing a unique greenish-blue glaze. The Koryo celadon pieces which survive today are eagerly sought by collectors and museums throughout the world.

According to documentary sources the Koreans were using movable metal type some 200 years before Gutenburg. This assertion was recently verified by the discovery at the French National Library in Paris of a Korean volume dating to the early 14th century and obviously printed from movable metal type.

The Yi Dynasty Period (1392-1910):

General Yi Song-gye was an eminent Koryo officer with a distinguished career against the Mongols but the poor judgement of the Koryo courts was causing him grave misgivings. Using his troops and popularity with the people he rebelled and in a surprise move captured the capital of Songdo. He supported the Neo-Confucian leaders who were tired of Buddhist favoritism, and wished to resume the traditional relationship with the Ming Dynasty of China. Like the founder of the Koryo Dynasty, Yi Song-gye was given the title of T'aejo by which he is known to history. The capital was moved to Hanyang (Seoul) and Buddhism was replaced by Confucianism as the major guideline, not only for government officialdom but for the private life of the nation.

The stability of the Yi Dynasty government was finally secured during the enlightened reign of the fourth monarch, Sejong (1418-1450), grandson of King T'aejo. One of the greatest literary achievements of Korea was the development of the phonetic alphabet called *han'gul* during King Sejong's reign. This alphabet is one of the most scientific and precise writing systems ever conceived. King Sejong was considered the greatest of Yi Dynasty kings who initiated impressive developments in scientific, philosophical, musical and technological fields.

In 1592 began the devastating invasion by the Japanese armies under Hideyoshi with the unsuccessful aim of conquering China. With little resistance Seoul fell within two weeks, while King Sonjo and his court fled north. Strangely enough the tide of war at sea created for Korea lasting fame. The Korean fleets with their superior mobility and firepower, inspired by the brilliant leadership of Admiral Yi Sun-shin, inflicted annihilating defeats on the large Japanese armada. Most dreaded for Japanese sailors was the fearless onslaught of a newly developed ironclad vessels called the "turtle." These turtle-shaped vessels were the world's first ironclad ships.

No sooner had the Japanese retreated than Korea found herself in another delicate position between the struggling Ming and Manchu powers of China. The Manchu armies invaded Korea twice, in 1627 and 1636, culminating in King Injo's surrender after a 44-day siege at South Fortress near Seoul.

Following these Manchu invasions Korea retreated into a stringent policy of isolationism and became known as the

Portrait of Yi T'aejo, Chonju City

"hermit nation." When a Dutch vessel a few years later was shipwrecked on Cheju, a southern island, the thirty-six seamen who survived were held as hostages. After many years several sailors escaped and one, Hendrik Hamel, wrote a book of his adventures.

Western influence began slowly through China and primarily through encounters with Jesuit priests. Books arriving through Chinese envoys were a mere trickle. However, the influence of Western religion began seriously to affect Korea in the late 18th century as it came into direct conflict with Confucian principles. The first Chinese Catholic priest to enter Korea in 1795 was later executed, along with about 300 persons practicing Christianity. In 1836 the first Western missionary, a French priest named Pierre Maubant, entered Korea, followed by several others during the next few years. They also were captured and executed. Andrew Kim was ordained in the Portuguese colony of Macao in 1845 and returned to Korea to become Korea's first recognized martyr.

Perhaps one factor that reinforced the Korean isolation policy was that Korea was "off the beaten track" without sufficient natural resources to attract Western merchants. The attempts to open Korea were only half-hearted. Had the Western powers given Korea's rulers a convincing demonstration of industrial power it is quite possible that the government might have adapted itself to reality and thus preserved Korean independence. Korean rulers remained secure in the belief that they could repel any foreign attack.

The year 1864 became a turning point. King Ch'oljong died and his successor was twelve-year-old King Kojong. The king's father became regent and received the title of *taewongun* and turned out to be one of the strongest personalities of the entire dynasty. He was an orthodox Confucian who bitterly opposed change. Unlike many of his contemporaries he was upright, honest and determined to do away with corruption and factionalism which so long plagued his country. The problem was that history had overtaken him before he was aware of it; in an earlier era he would have been a great ruler. In 1866 the persecution of Catholics began which cost the lives of 12 Western priests and over 8,000 Koreans.

Also in 1866 the American merchant ship the *General Sherman* sailed up the river toward Pyongyang but was burned with the loss of the entire crew and a missionary by the name of Thomas. In 1876 Korea reluctantly agreed to open her ports to Japan and in 1882 a treaty of friendship and commerce was concluded between Korea and the United States. This was followed by similar treaties with Germany, Austria, Russia, Italy and France.

Unfortunately Korea again became the arena for a power struggle, this time with Japan, China and Russia as prime competitors. Japan won against China in 1895 and then against Russia in 1905. When Queen Min, the wife of King Kojong, was coveniently murdered in a Japanese plot in 1895, the strongest of the political figures was eliminated from the Korean scene. Japan now met no serious foreign objection to her eventual annexation of Korea, which was officially concluded in 1910. Thus the dynasty ended with the abdication of King Sunjong, the 27th ruler of Yi.

Excavation of Silla tomb (Tumulus #98), Kyongju City

A village elder wears his horsehair hat and hanbok

Geography and Climate

The name of Korea or "Koryo" means high and clear, and is symbolic of the country's rugged towering mountains, clear blue skies and rushing streams which have earned the nation the nickname of "Switzerland of Asia." It is a beautiful country with simple grandeur but a land of amazing contrasts. The Republic of Korea is about the size of the State of Indiana.

The Korean peninsula extends southward from eastern Siberia and Manchuria to within seventy miles of Japan at the southern tip. On the north it is separated from the USSR by the Tumen River and from Manchuria by the Yalu River. The Sea of Japan and the Korean Strait separate Korea from Japan on the east while on the west the Yellow Sea lies between Korea and Communist China. The peninsula has more than six thousand miles of coastline dotted with over 3,000 islands. Approximately six hundred miles long and 130-200 miles wide, the peninsula has an area of 85,000 square miles. The Republic of Korea is 38,000 square miles in area and is slightly smaller than the northern half.

Korea varies in terrain. The spectacular Diamond Mountains run the full length of the east coast. Lashing tides of the Sea of Japan have chopped a rugged shoreline into rocky islets and sheer cliffs. Plains form the central region and slope to the western coast. In the south the mountains slope gradually to the sea and form many offshore islands, honeycombed with inlets. The tide at Inchon port is second highest in the world, exceeded only by the tides of the Bay of Fundy in Canada.

The rivers, though many, are mostly shallow, short and swift, with many sandbanks, providing little scope to navigation. The principal rivers of the Republic are the Naktong, the South and North Han and the Kum. There are few natural lakes and unlike Japan hardly any volcanoes. The Paektu (Ever-White) Mountain bordering northern Korea and Cheju Island in the south are sites of Korea's most famous volcanic craters.

The nation's climate is temperate. Moderately cold dry winters with long periods of clear skies, and hot humid summers are characteristic of Korea's climate. Temperature extremes range from $10°F$ in the winter to a maximum of $98°F$ in the summer. June, July and August have the heaviest rains, with July usually being the wettest month of the year. Spring and autumn are very pleasant with crisp weather and many days of sunshine. The milder winters of the Korean Republic are said to be characterized by three consecutive cold days followed by four warmer days. If you can choose the season, spring or fall are the times to visit Korea as the weather is good.

Traditionally the Korean people enjoy the fall season most. This has resulted in most of the country's holidays falling in this period. The weather is clear and bright, resulting in an often heard Korean expression, "The sky is high and the horse is fat."

In its physical features South Korea is a transitional zone between the continental land mass of northeast Asia and the island arcs rimming the western Pacific. Everywhere rugged mountains rim the horizon and ridge follows ridge in endless succession. It is said that three quarters of Korea "stand on end."

◁ *Overlooking Shilsang Temple, North Cholla*

The People

The people of Korea today might be considered the most friendly of all Asian people to the Westerner. They have a keen sense of humor balanced by earthy common sense .... quick to laugh and equally quick to show anger .... in a true Irish manner.

Koreans are descendants of several Mongol tribal groups which migrated from the north (present day Manchuria) in prehistoric eras and have now been fused into one separate, homogeneous group, independent of their neighbors to the east and west but with traits distinctive of both the Chinese and Japanese. The average man is taller than the Japanese while the women are usually small like most of Asia's women. Koreans are graceful yet robust and noted for their endurance under the most adverse conditions. They carry themselves with the dignity of a proud race.

Over the centuries the Koreans have stubbornly held to one language, one culture and an ancient tradition. Only recently have outside influences brought dramatic changes in the people and nation. Koreans all speak, understand and write the same language in basically the same way. This is an important factor conducive to the spirit of national unity and solidarity which has been a noted characteristic of Koreans for many centuries. The grammar of the language resembles that of Japanese but here the resemblance ends.

The family is the primary social unit in Korea and family relationships have a powerful influence in Korean society. Young people are still taught to show respect for parents and elders. When a Korean girl marries she leaves her family unit and becomes a part of her husband's. Though this custom is breaking down families are still careful to see that their children marry into families of equal or complementary social status.

Though Confucianism is a social factor of the past the tradition of this ethical historic force still strongly sways the thinking of the average Korean.

Traditionally, Korea had a fairly rigid class structure and a man could only attain a high position of influence through education in the Confucian classics and in correct social behavior. The upper class today has many of the old characteristics. Many of its members come from the traditional families of power and classical education. Education and academic scholarship are still considered important steps to top positions and social distinction, although now wealth has become an important factor in the class structure.

The old class system has been invaded by a new "in-between" group of businessmen and skilled workers in the towns and cities. Many are willing to pay to provide their offspring the education believed to be the prerequisite for success. With this dawn of modernization encouraging the aspiration for mass literacy and equality of opportunity, the *han'gul* (phonetic Korean alphabet) has come into universal use while Chinese characters are used sparingly. As a result the literacy rate in Korea is over 90%, one of the highest in the world.

The diplomatic approach is another major prerequisite in dealing with Koreans. A brusque, overly direct, manner is often resented. If you criticize do it in private and in a kind manner. Never criticize a Korean in public.

Kim, Park and Lee are the most common surnames in Korea, out of a

◁ *A Korean elder wearing the traditional topknot, Kyeryong Mountain*

total of only a few family names. Ee, Ea, Yi, Yih, Lih, Ri, Rii, Ree, Rhee and Le are only Western variations of the spelling of Lee (이) and are really the same family name of many Koreans. Koreans reverse their names. The family name comes first, followed by the given name such as Lee Sun-shin.

In the 1982 census the population of the Republic of Korea was 38,197,000, giving this country a population density ranking fifth in the world. Until recently the population growth had been a staggering 5.58% per year but through vigorous efforts in family planning programs the rate by 1979 became 1.5%. Approximately 800 thousand Koreans now live overseas with the largest number of overseas Koreans living in Japan and the United States.

◁ *A child in traditional* hanbok, *Seoul*
▽ *Koreans picnicking near a temple site*

The National Flag

The Koreans flag symbolizes much of the thought, philosophy and mysticism of the Orient. The red and blue swirl and sometimes the flag itself is called the "taeguk," a perfect balance of harmony.

The flag of the Republic of Korea is unique among the national emblems of the world. Its design symbol does not represent geographical or political division or a great historical event or even the aims and ideals of this country. Rather, it is meant to encourage contemplation and philosophic interpretation of the varied meanings of the universe. It has many interpretations.

In the center of a white background is a circle divided equally with each part resembling a comma. The upper (red) portion represents the *yang* and the lower (blue) portion the *um,* an ancient symbol of the universe in perfect balance and harmony. These two opposites express the dualism of the cosmos or the absolute: fire and water, day and night, good and evil, masculine and feminine, heat and cold and so on. The presence of the duality indicates that life is full of contradictions.

Occasionally the circle shows three comma-shaped whorls instead of two.

Odd numbers are considered more perfect than even and the concept of universality is not contradicted. The earliest Korean flag is depicted in this manner. This perfect balance and harmony in the cosmos is also seen in the Buddhist swastika (arms left or right) seen at all Buddhist temples.

The central thought in the *taeguk* form indicates that while there is constant movement in the sphere of infinity, there is also balance. As a simple example, the opposites of rain and drought may be taken for consideration. Crops must have rain for normal growth but floods will wash crops away, causing hardship during the dry season.

Three bars at each corner also carry the ideas of opposites and balance. Three unbroken lines represent heaven while the three broken lines represent earth. The bars in the lower left corner symbolize fire while the upper right bars represent water.

Rose of Sharon, national flower

Lotus blossoms, symbol of Buddhism

Flora and Fauna

Korea is botanically divided into five districts each with special differences: Cheju Island, Southern, Central, Northern Districts and Ullung-do, an island east of the peninsula.

A great variety of flora, pine, larch, spruce, juniper, oak, willow, maple, alder and birch trees, usual in temperate climates are found over the whole peninsula. Also large gingko and Chinese elm are scattered throughout the country. The world's largest and oldest fruit bearing tree, which is the gingko, is growing at the temple of Yongmun-sa, a two-hour drive from Seoul (trunk: 54 ft. circumference, height: 175 ft.). A Korean type poplar tree exists but the Lombardy poplar as well as the acacia have been imported and both are found widely spread as protection against erosion.

Flowering shrubs are numerous and grow profusely on the hillsides, such as forsythia, azalea, cherry, lilac, syringa and spiraea and many other varieties of wildflowers. The cypress, beech, maple and paulownia are found on Ullung Island. The soil and climate of Korea have proved most suitable for the cultivation of fruit trees and there are large orchards of apples, pears, peaches, and vine fruits.

Taegu City is called the apple capital of Korea. Dr. James Adams, an educator and Presbyterian missionary, who arrived in 1895, first introduced the Western apple to this country at the turn of the century. The walnut, chestnut and pinenut as well as persimmon are indigenous and produce good crops. Oranges and tangerines are now grown in the south but are still an expensive fruit.

Animals found on the peninsula are the boar, bear, deer, wildcat, wolf, hare, weasel, tiger and leopard, though now some of these animals are rare except in the mountains of Korea. The native horse is small but strong, while the cattle are large, useful for labor and beef, and widely distributed. The most common native birds are the crow, magpie, jay, kite, heron, crane, oriole, lark, sparrow, robin, tit, pheasant and quail while the migratory birds are goose, bustard, duck, teal, swan and rail.

A wide variety of water animals and fish have stimulated a vigorous fishing industry. Snakes of various kinds are found and hunted for medicinal value but few are venomous. Insect life has been well studied as many are harmful to trees and crops. Two hundred species of butterflies have been identified. Honey bees have made honey farming an important source of income.

As a measure of conservation of Korea's natural environment some flora and fauna have been designated as Protected Natural Resources (PNR) by the Cultural Assets Protection Law. There are now over 150 listed natural resources.

Certain birds such as the Tristram Woodpecker, Crested Ibis, Black Stork, Blackfaced Spoonbill and Great Bustard are registered and protected. A particular longhorned beetle found in Songni Mountain (PNR No. 218) is protected.

The Chindo dog (PNR No. 53) is protected as a pure breed on Chin-do, an island off the southwest coast of Korea. It is believed that this variety of dog was once widely distributed during the Neolithic Era. On the mainland the years of crossbreeding wiped out the unique characteristics of this dog.

Twentieth Century Korea

Emerging from the bleak conditions of a Japanese occupied protectorate, Korea has become a leader among Asian countries, progressive, modern and strongly supporting the free world.

Japanese Occupation (1910-1945):

A Protectorate Treaty was signed in 1905 conceding Korea's diplomatic rights to Japan and allowing a Japanese resident general to be stationed in Seoul. This signaled the beginning of strong Japanese encroachment on Korean independence and King Kojong was forced to abdicate in favor of his son in 1907. The Treaty of Annexation was signed in August 1910. Many Korean patriots went abroad and others went underground to fight for their country.

Upon the occasion of the public mourning for retired King Kojong, who died of unknown causes, a well organized people's demonstration erupted all over the country on March 1, 1919. A total of 33 representatives of the Korean people signed the Declaration of Independence, which had been drafted and printed for nationwide circulation, demanding restoration of the nation's sovereignty, to which Japan responded with brutality. However, Korea never abandoned its aspirations for national independence.

Establishment of the Republic:

When the Japanese surrendered to the Allied Powers in 1945 most Koreans took for granted that immediate independence of their fatherland would be granted. However, national jubilation soon turned to disappointment and indignation as the country was divided at the 38th parallel. The real cause of the partition was never clarified. Both American and Russian occupation authorities were to establish military rule in their respective occupied regions until a Korean provisional government was created.

The US-USSR Joint Commission met in Pyongyang in 1946 and Seoul in 1947 but failed to reach any agreement as Koreans wanted only immediate independence. The Korean question was then brought before the U.N. General Assembly in September of 1947 and a resolution was adopted to hold general elections in Korea to insure immediate independence and unification. However, the Russians and their followers in the north refused to comply with the U.N. resolution and refused entry to the selected U.N. Commission delegates.

An election under U.N. supervision was held in south Korea alone on May 10, 1948. The Korean Republic under the presidential system was officially formed and the first president, Dr. Syngman Rhee, was inaugurated August 15, 1948, to coincide with the anniversary of Korea's liberation from Japan. The north Korean communists set up their own regime headed by Kim Il-sung in Pyongyang the following month.

Korean War:

Then on June 25, 1950 the north Korean communists launched an unprovoked invasion into the Republic of Korea and captured Seoul in three days.

◁ *Toksu Palace, downtown Seoul*

Their attack penetrated to the outskirts of Taegu, far to the south. The United Nations branded the north Koreans as aggressors and troops of sixteen U.N. member nations were sent to resist the aggression.

The September Inchon landing by General Douglas MacArthur became one of history's most brilliant military maneuvers and marked the eventual defeat of the north Korean army in November. However, huge hordes of Red Chinese "volunteers" entered the battle to again push the U.N. forces back from the Yalu River. The Korean War was technically suspended on July 27, 1953 by an armistice agreement which the Republic of Korea refused to sign.

According to the armistice agreement northern and southern Korea were to be separated by a neutral Demilitarized Zone (DMZ) and reunification of Korea was to be brought about through political negotiations. These negotiations at Panmunjom have failed over the last 33 years as communist leaders of north Korea have refused to permit a U.N. supervised free election in their territory. Consequently there is no peace, and unification is still only a dream for the Korean people.

Student Uprising and Revolution:

The unparalleled destruction and misery in the wake of the Korean War were so acute that the worldwide image of Korea became one of helplessness and futility – a misleading image perpetuated in years immediately following by economic stagnation and political instability, all of which were the aftermath of the shattering experience of a war-torn people. Seoul, the capital city, had fallen four times in the course of one year.

President Rhee was re-elected in 1956, but his Liberal Party went too far when they attempted to re-elect him in 1960 for a fourth term through a rigged election. Nationwide student demonstrations resulted which caused martial law and eventual resignation of the president.

A new general election was held and elected Yun Po-sun as president. Contrary to public belief, however, it soon became clear that the political system in Korea was not effective in resolving the urgent national problems.

This chaotic state was ended on May 16, 1961 by a group of army and marine officers led by General Park Chung-hee who spearheaded the military revolution. This military government lasted two years. A new constitution was agreed upon in a national referendum which approved the presidential system. In the presidential election, retired General Park won the presidency of a civilian government.

Under the leadership of President Park Chung-hee and his Democratic Republican Party (DRP), many government reforms and rapid industrialization leading to economic stabilization finally began. A brighter image of a modern Korea emerged, proud and progressive, with a people optimistic and determined to shape their own destiny and build a better future no matter what the hardships.

This radically different image of Korea might surprise outsiders whose knowledge of the country's history is limited. Yet, there is little surprise for the serious students of Korea's four-thousand-year history.

On October 26, 1979 President Park Chung-hee was struck down by an assassin's bullet. Prime Minister Choi Kyu-hah became acting president according to the Constitution and was shortly, thereafter, elected President by the National Conference for Unification.

For many months the country went through a difficult period characterized by political, social and economic instability. In some cases unrest was fanned by student riots and overeager politicans. The horror of the "Kwangju Incident" created frightening feelings of impending disaster as the nation went under martial law and a special committee for National Security Measures was formed under the chairmanship of General Chun Doo-hwan.

Seoul City at night ▷

During the following months General Chun emerged as the logical choice to head the government in the days ahead. On August 16, 1980 President Choi resigned early to make the transition period as short as possible. General Chun, who had resigned from the Army, was elected President by the National Conference for Unification on Aug. 27.

In October a new Constitution, having been overwhelmingly approved in a referendum, introduced the Fifth Republic. Stronger political and civil rights were guaranteed than under the old Yushin Constitution. The presidency would be limited to a single seven-year term. Martial law was lifted and presidential election was held in February 1981. On March 3, 1981 President Chun Doo-hwan took office as the President of the Fifth Republic.

Within 18 months President Chun had a summit conference with President Reagon in the US, an Asian Pacific tour and an African/Canada tour. Also a summit meeting with North Korea was proposed by President Chun. The invitation of the 1986 Asian Games and 1988 Summer Olympics to Seoul promoted Korea internationally and elevated the people's pride.

Looking back on history's pages one can note the resiliency and fierce determination of the Korean people to maintain their national identity and freedom amidst frequent catastrophes. The Korean nation now has its future in its sights.

photo by Kang, Woon-gu

Downtown Seoul City from South Mountain

Hyundai-Hanyang apartments, south of Seoul

Subway construction, south of the Han River

Government

Rapid development in the economic field and attainment of political and social stability have given to the Korean people as well as government leaders a strong belief that they can successfully meet and overcome whatever challenges or aggressions may stand in the way of national progress, peace and unity.

Following the close of World War II the constitution of the Republic of Korea was first promulgated on July 17, 1948. President Syngman Rhee became Korea's first president on August 15, 1948.

Following the 1960 election of President Rhee to a fourth term the country was filled with uneasiness as the people became more aware of the fraudulent rigging of the election polls. Demonstrations began which reached a peak on April 19, 1960 when martial law was proclaimed. However, this did not silence the students and President Rhee finally resigned seven days later. An interim government was organized

On May 16, 1961 a group of army and marine officers led by Major General Park Chung-hee toppled the existing system. This military government, lasting two years, initiated many reforms and made significant achievements in both social and political life.

A new constitution was approved in a national referendum on December 17, 1962 which revived the presidential system. In the presidential election held on October 15, 1963, candidate Park Chung-hee, now retired from military service, won the presidency. Other candidates from his Democratic Republican Party demonstrated an impressive victory in the general election held the following month.

The changing mood in the international community toward peaceful coexistence and detente which began in early 1970 meant many changes for Korea. In 1972 this government began a

series of dialogues with the communist People's Republic of North Korea which were aided by the humanitarian Red Cross. However, these dialogues failed.

In November 1972 through a national referendum amendments to the constitution, referred to as a revitalizing reform, were approved. A unique democratic system giving the presidential office unlimited powers was implemented to further national security and fit the goals for a stronger defense posture on the peninsula. The efforts of the opposition NDP (New Democratic Party) were further curtailed as the question of human rights became a serious issue among Korea's intellectuals.

The government is divided into three major branches: the Administrative or Excutive Branch, the National Assembly and the Judiciary. The President serves as supreme Head of State with his powers and duties far-reaching. The President's term of office is seven years and no one will be allowed to pursue a second term in office. (Beginning with the 5th Republic, Oct 27, 1980.)

The State Council or Cabinet is the nucleus of the Executive Branch with the chairman being the President. There are 25 members represented by some of the following ministries: Economic Planning Board, Foreign Affairs, Home Affairs, Finance, Justice, National Defense, Education, Agriculture and Fisheries, Commerce and Industry, Construction, Health and Social Affairs, Transportation, Communications, Culture and Information, Labor, Unification

President Carter's visit to South Korea, 1980 ▷

Board, Science and Technology, Energy and Resources, Government Administration and Athletics. Also of ministerial rank are three ministers of State, Veterans Administration, Legistation and Academy of Korean Studies.

In addition to the Cabinet the President has had many agencies and councils under his direct control to help him formulate and carry out national policies. These included: National Security Council, Economic and Scientific Council, Audit and Inspection, Administrative Reform Committee, Agency for National Security Planning (formerly the Central Intelligence Agency) and Election Management. However, in Nov. 1981 the government abolished all of these agencies except the Board of Audit and Inspection and Agency for National Security Planning.

The Republic of Korea is divided into two special cities (Seoul and Pusan) and nine provinces. The provinces are further divided into *gun* (counties), *shi* (cities), *up* (towns), *myon* (districts) and *ri* or *dong* (villages).

The National Assembly exercises the right to approve or reject legislative bills, to inspect closing accounts of the national budget, to ratify or reject foreign treaties, and to concur on declaration of war.

In the Judiciary the Supreme Court is presided over by a chief justice who is appointed by the President. Its decisions are final and indisputable. There are three Appellate Courts in Korea located in Seoul, Taegu and Kwangju. There are also military courts and family courts. The family court system was established in 1963 as a new experiment to hear matrimonial cases and juvenile problems. There is no jury system in Korea.

The government of the Republic of Korea is constitutionally committed to democracy and the pursuit of peaceful domestic and international policies while denouncing aggressive wars. The constitution guarantees equality before the law regardless of sex or religion.

In 1973 the Republic of Korea announced a major foreign policy shift in stating that trade and contact with non-

Kwanghwa-mun in front of capitol building and Kyongbok Palace, Seoul

hostile communist countries would be welcomed.

On Oct. 20, 1979 the world was shocked and saddened by the assassination of President Park Chung-hee by his own KCIA chief. The late president had become a legend in the Far East as an economic miracle worker. With a stern hand he had ruled Korea for 18 years. The death of President Park ended a political era and brought about the disintegration of the Yushin movement. The transition period under martial law was headed by President Choi Kyu-hah who had been Prime Minister under President Park. The administration then attempted to solve the causes of growing social unrest, economic decline and increasing student demonstration following the assassination.

Preparation was begun to amend the Constitution to meet the demands of needed political reform. President Choi resigned on August 16 to make way for the new election. Chun Doo-hwan, former ROK army general, was elected President by the National Conference for Unification on August 27, 1980. The new Constitution was overwhelmingly endorsed on October 22, 1980 and the Fifth Republic under President Chun

Doo-hwan was officially established Oct. 27, 1980.

In the promulgation of the new Constitution of the Fifth Republic all political parties were abolished. However, on November 19 a new Political Party Law was passed by the Legislative Assembly lifting the ban on political activities. Almost immediately 12 parties registered.

The Democratic Justice Party (DJP) was organized by the ruling elite and presidential candidate, Chun Doo-hwan. In the National Assembly 151 seats were won. As the majority party, the DJP aims to establish a genuinely democratic government guaranteeing the well being of all citizens.

The Democratic Korea Party (DKP) was organized by former members of the New Democratic Party under Yoo Chi-song and the Korea National Party was organized by former members of the Democratic Republican Party under Kim Chong-chol. These minority parties hold 81 and 25 seats respectively in the National Assembly. Other parties gaining few seats were the Democratic Socialist Party, Civil Rights Party, Democratic Farmers Party, New Political Party and the Peoples Well-being Party.

Education

Koreans throughout history have had an unquenchable thirst for education which was initially motivated by the old Confucian school of learning where scholarly attainment could be achieved only through competitive examinations. Success in the exams held yearly in the capital would determine appointments and advancement to government civil service positions which during the dynasty were the most important posts in the nation.

Education during the Yi Dynasty was without exception limited to reciting and writing the lessons described in the Analects of Confucius, teachings of Mencius and Seven Chinese Classics as taught by scholars so that students might pass the civil service exams administered by the government. Usually sons of the ruling class were taught in private schools (*sowon*) or by tutors at home. Sungkyunkwan in Seoul was the only institution of higher learning in the nation.

Modern education, first introduced by the Western missionaries in the 19th century, was deeply influenced by the Western system. In 1885 King Kojong requested through the American Embassy that three young men be brought to Korea to establish a government school. Appointed were Gilmore from Princeton, Bunker from Oberlin, and Hulbert from Dartmouth. This first Western school was effective initially but did not prosper as the royal officials attached to the enterprise diverted school funds to their private use and the school had to be closed.

The world's largest women's institution which has an enrollment of over 8,000 students had its humble beginning in 1885 when Mary Scranton, pioneer Methodist missionary, purchased an unsightly strip of land consisting of nineteen straw huts. The first student was a high official's concubine. Her husband wanted her to learn English so

that she could serve as an interpreter for the queen. By 1888 the school enrollment grew to eighteen girls. The name of Ewha Haktang (Pear Blossom Institute) was given by the queen; thus began Ewha Womans University.

A group of missionaries from the Presbyterian and Methodist Mission led by Horace G. Underwood and Henry G. Appenzeller opened mission schools in Seoul before the turn of the century. Paichai and Kyungshin were the first boys' high school while Ewha Haktang became the first girls' high school in Korea.

Educational work in Pyongyang was begun by William M. Baird who founded Sungsil Boys' Academy. James E. Adams, brother-in-law of Baird, began the educational work in Taegu through the founding of Keisung Boys' Academy in 1906.

During this same period Yonhui College (later to become Choson Christian College and Yonsei) was founded in Seoul and Soongsil College in Pyongyang, both sponsored by Presbyterian Mission foundations.

The development of modern education was interrupted by Japanese colonialism that lasted for 35 years until 1945. Education was limited as only 30% of primary school children attended school and one out of thirty enrolled in high school. School children were forced to speak Japanese, adopt Japanese names and meet the educational requirements of a militaristic government.

The liberation of Korea in 1945 was a turning point for Korean education as it shifted from a totalitarian approach to a democratic one. For 35 years following the liberation, the number of schools increased from 3,000 to 10,000 with the number of students rising from 1½ million to ten million.

Korea today has adopted a school system dividing education into six-year elementary schools, three-year middle schools and three-year high schools. Undergraduate work in colleges and universities is four years. There are over ten million students (1/4 of Korea's population attend 10,500 schools served by over 240,000 teachers as of 1978). The need for classrooms and teachers is a problem for the Education Ministry. Double sessioning is common with even triple sessions in some areas. Classes of seventy or eighty students with one teacher are not uncommon in lower grade rooms.

The educational profession is still held in high regard though salaries are unreasonably poor. The status symbol of a teacher ranks high in terms of respect in the local communities. Emphasis is now placed on democratic education with the principle of equal opportunity.

In 1968 these ideals were set forth in the new National Charter of Education aimed at inspiring the young people with a high moral sense and mission for regenerating the nation. These goals are: to develop a new understanding of human relations through education in public ethics, to encourage scientific and technical education, to provide for balanced educational development, and to improve the educational environment and physical fitness of youth. The government is now giving first priority to the linkage of academic attainment with industrial development. Some of the recent educational reforms include the abolition of the middle school entrance examination and the establishment of a lottery system for assignment to school.

Primary school education is compulsory and a plan has been formulated to extend free education to nine years. There are now almost 7,000 primary schools in the country. Now the upward trend seems to be leveling off due to a general decrease of the population growth rate. In 1960 the population growth was 5.5% per year but through family planning projects the increase rate was lowered to 1.5% by 1979.

Though pre-school kindergarten education is not a part of the formal school system, the increasing demand has caused the Ministry of Education to begin experimenting with the idea of opening kindergartens attached to existing primary schools in the larger cities. At present there are over 900 kindergartens enrolling 66,400 children, accounting for 8 percent of the children 5-6 years of age.

Over the last several years there has been a sharp increase of elementary graduates entering middle school. This rose from 58 percent in 1969 to 96 percent in 1981. This brought about pressing problems for facilities and trained teachers available to meet the demand. Within a two-year period 8,600 new classrooms were built.

In 1945 there were only 165 secondary schools but in 1980 Korea had 2,000 middle schools and 1,353 high schools with a combined enrollment of over 4.1 million students with 105,800 teachers. Required courses in the academic high schools are: Korean language, social studies, ethics and morality, Korean history, world history, geography, mathematics, biology, physical education, music, art, and English. Elective courses offer a wide variety of subjects. The curriculum in the vocational high schools is divided into general and professional.

There are over 345 schools for higher education across the country including 85 four-year colleges and universities (19 are national). Within this category are the two year vocational colleges and teacher training colleges for elementary level. Other four-year training institutes such as nursing schools and seminaries are also included. About 70 percent of the institutes of higher education are

private. However, the appointment of presidents and board of trustee members is authorized by the Education Ministry.

Beginning in 1981, the main entrance examination was abolished, making only the qualifying high school examination effective. In lieu of the college entrance examination high school achievement and qualifying test score are considered on a 30-70% basis to determine eligibility. This reform was a step toward providing higher quality of education.

Some of the better known institutions in Seoul City are: Seoul National University (SNU), Korea University, Yonsei University, Ewha Womans University, Sookmyung Women's University, Sogang University, Sungkyungkwan University, Dongguk University, Chung Ang University, Kon-Kuk University, Kyunghee University, Hanyang University, Hanguk University of Foreign Studies, King Sejong University, Dankook University and Hongik University.

S.N.U. maintains branch universities in each of the provinces. In addition some of the better known private institutions outside of the capital are: Inha University in Inchon, Sungjun (Sungsill)

in Taejon, Choson University in Kwangju, Youngnam University and Kyemyung University in Taegu and Tong-A University in Pusan.

In the country's 85 colleges and universities there are over 402,000 students. The number of students accepted by the colleges and universities in Korea is regulated by the government.

Unfortunately the system still prevails that once a student is accepted into a university his chances of completing the courses are assured even though he may study haphazardly and often neglect class attendance. Now one person in 200 is a college graduate. The illiteracy in Korea is almost eliminated and is a much lower percentage than most Western countries including the United States.

In 1980 alone, a total of 235 Korean professors made overseas study tours of approximately one year's time. Also in this same year a total 578 foreign students enrolled in Korean universities and colleges. There were also 280 foreign professors and scholars residing in Korea either on invitation from Korean universities and colleges or

University library, Seoul (top) and Pusan vocational school (right)

on financial grants for research. In 1980 almost 17,000 Korean students were studying in institutions of higher learning in other countries (of these students almost 14,000 were in US study programs).

One form of adult education which has developed is the community education movement in which rural people are organized into classes. These classes conduct their sessions in the evening. Local school buildings are available for these evening classes.

Libraries in Korea are still in an age of infancy. School libraries are encouraged to be open to the general public but at present are seldom used on a lending basis. Many public libraries which receive financial support from city and central government are also subject to their direction and supervision. Unfortunately at present there is no lending system for the general public or students in Korea so that pleasure reading or research might be accomplished outside the confines of the library facilities.

In response to the growing complexity of the recent educational problems and demand for massive reforms, educational research has gained intensity. The Korean Institute for Research in the Behavioral Science (KIRBS), the Korean Educational Development Institute (KEDI) and the National Institute of Education were established to meet the needs of educational reform and the Academy of Korean Studies was established in 1978 to carry out in-depth studies concerning the heritage of the Korean nation. Since 1980 the Academy has offered MA courses.

In Korea today we see that education has turned away from exclusive concern with pure scholarship to emphasize technology, practical and productive skills needed for building the nation. Schools are encouraged now to specialize in fields which could best serve the interests of the people of that community. Human resources are necessary for the economic development of Korea. Many vocational schools are being established.

Economic Miracle

Despite the economic hardship experienced by Korea since the oil crisis of 1973 the nation has been able to score numerous achievements. There is still a steady growth in the economy as expansions have continued in pushing up Korea's exports while a firm basis has been formed for heavy industrial and chemical development. Through the "Saemaul" (New Community) Movement a revitalization of attitudes has become noticeable with general increases in the farmers' income and standard of living.

In the 19-year period from 1962 through 1981 the GNP grew from 12.7 billion to 57.4 billion, an increase of 452 percent. The per capita GNP at current prices rose from $87 to $1,506. A recent World Bank report stated: "From a position uncomfortably close to the bottom of the international income scale and without the benefit of significant natural resources, Korea embarked on a course of industrial growth that became one of the outstanding success stories in international development."

In 1973 Korea made an economic growth record of 16.5 percent for the year. This was primarily due to the U.S. involvement in the Vietnam War and other projects which had to be carried out with the U.S. role as "world policeman." When in 1971 President Richard Nixon worked out a new economic policy, brakes were applied to a prior free trade system. This caused other countries of the world to re-evaluate their own economic policies in respect to their own country's interest. The unfavorable monetary conditions in the West helped Korea to achieve an economic surge.

The oil shock which started in late 1973 forced the Korean economy to head down, though the recession was not as great as in other countries. Major industrial states recorded minus growth over two years.

Nation building through exports has been a major policy guideline of the Korean government from the early 1960's. During this first decade the annual export growth averaged 40% per year. This is truly a remarkable rate which can hardly be duplicated in world history. However, in 1973 the country's export attempts were adversely affected. Industrialization of Korea was crippled due to the lack of imported raw materials. Until 1973 one of the major accomplishments for the country was that exports always exceeded the yearly goals.

In 1975 Korea's exports fell under its target goal of six billion dollars (US) though it was still an increase of 15% over the previous year. However, Korean exports continued to snowball. In 1977 exports surpassed the ten billion dollar mark with the United States receiving 34% of total exports. The 1979 statistics show a total of over 14 billion dollars, which is a 14% increase over the previous year. Continuing effort has been made to further develop Korea's chemical and heavy industries. In 1973 following the dedication of the Pohang Iron and Steel Company five core industrial plants were built: a large shipyard in Ulsan, a copper plant in An'gang, a pig iron foundry in Pohang, a specialized steel plant in Yongdungpo and a heavy machine factory in Inchon. In addition many industrial centers developed, including a petro-

58

chemical complex in Ulsan, a copper refinery and an oil refinery at Onsan in
Kyongsang-namdo.

A large machinery industrial base
was developed in Changwon, Kyongsang-
namdo. A monumental industrial center
including Honam Oil and Dow Chemical
has developed in the Yosu area to the
far south. In addition to Hyundai Shipbuilding, one of the world's largest, at
Ulsan, the Daewoo Shipyards were
developed in 1978 on Koje Island. With
the opening in 1979 of the new east
coast expressway from Kangnung to
Pohang further development for industrialization is being planned for Kangwon-do. For some time the prospects for
discovery of oil off the Korean coast
have been good. Recent oil discoveries
in the Pohang area have further re-
confirmed to the world the bright
economic future of Korea. As far back
as 1968 a report from the U.N. Economic
Commission for Asia and the Far East
(ECAFE) made it clear that the geo-
logical structure of the ocean floor from
Pohang south had potentials for oil
similar to the Persian Gulf.

Prior to 1979 the *Saemaul* projects
have appreciably increased the income
of the average farmer. Starting in 1970
as a spiritual and educational renovating
campaign for rural communities, the
philosophy of the movement changed as
a result of the *Yushin* (revitalizing)
Movement in 1972. With the promulgation of the Constitution in
December, a new political order, referred
to as the *Yushin* System was born to
inaugurate the Fourth Republic.

The death of President Park Chung-
hee by an assassin's bullet brought an
end to the *Yushin* system. However, the
spirit of the *Saemaul Undong* continued.
The spirit of frugality and conservation
must be continued in daily activities in
order to overcome the economic difficulties of the 1980s. Under the *Saemaul
Undong* campaigns continue to urge
citizens to live within their means,
simplify various family rituals and
eliminate vanity and waste.

Though there was criticism raised by
intellectuals and urban dwellers, the

movement became a strong economic
drive for self-improvement with active
participation by the people. Beginning
with 1973 the *Yushin* Movement began
to stress projects which contributed to
boosting the income of the people.

Previously Koreans thought that
farmers were doomed to be poor and
the only way to get ahead was to go to
the big cities. Actually, farmers formerly
had little desire to push ahead.

Numerous other accomplishments
can be cited to further illustrate Korea's
continued economic growth. The "enterprise opening" program announced by
the government in May 1974, completion
of the Soyang Multipurpose Dam in
1973, four major river basin development programs, Asan Bay sea dike
completed in 1974, construction of the
Honam, Namhae, Yongdong and East
Coast expressways, modernization of
Inchon harbor in May 1974 and opening
of Korea's first subway in August 1974
are only a few.

However, with this remarkable progress problems were inevitably created.
These structural problems have become
particularily acute in recent years as
illustrated in the 1982 "curb-loan"
scandal involving members high in government and business. One serious problem
resulting from government efforts to
accelerate heavy and chemical industries
was increased inflationary pressure that
developed a vicious spiraling inflation.

A second serious problem had to do
with unbalanced growth among various
firms and industries. Government
favoritism caused certain aspects of the
economy to suffer. This resulted in a
third problem of weakening the com-
petitiveness of Korean industry. A
fourth problem is related to excessive
concentration of the population in large
urban centers and difficulty in adequately meeting the basic needs of
housing, education and utilities.

Another problem concerns the
deterioration in income distribution and
growing disparity in living standards of
different social groups. By 1980 the
top 20% of the population claimed
45.4 percent of the national income

Hyundai Shipbuilding at Ulsan ▷

and the lower 40% of the population claimed only 16.1 percent. The sixth and final problem is related to excess caused by rise of oil prices. Recession produced a sudden decline in demand and Korea may have produced an over-capacity.

But in spite of these serious problems the national will power did not falter in its steps toward economic development even with harassment from the north Korean communists. Amidst international economic turmoil the nation could still witness steady growth and this could not have been accomplished without the devoted efforts of the people.

On the economic front Korea's future still holds an image of a continuing struggle against the hard odds of inflation with short supply of natural resources and rising trade barriers. The galloping pace of growth has slowed to a walk over the last two years.

The government started sweeping campaigns to clear up irregularities and tighten discipline in the bureaucracy.

Increased efficiency and fair management have become a major policy objective of the government.

The government continues to view heavy and chemical industries as Korea's chief line of export. Stress will be laid on machinery, electronics, shipbuilding, petrochemicals, steel and fertilizer. Expansion of the Pohang iron and steel mill since 1973 has now placed Korea among the world's top ten countries in the production of steel. The production of POSCO for 1980 was 9.3 million tons. A massive plant to supply two hundred thousand tons of water to industries of Changwon Industrial Complex was finished. In 1980 Korea attained fourth place among the world's shipbuilding nations.

The nation's ten top export companies for 1979 include: Daewoo Industrial Co., Samsung Co. Ltd., Hyosung Corp., ICC, Bando Sangsa Co., Hyundai Corp., Ssang-yong Corp., Hanil Synthetic Fiber Industrial Co., Sunkyong Ltd., and Kumho and Co.

The number of tourists continues to

60

increase over the years to bring in foreign dollars. In 1975 only 640,000 foreign tourists visited Korea and spent some $140 million. By 1978 Korea surpassed the one million mark and by the following year realized 1.2 million tourists visiting the country. Effort was made to upgrade the tourist hotels to meet international standards. Korea now has over 130 tourist hotels with Seoul boasting seven deluxe hotels: the Hyatt Regency, the Sheraton-Walker Hill, the Lotte, the Silla, the Chosun and the Plaza. The Hilton Hotel

will be completed in the fall of 1983.

There are in addition three luxury hotels in Kyongju, two in Pusan and two on Cheju Island. By the end of 1980 there were almost 19,000 hotel rooms in Korea but there is still a demand for more. Following the assassination in 1979 there was an immediate slump in tourism for about a year. Now with the Asian Games and Summer Olympics in the future the tourist industry is optimistic about the 1980s. To help meet this increasing demand, six universities and fifteen

Ssangyong cement factory

colleges now offer majors in hotel management and related tourist activities.

In 1979 Korea hosted the PATA conference in Seoul and Kyongju City, the capital of the ancient Silla Dynasty. Over 3,000 delegates attended. As a major international tourist attraction the Pomun Lake Complex was completed near Kyongju City at a cost of $57 million.

In 1970 over 32 percent of the 55,000 tourist were Western with Japanese the second largest group next to Americans. However, in 1980 visitors from Asian regions comprised 77% of the total. This indicated that the nation's tourist market has been shifting from the Americas to the Asian region.

Due to the Summer Olympics of 1988 Korea is developing tremendous programs for the tourism industry. All aspects including transportation, hotels, recreation and sightseeing are being scutinized closely. Tourism is a promising industry and Korea has so much to offer. And apparently now the government is definitely planning to tap the nation's cultural resources.

Daewoo heavy industry factory

Centennial Year in Korean-American Relations

The relations began with mutual entanglement in the late 19th century, characterized by mistrust and ignorance; this unique partnership which binds Korea and America go back a century to 1882 and a treaty which formalized the improbable alliance that opened the "Hermit Kingdom" to the west and a variety of interchange with the United States.

The origin of official Korean-American relations dates to 1882 when the "Hermit Kingdom" of the Yi Dynasty first entered into a formal diplomatic relationship. It is unique that Korea decided that the United States would be the first foreign partner in international relations of equal nation-status that was not associated with the Sino-centric world view that Koreans had maintained for many centuries.

This Treaty of Amity and Commerce between the two nations, usually called the "Shufeldt Treaty," was signed at Chemulpo (Inchon) on May 22, 1882 by US Navy Commodore Robert W. Shufeldt and two Korean ministers plenipotentiary, Shin Hon and Kim Hong-jip.

At this time most Americans knew little about this distant "Land of Morning Calm," nor did Koreans know anything about *miguk* (Beautiful Country) as America is called. As the centennial year was marked, the relationship between the United States and Korea is still characterized by geographic distance, yet the people on both sides of the Pacific feel close psychologically.

The importance of the United States to Korea during this early period was simply to recognize another barbarian country to help balance the many barbarians clamoring for recognition, as Korea's isolation policy appeared no longer viable. The Chinese-Japanese rivalry, which followed the rise of the Meiji era in Japan, brought Korea into direct contact with the outside world.

America was basically interested in opening commercial doors in East Asia and Korea was a logical beginning.

Already two abortive American attempts to open ties with Korea through "gunboat diplomacy" had been shattered. In 1866 the *General Sherman*, an American merchant schooner, was burned with the entire crew and passengers killed, including a Scottish missionary.

The second clash took place on Kanghwa Island in 1871 when marines from the ship *USS Colorado* and four other ships captured Chojijin Fortress, resulting in 350 Koreans killed and 13 American deaths.

By 1873 the boy ruler King Kojong had reached maturity and assumed full rule from the *taewon-gun*, his father-in-law. King Kojong pursued a more flexible foreign policy, particularly toward the United States. Korea signed its first Western-style agreement with Japan in 1876.

China then decided that they must negate Japanese encroachment on the Korean peninsula. Encouraged by the great Chinese statesman, Li Hung-chang, Korea was persuaded to negotiate with the West to help contain Japanese designs on the country.

In the 1880s Commodore Shufeldt on the *USS Ticonderoga* had been sent to the Far East for the purpose of expanding US commercial interests and possibly writing treaties of friendship. Through the Chinese statesman Li, the

◁ *1982, Korea-USA centennial celebration, Inchon*

Koreans and Americans were brought together and, after two years of secret diplomacy and correspondence with Peking, Seoul and Washington, the 1882 Treaty of Amity and Commerce was signed and later ratified by Congress.

Encouraged by King Kojong's pro-American feelings, the United States dispatched Lucius H. Foote as its first envoy to Seoul on May 12, 1883. In reciprocation for prompt American action for the betterment of ties, King Kojong in August of the same year sent a seven-man friendship mission led by Min Yong-ik, Queen Min's nephew. The first Korean legation in Washington opened in January 1888 with Pak Chong-yang as first minister.

Possibly due to lack of territorial ambitions in Korea, the United States demonstrated a rather lukewarm attitude toward Korea, though Korea attempted many positive actions toward closer amity. In the rivalries for the domination of Korea between China, Japan and Russia, the American position was usually strict neutrality.

Major foreign policies under President Theodore Roosevelt changed dramatically as to Korea following the Russo-Japanese War. American envoy Horace Allen, who was a former Presbyterian missionary to Korea, found no sympathy in Roosevelt's pro-Japanese cabinet. The United States now supported Japan's domination of Korea as a means to check Russia's drive south.

At a time when Korea needed American help desperately from a treaty where it was promised, secret agreements were being made with Katsura, the Japanese Prime Minister, and William H. Taft, US Secretary of War, which sanctioned Japan's occupation of Korea in return for Japanese disinvolvement in the Philippines.

Through this Taft-Katsura Agreement the 23 years of official relations between the United States and Korea were finally severed in 1905. With forced annexation in 1910, the Korean peninsula receded into near oblivion until the end of World War II. The people of Korea lived under a bitter Japanese colonial rule for over thirty-five years. During this period the Korean people's desperate cries for liberation went unheeded following America's literal "sell out" of the country.

When Korea received independence in 1945, Korean-American relations were renewed. At the time when President Franklin D. Roosevelt and his military advisors were planning post war strategy, Korea was still considered unimportant, though the Cairo Declaration of 1943 provided that Korea would become free as an independent nation.

Alarmed by Russia's encroachment into northern Korea, Washington, hurriedly and without thought, selected the 38th parallel as a temporary demarcation line to facilitate the surrender of the Japanese forces in Korea. Announcing its intention to repatriate Japanese south of the 38th parallel, the United States opted to curb Soviet occupation of Korea, though it had no concrete plan for American occupation of Korea at that time.

General John Hodges with the American Occupation Forces to Korea found a nonexistent economy with no industry, barren hills, infertile farms and fisheries exhausted by exploitation and a people brutalized by unchecked colonialism. Unfamiliar culture with language barriers in addition to lack of experience and training in military government caused serious difficulty and aroused suspicion and discontent.

The dismal failure of the joint American-Soviet Commission responsible for unifying the Korean peninsula was another setback when they indefinitely adjourned in May, 1946. Shortly thereafter, the UN General Assembly adopted a resolution calling for a United Nations supervised election throughout Korea.

However, the Soviets denied UN entry to northern Korea and as a result the Republic of Korea was established in the south on August 15, 1948. In defiance of the UN resolution, the Soviets established the Democratic People's Republic of Korea with its capital in Pyongyang, thus splitting the nation in two.

Because of American lukewarm

Robert Wilson Shufeldt IV, grandson of the Commodore (bust at right), at the Korea- ▷
USA centennial ceremony, May 22, 1982, Inchon

commitment and failure to perceive the real threat of communism in the north, the Republic of Korea was totally unprepared for the communist aggression launched on June 25, 1950. What began as an arbitrary demarcation line solidified into a political barrier and center of world tension.

Before the Armistice Agreement was signed on July 27, 1953, over 36,000 American lives were lost, with estimated civilian deaths in the millions. The contemporary Korean-American relationship was born and nurtured in the dark days of the Korean War. Korean-American friendship was transformed into "bonds born with blood" through their joint efforts over the years to resist the communist threat.

American economic assistance and emergency relief efforts helped to raise the country from the tragic ashes of war and later became the impetus for Korea's unprecedented economic growth two and three decades later. Korea's rapid recovery and development was unpredictable. Exports grew from $50 million to $21 billion, with a per capita GNP from $80 to more than $1,700. In the 1950s few would have anticipated the development of an enormous and mutually beneficial investment and trade relationship between Korea and the United States.

In the three decades following the Korean War, Korean-American relations have become solid and constructive, with a major emphasis on security. Close cooperative efforts based on the Mutual Defense Treaty have played a vital role in maintaining peace on the Korean peninsula.

The Centennial Anniversary of the opening of diplomatic relations between Korea and the United States has special meaning in view of the numerous historic events of the last century. A mature friendship of interdependence and partnership has developed, and now Korea's economy is inseparably interwoven with the United States as its 12th largest trading partner.

During the Centennial Week in May, 1982 the grandson and great grandson of Commodore Robert W. Shufeldt arrived in Korea to attend the numerous ceremonies. They assisted in the unveiling of a bronze bust of the Commodore in the port of Inchon (Chemulpo) where the treaty was signed.

Though the world is shrinking in many aspects, still the Pacific Ocean is a vast expanse that separates the two countries. Equally pronounced are the different cultural origins which may seem almost insurmountable. Yet the relationship between Korea and America continues to grow with mutual determination and a common dedication for freedom, peace and prosperity.

Chapter II.
Seoul the Capital

◁ *Ch'angdok Palace, Seoul*

Historic City Within a Wall

Established one hundred years before Columbus discovered the Americas, Seoul is an ancient city by New World standards but compared with the antiquity of Korean history, Seoul is a relatively new city spanning only five hundred years . . . . now a city of ten million people.

For more than five hundred years Seoul has served as the capital city of Korea. Before the modern era this city was called Hanyang, the seat of Yi Dynasty government from 1392 to 1910. The name "Seoul" itself is a native Korean word meaning "capital" and cannot be written in Chinese calligraphy. Probably the word was derived from the ancient Silla word *sorabol* which was the name given to the early kingdom founded in the Kyongju valley by Pak Hyokkose in 57 B.C.

When King T'aejo founded the Yi Dynasty in 1392, his first aspiration was to build his capital near the present city of Taejon below the slopes of Kyeryong Mountain, but the king was advised to move to the north bank of the Han River called Hanyang because the Kyeryong-san region was reserved for the Chong family and its future dynasty's capital. There are many interesting legends relating to the founding of the capital and the close association of King T'aejo with Priest Muhak. The famous Priest Muhak was a geomantic prophet and many of his prophecies came true in ensuing years.

A ten-mile wall was built around Seoul which contained nine gates; five of the city gates remain and have been repaired by the city government. Also many of the ancient palaces and gardens still exist to provide for tourists numerous hours of pleasure as the ancient structures with their many intricate architectural designs are viewed, studied and photographed.

Seoul is truly a city of contrasts. The din and rush of traffic past modern skyscrapers seem strangely out of place as only a block away a lazy stream meanders under a stone bridge many centuries old. You rest in a palace garden while the late afternoon shadows accentuate the eerie stone face of the guardian spirit of the waters. The great South Gate sits with stoic majesty in the center of a swirl of traffic.

At the turn of the century Seoul was no more than a sleepy town with thatched-roof houses and then a population of about 150,000. Before the Korean War the estimated population was about 500,000 people. In 1953 Seoul was still a mass of rubble, pathetic to see. The term "Phoenix City" has been given to Seoul for out of the ashes caused by four invasion armies sweeping through Seoul's streets emerged one of Asia's most modern cities, clean and delightful. The population has leaped to almost ten million. In 1974 the country's first subway through the center of Seoul was opened. Korea became the third nation in the Orient to develop a subway system.

Seoul was once a city for kings. But now the capital has become the hub of the entire nation while its rich culture is displayed and noted every day by increasing numbers of tourists. Seoul has always been the center for educational opportunities, and aspiring men looking for professional preparation and leadership. Living in Seoul still engenders personal prestige and so throughout the

◁ *Restored city wall, northeast Seoul*

centuries the young and old would migrate to Seoul if possible. From these converging people have come the chief characters of Korea's historical drama lasting over five hundred years of Yi Dynasty rule.

Into Seoul's rich history, a heritage has been woven which is evidenced by the palaces, shrines and monuments still standing throughout the city. For the serious student of Korean history or the casual sightseer there is in Seoul a wealth of lore and knowledge about Korea and its people. There are few cities in the world, much less capitals, where the very new and the ancient exist side by side in perfect harmony for one to enjoy.

Today we find Seoul a fully modern metropolis with seven hotels classified as deluxe, meeting international standards. Just a few steps from the major hotels in the center of the city is the Toksu Palace which is now a public park. The ancient tile-roofed throne hall and annex buildings where the king once received foreign envoys stand near two Grecian-style buildings that might have come from Versailles, an example of Seoul's unique blend of old and new.

In the National Museum located on the grounds of Kyongbok Palace a visitor can see priceless treasures of Korea's antiquity. The *5000 Years of Korean Art* exhibition which began a two-year tour of the U.S. in 1979 displayed a few of the numerous objects on exhibit at the National Museum of Seoul and the four branch museums in Kyongju, Kongju, Puyo and Kwangju.

Also nearby in the Kyongbok Palace is the National Folklore Museum. If a visitor to Korea is unable to see the Folk Village near Suwon then it is highly recommended that the National Folklore Museum be visited.

East of the main palace grounds is the Ch'angdok Palace and the famous Secret Gardens, a fairyland of intertwining paths linking wooded slopes, lotus ponds and pleasure pavilions. Always bustling with people and the center of recreation during the cherry-blossom season is Ch'anggyongwon with its municipal zoo and amusement park.

For those with classical tastes, Seoul offers a variety of symphony concerts, operas and recitals by local and visiting musicians, as well as special tearooms where recorded music from huge disc collections may be enjoyed. Visitors should not neglect to take the opportunity to visit the National Theater and Institute of Classical Music on South Mountain. Here traditional as well as modern programs are frequently performed for the general public. As a center for the performing arts of Seoul the new Sejong Cultural Center opened in 1978 as one the largest auditoriums in Asia.

A ride to the peak of South Mountain (Nam-san) by cable car and up the elevator of Namsan Tower for a panoramic view of the city is a short adventure, while a leisurely tour over the scenic Skyway Drive of Pugak Mountain will again provide unsurpassed pleasurable memories as one gazes over this vast city of Seoul with its many contrasts. If children are in your group a visit to Children's Park will easily provide numerous hours of pleasure and enjoyment for both the young and old. Excellent science displays and botanical gardens are available.

Korea House which was recently renovated is located along the lower slope of South Mountain off Taegye-ro and is a cultural center for foreigners to promote insight into the beauty of Korean tradition and customs. Operated by private management, traditional Korean music, dance and drama are provided six days a week. An excellent buffet of Korean food gives the tourist or newcomer to Korea an opportunity to sample typical Korean dishes. As the facilities are often crowded it is recommended that reservations be made well in advance. Korea House offers a chance to glimpse a "slice of tradition" of old Korea.

The 1980 publication of *Art Treasures of Seoul* is highly recommended for its numerous pictorial scenes of the capital city. This and many other publications are on sale at Korea House.

Seoul city wall in winter ▷

South Gate (National Treasure No. 1)

Downtown Seoul with South Mountain in background

Independence Arch in western Seoul

The Palaces and Seoul's Heritage

Seoul's special lure and charm are its palaces with its traditionally classic breath-taking architecture, representing a colorful history of turmoil during 500 years. Whether it comes from the silence of winter's snow-laden tile roofs or during a congested autumn Sunday afternoon . . . . hidden paths among painfully silent garden walls or a bustling courtyard before the great throne room . . . . the palaces of Seoul, the city's major attractions, provide a glimpse of Korea's traditional past before submersion into modernization.

For the average tourist with minimal time to spend in Korea, a half day visit to one of the palaces is highly recommended. The palaces are the most obvious sightseeing attractions in the capital and fortunately all are conveniently located near the downtown center. For a brief moment a foreign visitor may catch glimpses of Korea's magnificent heritage from the worn paths leading by intricately patterned wall murals or from under the clay figures which sit in eternal vigilance, warding off evil, on roof ridges.

The palaces still continue to be a source of enjoyment to Koreans who frequent the park-like grounds throughout the year. Here you will meet the people in an informal setting . . . . a people who are quick to laugh, frank and willing to become your friends. What better place than within the palaces to make an acquaintance? The spirit of the Korean people will begin to show, a people proud of their heritage, progressive and willing to keep it but also willing to share it with you if interest is shown.

Kyongbok: Palace of Shining Happiness

When Hanyang (Seoul) became Korea's capital city established by Yi T'aejo in 1392, Kyongbok Palace was built to be the residence of the king and hub of dynastic power for the Yi family. Serving Korean rulers for two hundred years, Kyongbok Palace was burned during the Japanese Hideyoshi invasion of 1592, not by the enemy but by Korean slaves who wished to destroy the official records of their serfdom. The Palace of "Shining Happiness" was then left in ruins for over 270 years. In 1867 it was rebuilt by the regent Taewon-gun for his second son, Kojong, who became 26th ruler of Korea. Using the old palace plans, buildings were then reconstructed on the old foundation stones left on the site over the centuries.

After Queen Min's murder in 1895 at her private villa in the palace, King Kojong and his son fled in a woman's palanquin to the Russian Legation. The palace was never again used as an official residence. After the Japanese annexed Korea in 1910, all but ten of the five hundred buildings that once formed Kyongbok Palace were torn down. In 1926 a new capitol building was erected on the palace grounds in front of the throne hall while Kwanghwa-mun, the great south gate of the palace, was moved to the east wall.

In 1969 Kwanghwa-mun was restored and then returned to its original location in front of the capitol building, though it is now entirely constructed in concrete rather than wood. One minor change, reflecting a modern trend, is that the name plaque on the gate is

◁ *Tonhwa-mun, main gate to Ch'angdok Palace, Seoul (Treasure No. 383)*

The lotus pond of Hyangwon and multistoried Koryo pagoda (National Treasure No. 86) are popular attractions in Kyongbok Palace, Seoul

Kyonghoe-ru and Koryo pagoda (National Treasure No. 100); Kyongbok Palace, Seoul

Koryo pudo for Chingong (Treasure No. 365)

Silla pagoda (National Treasure No. 99)

written in *han'gul* and not in Chinese characters, the only major gate of the city where this has been done. This calligraphy was done by the late President Park Chung-hee.

In front of the Kwanghwa-mun stand two large stone *haet'ae* which are remarkable mythical beasts, having become a symbol of justice. They can tell right from wrong, destroy evil and also have the ability of eating fire. When King T'aejo initially built Kyongbok Palace he was warned by court geomancers that Kwanak Mountain, located across the Han River, was exerting a fire influence on the palace. One way to counteract this evil was to place the *haet'ae* before the palace. This, of course, was done.

The palace is now entered by the east gate after passing the busy intersection where the remains of one of two corner watchtowers stand forlornly isolated from the palace wall. The west tower was destroyed in 1908. Inside the entrance gate a majestic thirteen-storied intricately sculptured pagoda of late Koryo greets the visitor. It was built in 1348 in honor of a royal wedding at Kyongch'on Temple near Kaesong, the former capital of the Koryo Dynasty.

In a spacious stone paved courtyard enclosure is the main throne hall called Kunjong-jon (Hall of Government by Restraint). Around the corridors are many stone and bronze remnants of tablets and images brought for safekeeping from many historic sites throughout Korea. The tablet erected in 569 by King Chinhung of Silla was brought from Pi-bong, a peak near Seoul. Now on display and listed as National Treasure No. 3, this treasured preunification Silla stone contains some of the oldest written inscriptions found in Korea.

To the west is magnificent double storied Kyonghoe-ru, a unique pleasure pavilion by a large lotus pond. Chogyong-jon, where the Dowager Cho lived until her death in 1890, exemplifies a typical residential palace villa. Intricate patterns and scenic designs of clay and brick still remain on the compound walls. Hamhwa-dang was originally used as an audience reception hall for foreigners.

The pavilion of Hyangwon located in the center of an island joined by an ornate wooden bridge portrays a unique charm and innate beauty during all seasons. Beyond this pond is a Western style building often used as a gallery and now designated as a folklore museum. It is located on the site of the former Konch'ong Villa which served as the private residence of the king and his family. It was here that Queen Min was murdered and a stone marker was erected in 1954 at the site of the folklore museum. Now many stone tablets, pagodas and lanterns which are designated treasures are located throughout the palace grounds. Most were moved from remote temple sites during the Japanese occupation to help beautify the bare palace grounds after so many buildings were demolished.

Now Kyongbok Palace is a beautiful park region with pleasant shady surroundings, though it has lost its former regal spirit and grandeur. Nevertheless, the heritage of this country's rich culture and proud achievements can be sensed in the few remaining structures of this greatest of Yi Dynasty palaces.

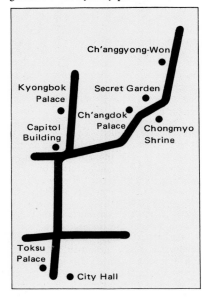

Ch'angdok: Palace of Illustrious Virtue

Ch'angdok Palace, which was originally constructed in 1405 as an eastern detached palace, is the best preserved of Seoul's five palaces. It is now considered the favorite for most tourists. The other palaces are Kyongbok, Toksu and Ch'anggyong, while the fifth palace of Kyonghui (known as the Mulberry Palace), formerly located near the West Gate of Seoul has completely disappeared. Originally Ch'angdok Palace was smaller and inferior to the central Kyongbok Palace. This palace was also burned during the Japanese Hideyoshi invasion of 1592 but was rebuilt in 1611 with more color and a slightly different style of architecture. It was used as the royal residence until the construction of Kyongbok Palace in 1867. The main throne hall, Injong-jon, was burned in 1803 and rebuilt the following year.

After renovation in 1907 Ch'angdok Palace was used by Sunjong (27th king) until his death in 1926. Queen Yun retired to Naksonjae, an annex of Ch'angdok, until her death in 1966. Naksonjae is now being used by Princess Yi Pangja, wife of the last Crown Prince Yi Un, who died in 1970. Also Princess Tokhye, daughter of Kojong (26th king), lives in retirement at Naksonjae.

Covering over 105 acres of land, Ch'angdok Palace can be divided into four major areas: the central palace buildings, Secret Garden, Villa of Naksonjae, and Sonwon-jon, a pavilion for royal birthdays.

The classic entrance gate to Changdok Palace, called Tonhwa-mun, is possibly the oldest original gate in the city as it is now thought that Tonhwa-mun survived the conflagration of 1592. A stone bridge is crossed immediately upon entering the palace. Called Kumch'on (Beautiful Silky Stream) it is believed that the reformists in the 1884 coup hid under this bridge.

East of the main throne hall is a smaller audience chamber called Sonjong-jon, the only palace building covered by a blue-glazed tile roof typical of the earlier Koryo period. The halls of Huijong-dang and Taejo-jon were rebuilt in 1920 using materials from buildings moved from the Kyongbok Palace. This residential portion is semi-European in style and furnishings. Taejo-jon is different from others as it has no central ridge roof beam as do the other palace buildings. Taejo-jon was used as sleeping rooms for the royal monarch: Curiously symbolic, the intent was to prevent any birds from perching on the roof beam, thereby degrading the royalty sleeping below.

Naksonjae is located east of the main palace buildings. Behind these walls Yi Dynasty history lingers on as the few remaining occupants provide a living link between modern and traditional Korea. Naksonjae was first constructed in 1846 by order of Honjong (24th king) for his concubine, Kim Kyong-bin, who was then fourteen. It was to be later used as a retirement home for queens. Queen Yun, the last queen of Korea and wife of King Sunjong, lived here until her death on February 3, 1966. The last crown prince, Yi Un (Yongch'in-wang),

Wall designs, Naksonjae, Ch'angdok Palace

passed away behind these walls on May 1, 1970. The private entrance to Nakson-jae Villa was changed in 1979 to a small gate east of Tonhwa-mun.

Behind Ch'angdok Palace is the tranquil woodland called the Secret Gardens (*piwon*) covering 78 acres of hills. From 1977 to 1979 the Secret Garden was closed to the general public. Now one can only enter by scheduled tours with guides. Further information can be obtained through tourist agencies or hotels.

During the Yi Dynasty *piwon* was reserved for the royal family and palace women. Forty-four pleasure buildings are scattered among the myriad ponds, bridges and streams of this royal park. Throughout the year the seasonal changes are mirrored in the placid pools, while fanciful pavilions continue to enthrall all ages. Tales have been tattled through the years concerning the prodigal ruler Yongsan-gun and the unbelievable orgies he held behind these garden walls. Entertainments held in the Secret Garden

would feature graceful dancers who would perform along the terraces and walls beside the ponds.

The first cluster of buildings is called Yonghwa-dang, with Chunhap-ru and the unique "Fish Water Gate," supporting a heavy roof by only two pillars. Over the hill is Yon'gyong-dang, a villa built in 1828 in the style of a typical *yangban* villa which was permitted to have an area of 99 *kan* by law. Considered the most picturesque pond within the Secret Garden is Pando-ji, famous for its shape, likened to the peninsula of Korea. It was first envisioned by Injo (16th king) in 1644 as a fishing hideaway.

Situated west of the Secret Garden and reached after entering an impressive gate and tree-lined path is another cluster of palace buildings called Sonwon-jon. The structures came originally from Kyonghui Palace. Previously the portraits of the kings were on display and their respective birthdays were recognized with honor. Normally the compound of Sonwon-jon is not open to the public.

Chuhap-ru

Yon'gyong-dang

Puyong-jong

Ch'anggyong: Palace of Bright Rejoicing

Now a delightful park once containing Seoul City's zoo and an amusement facility, only a few buildings remain which suggest that this area served as a detached palace during the Yi Dynasty. The main entrance is through Honghwa-mun opposite the Seoul National University Hospital. During the Koryo Dynasty King Sukchong tried to establish a second capital in Seoul and constructed a palace on this site, thus giving Ch'anggyong the oldest history of any of Seoul's palaces.

The main hall of Myongjong-jon is single roofed and small, but the oldest, as it was built in 1483. Most of the other buildings were rebuilt in 1833. A botanical garden was established on the grounds in 1907 by order of the king. The title was changed from *kung* (palace) to *won* (garden) at this time. The Japanese authorities developed Ch'anggyong-won into a zoo with the subtle intent to weaken the influence of the king, by humbling him in turning over his domain to animals and birds. However, the wooded area of Ch'anggyong-won was made into one of the finer zoos of Asia and was greatly expanded ever, after the war years. This park is well worth a visit, especially in the spring, as the many paths are lined with flowering cherry trees. The Seoul City's new zoo will open in 1984.

Toksu: Palace of Virtuous Longevity

These familiar gardens and palace buildings situated between the capitol building and South Gate in the center of the city do not exhibit the true traditional style of a Yi Dynasty palace, yet these remaining historic buildings will provide a rewarding photographic afternoon for any visitor. In the Toksu Palace the five hundred years of Yi Dynasty

Honghwa-mun, main gate to Ch'anggyong Palace (Treasure No. 384)

Sokjo-jon and gardens, Toksu Palace

rule drew to a painful and tragic end as Japanese domination finally resulted in annexation in 1910.

Toksu Palace was originally a royal villa built to appease a grandson of Sejo (7th king) who was passed over twice for king. This Prince Wolsan was loved and respected by all, including his younger brother who became Songjong (9th king). He was an avid reader and patron of the arts. After the Hideyoshi invasion Sonjo (14th king) returned to Seoul and took up residence within this villa as the other palaces had been burned.

Following the murder of his queen, Kojong (26th king) fled in February 1896 to the Russian Legation located behind this palace. He remodeled the palace and finally moved in to make it the seat of government. After abdicating in 1907 he also used these buildings for his retirement. During this period Sunjong (27th king) renamed the palace *toksu* to honor his father Kojong. Hamnyong-jon contains the royal bedroom where King Kojong died on January 21, 1919. The palace was closed until 1933.

In 1909 Sokjo-jon was completed. The architecture is Renaissance in style. Henry W. Davidson, a British businessman, supervised the construction. The daughter of Davidson later married Horace G. Underwood, now serving the Presbyterian Mission at Yonsei University. Retired King Kojong used Sokjo-jon to entertain ranking foreign diplomats. After World War II it served as headquarters for the American-Soviet Commission for the Unification of Korea. From 1955 it was used as the National Museum until 1972 when the museum was moved to the new site in the Kyongbok Palace.

The former museum buildings are still being used for various art exhibits throughout the year.

Sogo-dang, Toksu Palace, downtown Seoul

Chongmyo: Shrine of Royal Ancestors

In a secluded garden southeast of Ch'angdok Palace in the heart of Seoul lies Chongmyo, housing the ancestral tablets of Yi Dynasty kings and their queens. It is here that one can visualize the pomp and the ceremony of the Confucian style memorial services held five times yearly during the dynasty period. Recently the ceremonies are being reenacted every year by the Yi Dynasty Association in an attempt to keep alive the culture of this earlier period. Traditional colorful clothing and ancient instruments are used in this ceremony which is open to the public.

On the well-forested grounds are two buildings, Chong-jon and Yongnyong-jon. The more spacious main shrine of Chong-jon is where the tablets of eighteen most significant Yi rulers are enshrined from T'aejo (1st king) to Sunjong (27th king), the last ruler, who abdicated in 1910. On October 24, 1968 the tablet of Queen Yun was officially enshrined in Chong-jon. Food and three chalicer of wine were offered to the spirits represented by each tablet.

This smaller shrine building of Chongmyo, called Yongnyong-jon, is architecturally different as the ridge beam is not continuous. The higher portion in the center houses the four ancestors of the dynasty's founder, while on either side are twelve minor rulers and their queens. (Some were designated crown princes but actually did not rule.) The buildings were burned in 1592 and rebuilt in 1608. In 1972 the tablet of the last crown prince, Yi Un (Yongch'in-wang), was placed in this smaller shrine building. Chongmyo was first opened to the public in 1960.

The 1982 edition of *Palaces of Seoul* is recommended for those wishing to know more about the palaces. The 128 color plates, album of old royal photos, maps and charts make this book the most popular concerning palaces of Seoul.

Confucian ceremony at Chongmyo honoring Yi royalty, Seoul

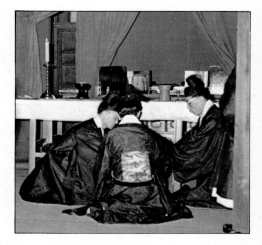

The family descendants of the Chonju Yi clan gather for the royal Confucian ceremony held yearly at the Shrine of Chongmyo, Seoul

*Yi Ku, royal family head (above) and
brocade crane pattern on ceremonial
official's robe, Chongmyo, Seoul (right)
Ceremonial instruments used during
Confucian ritual, Seoul (next two pages)*

李垠

Crown Prince Yi Un (Yongch'in-wang) in 1935 (1897-1970)

Meeting Korean Royalty

Prince Kyu Lee is a thin, soft-spoken man with glasses and a personable smile. Should you meet him you would be surprised to learn that this man might have been the 29th king of Korea if the Japanese had not forced his uncle King Sunjong to abdicate in 1910. As an American-trained architect from MIT we find him a thoroughly modernized Westerner who lives in two worlds, that of rigid ancestral tradition as well as elasticized economic and social fluidity.

Let's look for a moment at the ancestral home located behind the walls of Naksonjae (Mansion of Joy and Goodness), an annex mansion adjacent to Ch'angdok Palace where Korean dynastic history has come to a slow halt. Here the few remaining occupants now provide a living link between progressive Korea and the traditional Yi Dynasty which has left an indelible mark over the last five hundred years. This is where Princess Yi Pangja lives in retirement. She is the widow of the last Crown Prince Yi Un who passed away in 1970.

Down the rambling corridors the echoes grow faint and almost oppressive, yet in the picturesque gardens of forsythia, azaleas and cherry, birds still twitter among the eaves of the pavilions and numerous gates which join the three

Princess Yi Pangja in her home at Naksonjae, Ch'angdok Palace

98

court gardens of the villa of Naksonjae.

Until only a few years ago three old and fragile court ladies called *sanggung* might still be noticed slipping in and out of the front gate of Naksonjae. They once served Yun-bi, the last queen of Korea, who passed away in 1966. The eldest *sang-gung*, Kim Myong-gil, began her training in 1906 when she was only thirteen and entered the palace with Queen Yun who was then a twelve-year-old bride. In traditional court dress for mourning, the son of the last Crown Prince led the other members of the Dynasty Association in the customary ceremonies for the departed queen. She was buried beside her husband King Sunjong, east of Seoul at Kumgok.

Queen Yun was born in Myong-dong, Seoul. Her elder brother who studied in the United States had obtained a doctoral degree. One younger sister of Queen Yun married Yu Ok-kyom who held the office of Education Minister and president of Choson Christian College (now Yonsei University). Queen Yun possessed an unusual aptitude for languages, being fluent in Chinese, Japanese and English. She also studied piano and voice. The tragic story of the heroic hardships she bore during the Korean War portray the brave and courageous spirit of this gentle woman. She was permitted to return to Naksonjae in 1960 and often received visitors during her final six years of life.

Also living in Naksonjae in quiet seclusion is Princess Tokhye, the only living child of a Korean king, daughter of King Kojong's seventh wife, Yang Pongyong-dang. Princess Tokhye was born in 1912. Forced to marry a Japanese aristocrat in 1928, she had one daughter who died following World War II. After liberation she was given permission to return to Korea and now at the age of seventy has found a place of peace for her remaining years.

The addition in front of Naksonjae was built by the Japanese in 1927 and is now the official home of Princess Pangja (Masako), the mother of Kyu Lee (Yi Ku). The story of this amazing woman is told in her autobiography *The World Is One,* in which she relates how as a Japanese princess she woke up one morning to read in the papers that she was to marry a Korean prince. Princess Masako's personal happiness was sacrificed for political expediency and she was powerless to resist. Born of noble lineage, she had been considered as a possible bride for the crown prince of Japan, but suddenly at the age of seventeen she was plunged into the maelstrom of political intrigue.

Her husband was Yongch'in-wang (Yi Un), younger half-brother to King Sunjong, who had abdicated a decade before. Their first child died suddenly and tragically on a state visit from Japan to Korea in 1922. Their second son, Kyu, was born and educated in Japan. In 1950 he departed for the United States where he completed his master's degree in architecture at MIT, eventually became a naturalized U.S. citizen, and married Miss Julia Mullock.

The paramount desire of Kyu Lee's father, Yongch'in-wang, was to return to Korea, his homeland. Though the dynasty had ended he had been given the title of Crown Prince because King Sunjong had no children. In 1963 the Korean government gave permission for Yi Un (Yongch'in-wang) to come to Korea with his family.

Tragically, Yongch'in-wang returned to his homeland too late. He was an invalid and had to be confined to the hospital for the next seven years. A few hours before his death on May 1, 1970 the Crown Prince was taken to Naksonjae. The Crown Prince and his wife Pangja had recently observed their fiftieth wedding anniversary only two days previously.

At the age of eighty-two when most people are enjoying retirement Princess Pangja (Masako) is still active in promoting vocational education among the physically handicapped of her adopted country by means of the *Myonghui Won* an association she started. In 1972 the Korean government conferred the Order of National Merit on her for her achievements in this field of social work.

Yi Ku, son of Yi Un, in Chongmyo Confucian ritual, Seoul ▷

Countryside Near Seoul

Seoul has a wealth of history and culture and even now beyond the gates of Seoul tradition and custom still abound at tomb sites and temples. For the energetic hiker mountain peaks touch the blue sky almost within the city limits where crumbling walls of a dynasty's fortifications meander over the sharp ridges. When one knows what's there . . . . there is so much to see with such little time.

For those willing only to sample the rich culture outside the city walls the average tourist agency will accommodate by providing tours to the better known attractions. For more detailed information with maps to direct one to little known and unique historical sites in the Seoul vicinity the two-volume book *Through Gates of Seoul* is recommended for your pleasure.

Suwon is the provincial capital for Kyonggi Province, and is also a city walled as a fortress (pop. 200,000). Located only thirty miles south of Seoul, its massive stone gates are picturesquely stark against the clear blue skies. An unusual water gate and numerous pavilions add historical luster to this rapidly industrializing city. Near Suwon is Yongju-sa, a historically impressive temple which houses a National Treasure (Bell: No. 120). Nearby are two royal tombs belonging to the tragic "coffin king" Sado Seja and his son Chongjo (22nd king) who ruled in the 18th century. King Chongjo's desire was to move the capital from Seoul to Suwon. He was responsible for fortifying the city. Near the Suwon exit on the Seoul-Pusan Expressway is the Korean Folk Village. To experience the rich heritage of this beautiful country, a trip to this village is a must.

There are two major mountain fortresses near Seoul, Namhan-sansong (South Fortress) and Pukhan-sansong (North Fortress). South Fortress can be reached by a paved road 23 miles southeast of Seoul, beyond Walker Hill

toward Kwangju. Believed to have been used as a fortress site as early as the 1st century by the founder of Paekche, the city's present walls and gates were completed in 1626 as a protective measure against the Manchus. Along the five-mile wall are seventeen small gates. The east gate and west gate are still in excellent condition and now easily reached by a paved road. In 1636 Injo (16th king) with his court fled to this fortress and finally surrendered after a 45-day siege. The view from the peak is spectacular on a clear day as it overlooks the Han River valley.

North Fortress can be reached by taking the Munsan highway past the West Gate circle of Seoul. The wall encircles the large impressive peaks north of Seoul which are called Samgak-san (Three Corner Mountain). Many hiking courses crisscross these peaks but because of military restrictions in some areas it would be best to gain hiking permission first through police authorities. Normally the southern sides of these peaks are more accessible than the northern sides. Except for the West Gate, most of the eleven remaining gates are reached only after a hard climb. The view from the wall is especially rewarding. The present five-mile wall, still meandering over ridges and jagged cliffs, was constructed in 1711 by Sukchong (19th king). Many temples and temple sites abound on the slopes of these mountains.

A third famous fortress area for Seoul is Kanghwa Island, fifth largest

◁ *Silla pagoda near Ulsan (Treasure No. 382)*

island in Korea, located at the mouth of the Han River only 25 miles west of Seoul. Kanghwa Island is reached by a well-paved highway. Buses depart hourly from the Shinch'on Rotary in Seoul. Historical accounts of this island span the entire spectrum of Korean existence, from the period of Tan'gun to the opening of Korea to the Western world. Dolmens, pagodas and fire signal towers can be seen near Kanghwa City, another walled town with two remaining city gates.

Chondung-sa, the main temple on the island, is the center of recreational as well as cultural interest. A one-mile wall, consisting of four gates encompassing this temple valley, was legendarily built by the sons of Tan'gun who established Korea's first kingdom four thousand years ago. For the enthusiastic hiker, a climb to Mani-san to see Tan'gun's altar, or a shorter hike to Chongsu-sa on the other side of the mountain, will offer unparalleled coastal and island scenery.

Within the nearer vicinity of Seoul among the rolling hills are many royal tombs which provide a fascinating study of architectural design and transitory culture. Tombs are well suited for picnic pleasures on a sunny day. The tomb regions with spacious grassy areas are generally well forested with evergreens. Often on holidays and weekends during the spring and fall tomb sites ring with laughter and gaiety from picnic crowds.

The two scenic tomb regions of Kumgok and Tonggu-nung in the countryside northeast of Seoul offer the most concentrated assemblage of royal Yi Dynasty burial mounds, from the oldest to the most recent. Both of these favorite recreation sites can be reached easily by a paved road. King T'aejo, founder of the dynasty, was buried at Tonggu-nung in 1408, while the last two kings, Kojong and Sunjong, were buried in the twentieth century at Kumgok. As recently as 1970 the last crown prince of Korea and son of King Kojong, Yi Un (Yongch'inwang), as well as Samch'uk-dang Kim-ssi, the last concubine of Kojong (26th king), were buried with

Suwon City's fortress remnants (Treasure No. 403)

royal ceremonial tribute within the vicinity of Kumgok.

Other tomb sites that are fairly close to Seoul are the West Five Tombs (So-o-nung) and West Three Tombs (So-sam-nung).

So-o-nung is closer to Seoul and has recently been well developed for sightseers. The rolling hills of this area are ideal for picnics. There is a charge to enter the tomb grounds. The famous Sukchong (19th king), considered to be the fortress-building king of the dynasty, and his two queens are buried at So-o-nung.

South of the Han River near the Yongdong Bridge and beyond are two other major tomb areas near Seoul (Son-nung and Chong-nung; In-nung and Hon-nung). Both sites can be reached by paved roads. Taegang-nung east of Seoul near the Army Military Academy is also a popular tomb.

Further out from the city in the National Forest district of Kwang-nung (20 miles) is the tomb site of the infamous ruler Sejo (7th king), a younger son of Sejong (4th king), who ursurped the dynasty's throne in a blood bath of political rivalry peaked by the tragic murder of the boy King Tanjong, a nephew, who had been exiled to the mountainous interior of Yongwol. In the Kwang-nung forest is the temple of Pongson-sa which was burned during the Korean conflict but has now been rebuilt.

Yoju, which can be reached by the Seoul-Kangnung Expressway within one hour, is the site for the tomb of King Sejong (1418-1450). This fourth king is considered to be the greatest of all 27 rulers of the dynasty. He was grandson of the dynasty's founder and third son of T'aejong (3rd king). His brilliant rule was marked by many scientific inventions and high literary development climaxed by the *han'gul* (Korean alphabet) invention. His tomb, called Yong-nung, is located two miles out of Yoju town on an extremely picturesque hillside of woodland and streams. Also buried here is Hyojong (17th king).

Located at Yoju, the large temple of Silluk-sa which dates to the Silla period

is one of the major temples near Seoul. On the premises are seven designated cultural treasures which include tablets, lanterns, pagodas and buildings. From a bluff near this temple a breathtaking panoramic view of the South Han River adds a pleasant ingredient to this pleasing temple site.

Eight miles from Yoju is the abandoned temple site of Kodal-sa where on the hillside still remains a large sculptured stupa now listed as National Treasure No. 4. The massive turtle head and four writhing dragons exquisitely sculptured in stone are truly works of art. Nearby in the fields are three other designated cultural treasures. On the outskirts of Yoju town is the ancestral home of Queen Min who was ruthlessly murdered in 1895 in the Kyongbok Palace.

Actually there are few large temples within the Seoul vicinity, possibly resulting from the fact that Buddhism was ignored and occasionally persecuted during the Yi Dynasty. There were periods when Buddhist priests were not even permitted to enter the capital city. Located west of Seoul near Yonsei and Ewha Universities is the prosperous temple of Pongwon-sa which was first established in the 10th century by the well-known prophet Priest Toson Kuksa. This temple is now headquarters for the married sect of the Buddhist clergy.

The only temple of any significance located in the heart of Seoul is Chogye-sa. It can be reached by an alleyway between Chong-ro and the U.S. Embassy Residence Compound No. 2. It serves as administrative headquarters for over 1,500 affiliated temples throughout Korea and touches the lives of over 10,000 priests and 3,000 nuns who live in remote monasteries deep in the mountains. In 1970 a split between the married and celibate priests came about, with the former moving its headquarters to Pongwon-sa.

On the outskirts of eastern Seoul is Korea's largest nunnery, called Pomun-sa. Recently a *sokkuram* grotto was constructed on the hillside behind this temple. Though it is smaller in size than the famous Sokkuram behind Pulguk-sa in Kyongju, an attempt was made to duplicate the style. The sculpturing is pleasing. Pomun-sa is one of the more properous temples in Seoul.

Possibly the most picturesque in terms of temple landscaping beauty is Kyongguk-sa in Chong-nung Valley. It is easily reached by road northeast of Seoul near the entrance of the Pugak Skyway. In spring the azaleas bloom in riotous profusion. The serene beauty of the surroundings isolated from the bustling capital city presents a truer image of the meditative tenets of Buddhism. Nearby is the tomb of Queen Kang, second wife of the dynasty's founder, who was buried in 1396.

Along the Uidong route north of Seoul are the two impressive temples of Hwagye-sa and Toson-sa. Toson-sa claims today that more pilgrims come to this temple than any other temple near Seoul. There is a large relief image of the Miruk in stone behind the temple buildings which supposedly has miraculous healing powers.

Across the Han River near Yongdong bridge is one of the oldest and largest temples within the Seoul City vicinity. Pongun-sa was established during the closing years of the 7th century, and during later periods continued to receive favor from some of the dynasty queens. In front is a large impressive *sach'onwang* gate containing the four deva guards who traditionally watched over the Buddha through life and continue to protect the heavenly mountain of Sumi. Once isolated, the temple is across the street from the Korea Exhibition Center (KOEX).

For the many in Seoul interested in hiking courses the craggy mountains encircling the city offer numerous trails for the beginner as well as the avid alpinist. Samgak-san or the North Fortress slope is probably the most popular with Paegun-dae (2820 feet) Seoul's highest peak. Next to Paegun-dae is Insu-bong with treacherous cliffs scaled only by use of ropes. Almost yearly lives are lost by those attempting to scale Insu-bong without enough experience. Trails along the ridge's fortress wall can lead to Pohyon-bong, passing several gates. Beyond are the mountain temples of Munsu-am and Sungga-sa.

Within the fortress (north side) are other small temples such as Hungguk-sa, Wonhyo-am and T'aego-sa, scenically located on the forested slopes. Also on this northern slope is Chin'gwan-sa, a larger temple with an early origin. The vicinity of Chin'gwan-sa is known for its large concentration of Korean *mudang* (sorceresses) who keep alive the cult of shamanism, the original primitive religion of Korea. To the north, To-bong mountain range offers further hiking courses and many small temples hidden in the upper valleys.

South across the Han River Kwanak Mountain's peaks rise as a sawtooth silhouette against the sky. The hike to Yonju-am on the north side or the trek to Sammak-sa from the Anyang pools are both popular courses, well rewarded by spectacular views for those who reach the top.

On the Munsan route from Seoul, Freedom Bridge can be reached by an impressive paved four-lane highway. Tours can also continue over this bridge to Panmunjom, the negotiation site on the DMZ, if arrangements are made with the Korea Tourist Bureau. Also a paved road continues behind Samgak Mountain range to Uijongbu City and back to Seoul, making a delightfully scenic circuitous trip by auto. Many pleasure resorts have recently sprung up along this route.

Along this route a side trip to the Paju Miruk, large stone relief images sculptured in the Koryo period, and the temple of Pogwang-sa with royal tombs nearby can be an enjoyable afternoon excursion.

Beyond Uijongbu City is the resort of Sanjong Hosu, a lake where once stood the summer villa of Kim Il-sung, the north Korean dictator. This area previous to the Korean War was located north of the 38th parallel. Several miles from Uijongbu is the Oknyu Waterfall with the small hermitage of Naewon-am on Surak Mountain. Over the ridges is

Hungguk temple which is also beautifully landscaped, as is Kyongguk-sa near Chong-nung. Hungguk-sa can be reached by road from Oknyu Waterfall, yet a better road can be taken through Taegang-nung. Further north from Uijongbu is Soyo-san, another favorite resort site nearer the DMZ. A small hermitage nestled among weird rock formations and fleecy waterfalls makes this valley comparable to the famed Sorak Mountains on the east coast.

During the summer, recreational water sports become popular as Seoul's inhabitants seek the many resorts near the city. On the northern Han River is Chongpyong Dam with a reservoir. Along the banks of the ten-mile stretch of clear water are many resorts, tourist hotels and private villas. Boating, water skiing and sailing are popular. Though sandy beaches are few because of the steep hillside, several swimming pools have been constructed by the more affluent resorts. Nami-som, a small island in the river, has become exceptionally popular over the last few years and is located on the way to Chunchon. Chunchon City also has a large dammed lake and is well established as a summer resort town. Several tourist hotels are available and arrangements can be made in Seoul for reservations.

Continuing further up the North Han River toward the east coast, Soyanggang Dam has been recently constructed which will soon develop this area into Korea's largest man-made lake. This large reservoir completely covers the former 38th parallel on the main route from Wonju to Injae and Sorak-san. Many recreational resorts are developing in this area as it is relatively close to Seoul by good roads through Chunchon or Wonju.

Near Seoul, at the junction of the north and south Han River, is Palt'ang Dam, completed in 1974 by a French and Korean joint venture team. The water behind this dam almost reaches Chongpyong Dam further up river. As this area has only recently been developed there are fewer resorts than at Chongpyong Lake; however, Palt'ang will undoubtedly develop quickly as the lake is closer to Seoul and can be easily reached by good paved roads. Beyond Palt'ang Dam is found the famous temple of Yongmun (Dragon Gate) where the world's largest and oldest fruit tree, the giant gingko, is growing. In the fall its leaves turn to brilliant golden yellow.

Kanghwa Island's Historic Culture

For a foreign tourist wishing to leave the smog and noisy traffic confusion of Seoul and see glimpses of pastoral beauty in the Korean countryside, Kanghwa Island is to be recommended. Situated in the estuary of the Han River north of Inchon port, this fifth largest island of Korea is rich in history and natural beauty. In 1973 the road was completely paved to Chondung-sa, the island's largest temple and one of the thirty major temples in Korea. The driving time from Seoul to the temple is about 1.5 hours. An express bus can be taken from the Shinch'on Rotary.

The entire spectrum of Korean history, from the hazy era of the legendary Tan'gun to the opening of Korea to the Western world, can be observed and studied on this island. In the twelfth century Korean celadon reached its highest level of artistic distinction and one of the major regions for this production was on Kanghwa Island. During periods of frequent invasions from Japan, Korean artisans were transported to southern Japan where they developed the famous Japanese pottery industries of today.

Numerous fortresses were constructed along the mainland side of the island. A wall was built across the ridges of Munsu-san, near where the bridge now crosses to the island. Remnants of these fortifications seen today date from as early as mid-thirteenth century, when Kojong (23rd Koryo king) fled to this island from the capital Songdo during the Mongol invasion.

Kanghwa City is reached within three minutes of crossing the bridge. Remains of the old city wall and gates are still observed. The West Gate is the best preserved, while the South Gate on the route to Chondung-sa has been recently reconstructed.

The story is told that during the Manchu invasion of the seventeenth century a retired prime minister, Kim Sang-yong, heroically helped in the defense of the city. As the Manchu soldiers swarmed through the South Gate after a long siege, Kim destroyed the gunpowder stored in the gate's roof and perished in the frightful explosion. His memorial tablet is located near the city bell which is a designated treasure (No. 11).

The bell, weighing over four tons, was cast during the reign of Sukchong (19th Yi king) and when the French attacked in 1866 and burned the city, the bell was carried to the outskirts of town. However, the French soldiers found it too heavy and abandoned it. Also in Kanghwa City is the birthplace of Ch'oljong (25th Yi king). This boy, born in 1831, grew up on this island as a son of Chongye *taewongun*, a nephew of Chongjo (22nd Yi king) who had fled for his life from Seoul years before.

Probably one of the most interesting buildings situated on a hill is the old Episcopal Church considered one of the oldest churches in the country. Bishop Corfé who arrived in Korea in 1890 ordered the building of this present structure ten years later. At the dedication ceremonies a *bodhi* tree was planted which is still seen in the southwestern corner of the compound. It was this type of sacred fig tree (belonging to the mulberry family) that the Gautama Buddha sat under when he received enlightenment. The nuts from the *bodhi* tree are used for making Buddhist prayer beads.

◁ *Yongin Familyland, south of Seoul*

A short distance west of Kanghwa City, amid fields of ginseng, lies a prehistoric dolmen and the remains of at least one other nearby. Man's habitation of the Korean peninsula may date to the paleolithic period, according to recent archaeological findings near Kongju. The legends in history push back this country's kingdoms over four thousand years to the mythical founder Tan'gun. This foundation legend is deeply embedded in Korean culture. In the southern region is the island's highest peak, called Mani-san.

At the summit is an altar which Tan'gun first established for worship in 2333 B.C. Ancient records tell that the heavenly being Ung while visiting earth transformed a bear into a woman and then married her. Their child was Tan'gun who later migrated south from Ever-White Mountain along the Yalu River to Pyongyang, where he established Korea's first capital and called his kingdom *choson* meaning "morning freshness."

Also in the southern part of the island is the famed temple of Chondung-

sa. Circumscribing the temple grounds is a one-mile fortress wall which was first built according to legends in only one day by the three sons of Tan'gun. Many elegant pines, gingko and flowering cherry trees grace the slopes near the temple. It is believed that a temple in this valley was first built during the early Koguryo period when Buddhism was introduced to the peninsula. However, a later temple came into prominence during the late Koryo era when Kojong (23rd king) commissioned the famous *Tripitaka* wood blocks to be made which are now stored at Haein-sa.

These wooden blocks, consisting of over eighty-one thousand pieces, were carved as a religous endeavor for Buddha to plead for aid in driving out the invading Mongols. King Kojong had fled from the capital and the Koryo court was using Kanghwa Island as a sanctuary. This king is buried on this island and his grave can still be seen near Kanghwa City. Today the *Tripitaka* are the oldest and best preserved of any complete Buddhist scriptures in the

Chondung Temple (left page) and prehistoric dolmen of Kanghwa Island (above).

world. In 1299 the queen of the ruling Koryo king and grandson of King Kojong donated a rare jade lamp to this temple thus giving the temple its name of *chondung* which means "Inherited Lamp." Unfortunately the exact whereabouts of the lamp is unknown.

A nine-hundred-year-old bell which is Chinese in origin as well as the two buildings of Taeungbo-jon and Yaksa-jon are listed as government-designated treasures (Nos. 178, 179 and 393). The Yaksa-jon is dedicated to the Buddha of Medicine. The main hall is the Taeungbo-jon enshrining the Sokkamoni (Historic Buddha) and his two *posal* attendant, Munsu and Pohyon.

Under the eaves at the four corners of the Taeungbo-jon are rather curious human figures squatting with their knees under their chins. Each face portrays an anguished look. These unique carved wooden images are found only at Chondung-sa.

An unusual tale is told that during the reconstruction of the hall after the Japanese Wars of the 1590's the builder fell in love with the daughter of the wineshop owner in the town. There was no place to stay on the temple grounds so he had rented a room next to the wine shop. As the builder had no money he promised the girl that as soon as the temple was completed they could leave and get married.

After some time the day finally came and proudly the carpenter brought the money and preparation was made to depart soon. However, unknown to the simple carpenter, the girl had made other plans with a younger boy of the town and during the night slipped away with the money. One can imagine the anger and frustration of the builder the following morning when he knew what had happened, realizing that he had been duped over the past years.

He sullenly went back to the Taeungbo-jon of Chondung-sa which he had just completed to meditate over his losses. An inspiration came and he began his final project in revenge for his frustrations. He carved four nude images of his faithless girl and placed them in a crouching position with the heavy beams of the roof pressing her head to her knees.

Here she continues to sit in abjection, appearing to plead for forgiveness from outside the Taeungbo-jon. The builder slipped into oblivion leaving behind this legend and images illustrating his regrets.

Symbol of Communist Aggression

Representing an impasse in the Korean War of 1950-53 Panmunjom still provides a revealing window into the Communist world of deceit and false promises on the Korean peninsula. For over thirty years the north Korean's unwillingness to reach a lasting peace agreement has become a matter of historical record.

Located only thirty-five miles from Seoul, Panmunjom still is an arena for the negotiating armistice combatants representing two antagonistic ideologies. Tours can be arranged through KTB and will give you a lasting impression of the evil force of communist aggression still determined to conquer the free world. Today Panmunjom is a symbol of this struggle, the drama of which is seen every day. Devoted to world revolution, one side continually strives to impose its ideals by force and subversion, while the other side attempts to protect its own cherished ideals of individual freedom and rights, inherent in a democratic society. Panmunjom not only served as a culmination of the Korean conflict but as a turning point in the struggle between the communist and the free world. This entanglement continues to attract world attention.

On July 27, 1953, after two years and seventeen days, 575 major meetings, and eighteen million recorded words, the Korean Armistice Agreement was signed at Panmunjom, making this the longest truce talk in history. Many books have been published on the negotiation talks. Encouraged by this the chief negotiator for the United Nations Command, Admiral C. Turner Joy, once stated that − "the more books published on the Korean Armistice the better will be the chances of getting the American public to understand the dangerous nature of our communist enemies and the difficulty of dealing with them."

Korea has traditionally been a weak power sandwiched between stronger nations. The entire history of Korea reflects a series of attempts to maintain its identity and independence. Often Korea has been a pawn of rivalry between China and Japan.

Even thirty years following the outbreak of the Korean War, words and accusations still fly across the conference table and a peace treaty has never been signed. The north has continually harassed the south, while claiming they are only being provoked. During Red Cross talks that commenced in 1972 communist authorities were constructing illegal tunnels under the demilitarized zone, to be later discovered in 1975. Several Korean and U.S. military men lost their lives through "booby traps" in the investigation of these illegal tunnels. Assassination attempts on the former President Park Chung-hee as well as hit-and-run attacks among the offshore islands have all been a part of a careful north Korean strategy.

The impasse of the Korean War, witnessed in the armistice meetings in Panmunjom, illustrates to the Free World the lurking dangers of trusting the communists. The lesson of 1950-1953 ending in a shaky cease-fire agreement should have left some lasting attitudes concerning diplomacy with the communists. Negotiation for the communists is only another lethal weapon in their arsenal for war. Truth and what is ethical for the communists are always considered in light of what it contributes to the final goal of world domination.

◁ *Mani-san, Kanghwa Island*

Peace as viewed by the communists can be achieved only in a completely communist society.

In gazing past "Freedom Bridge" and "Bridge of No Return" the visitor who comes for the first time will be profoundly impressed. Here on the hills of the Korean countryside the frustrations of a stalemate war came to fruition.

On August 18, 1976 the cold calculating aggression of the north Korean communists reached shocking proportions when two American military officers were hacked to death in cold blood with axes in a surprise attack at Panmunjom. Certainly the aggression which occurred on June 25, 1950 must never be repreated. Yet, as constantly seen daily in the Panmunjom area, the threat from the north still remains.

The constant negotiations continue across the table while within the region of the no-man's-land of the DMZ (Demilitarized Zone) reminders of war rust on their sites half covered by grass and foliage. Korea is still divided between north and south while the anguish of

the people has not dimmed over the many years. The Republic of Korea always remains alert and ready, for the memories of the Korean conflict with all its horror are still vivid.

Glimpses Into the Past

A traditional Korean Folk Village located thirty minutes south of Seoul near Suwon maintains all the rural enchantment of life in Korea hundreds of years ago.

An old gentleman with a slender bamboo pipe in hand and wearing a wide-brimmed horse hair hat strolls between the low straw thatch of several homes. His flowing *turumagi* (topcoat) draws attention to the serene surroundings. The rhythmic clacking of two sticks is audible behind the walls.

The curious tourist may wonder and wander at Korea's Folk Village yet need not be shy in poking his head into the many private homes. On her porch a woman is ironing clothes by beating them with two sticks, while in the next courtyard another housewife is spindling silk thread from a small white cocoon simmering in a cup of boiling water.

This cultural Korean village was erected in 1973 and now includes aspects of almost everything uniquely Korean from days gone by. Homes typical of the various provinces of Korea can be identified. In the village square tight-rope walkers, weddings or funeral processions, kite flying contests, and graceful dance troupes are seen periodically.

The blacksmith, furniture carpenter, potter, or instrument craftsman can be visited in their shops. A *yangban* house, a watermill or the clean but humble farmer's home can be entered so as to see all the furnishings representative of an early era.

Don't mistake the young chap for a maiden with a long single braid down his back. The boy is simply not married yet and will only cut his hair for the wedding ceremony. A top-knot will then be made which will fit comfortably under his new horsehair hat, a symbol of

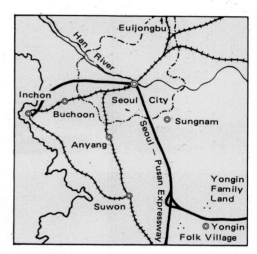

married life.

The village offers over 70 exhibitions of life styles of the past, and includes restaurants both traditional and contemporary. Real artisans daily practice such traditional skills as paper making, pottery, pipe maker, hat maker or brass making. The village is an actual working community representing all the regional areas of Korea including Cheju Island.

If you are to be in Korea for only a few days then a trip to Folk Village is highly recommended. Most of the tourist agencies can arrange tours; however, if you travel on your own it is best to take an express bus from Seoul or train to Suwon City. From Suwon City the taxi fare is about $5.00 one way. Plan to spend an entire day.

◁ *Panmun-gak (top) and the 'bridge of no return' across the DMZ*

Korean
Folk
Village

Museums and Cultural Assets

Preservation and promotion of the nation's historic treasures and cultural legacy has become an increasing concern in the development of Korea's many museums both national and private. Ancient art and archaeology were the earlier principal targets of research and display but now greater concern is being given to folk culture exhibits.

The government-sponsored National Museum of Korea maintains the largest museum in Seoul with branch museums in Kyongju, Kwangju, Puyo and Kongju.

On Aug. 25, 1972 the new National Museum of Seoul was opened with the late President Park cutting the ribbon. The striking new building can now easily be seen on the grounds of Kyongbok Palace behind the domed capitol building. Replicas of three architectural structures which are listed as national treasures of Korea dominate the skyline. The five-storied pagoda is a replica of Palsang-jon at Popchu-sa, while the other two buildings are to be found at Hwaom-sa and Kumsan-sa. Ample time is required to see all of the displays. Resting areas are provided among the many wings of the museum.

The Kyongbok Palace grounds display many stone remains of historical value and during good weather provide a serene environment for the stroller to leisurely wander about.

To better understand the folk culture of rural Korea a visit to the National Folklore Museum is a must. Also located in Kyongbok Palace, the museum exhibits patterns of life and working conditions from the earlier eras in authentic lifestyle settings and explained for the foreign visitor. Nine large display rooms exhibit over 5,000 folklore articles. It is here that the disappearing folk culture of Korea can be preserved for generations to come.

The provincial museums at Puyo and Kongju were constructed in 1971 and 1973 respectively. Though smaller displays, the two museums emphasize many of the archeological findings within the vicinity. As these two cities once were Paekche capitals most of the displays relate to Paekche history which terminated in the 7th century. Many of the articles coming from King Muryong's tomb, which was accidentally discovered in 1971, are displayed in the Kongju museum.

Puyo is where the Paekche Dynasty came to a close in 660 A.D., and many historical sites are to be found in and about this city. The famous cliff of "falling flowers" where many maidens leaped to their death rather than be ravished by conquering troops is within walking distance of the museum.

The third local museum which was dedicated at a new site in 1975 is situated on the outskirts of Kyongju City. Though smaller than the Seoul museum, nevertheless it is one of the finest museums of the country. Here the abundant remains of Silla are centrally located, including the world-famous Emillie Bell. The museum itself was constructed on a Silla building site which was accidentally discovered in the course of ground preparation. An ancient rock well was discovered and can now be seen.

The entire vicinity of Kyongju is an open-air museum. Though principal attractions are well defined, still over 80% of Kyongju's hillside treasures are unknown to the average person. Even today stone remains are often lost among

◁ Seoul's National Museum, Kyongbok Palace

the rice fields or rocky valleys of mountains such as Nam-san. The recent 1979 publication of *Kyongju Guide* (both Japanese and English) is the most comprehensive study of the Kyongju vicinity.

In December 1979 Kyongju was picked by UNESCO as one of ten historic cities in the world during a regional meeting held in Thailand. UNESCO plans to make a large-scale cultural survey of the ten cities as part of its preservation program of the world's most important historic sites.

In 1978 a new provincial National Museum was opened in Kwangju and next to Kyongju is the largest outside of Seoul. The exhibits include the entire spectrum of Korean history from the paleolithic period. It is noted for its 21 Yi Dynasty paintings as many of Korea's famous painters came from this region. Many of the ceramic kiln sites were located in this southern area so the Koryo wares are especially abundant.

In May 1975 a 14th century Chinese ship was discovered with a submerged cargo of ceramics off the Korean coast at Shinan. Divers raised over 12,000 artifacts to make this find the largest collection of Chinese ceramics ever excavated outside of China. The Kwangju Museum has the only permanent display of these Shinan relics.

In addition to the national museums there are several private and municipal museums, and over thirty university museums.

Of the numerous campus museums to be found in Korea, many of which contain valuable art objects of national merit, the Sejong University Museum in eastern Seoul is one of the largest. Completed in 1974, it serves as one of several folklore museums in Korea.

The finest collection of Korean apparel is found in Suk Joo-sun's collection located in the Dankuk University Museum dedicated in 1980. Her collection totals almost 3,500 pieces.

The Korean Christian Museum had its origin in the private collection of the late Rev. Kim Yang-son which was put on public display in 1948. In 1967 the collection was donated to Soongjon University.

In addition the Seoul National University Museum, the Yonsei University Museum and the Ewha Womans University Museum have excellent and well known collections.

Museums specializing in embroidery, medicine, Korean alphabet, stone carving and ancient books are available in Seoul.

Unfortunately the fine collections held by the Kansong Museum are difficult to see as the museum opens for only two week each year.

On April 22, 1982 the Hoam Museum opened its doors to the public. This museum on the grounds of Yongin Family Land is excellent and worth the trip of one hour out of Seoul. Known for its pottery and paintings, this collection belongs to Lee Byong-chull, a well-known tycoon and chairman of the Samsung Group. The sculptured monuments on the grounds surrounding the Hoam Museum are pleasing pieces of modern art.

By far the finest folk art collection in the country is housed at the Onyang Folk Museum, about a two-hour drive from Seoul. This collection of over 15,000 pieces is owned by Kim Wondae, president of Kyemong Publishing Company. Captions are well done in English. This collection is recommended over the collection housed in Kyongbok Palace. Also excellent publications produced by this museum are available in the bookstores.

Possibly one of the most interesting of the private museums is the Emileh Museum which moved in the spring of 1982 to *Sokni-sa* near the temple of Popchu-sa. The drive is about 3 hours yet the scenery is spectacular and the road is paved the entire way. Zo Zayong who developed this private collection of folk art can enthrall visitors with stories of pesky sprits and tigers. An architect by profession, Zo, who is known as the "Korean tiger man," has spent a small fortune in attempting to educate people in a forgotten aspect of Korea – the folk art.

The terms "national treasure" or

Traditional scenes in the National Folklore Museum, Kyongbok Palace ▷

kukbo and "treasured thing" or pomul in Korea are often used in reference to many historic objects or remains. This system of classifying cultural objects and giving them numbers is often baffling to foreigners. The actual numbered cultural assets of Korea are now well over one thousand.

These assets generally include things that are products of human skill, with the highest rank being "National Treasure – kukbo." Presently there are 206 national treasures listed for the Republic of Korea. Those historic relics of secondary importance are called "Treasured Things – pomul" and now number 734.

This designating system began under the Japanese occupation and following independence was continued. The last major reclassification took place in 1958. As new discoveries were made over recent years, additional treasures in all categories have been listed. Now in the countryside the old stone designating markers might still be seen beside the new stone markers.

Korea's cultural assets are a part of her spiritual heritage and have been passed on from ancient days. These assets are classified into eight major divisions. The first three are listed as Objects and Sites with Historic and Artistic Value, and are by far the greatest in number as they include the National Treasures (kukbo), Treasured Things (pomul) and Historic Sites (sajok) which include 292 sites. Other categories include Natural Protected Resources (235), Intangible Cultural Assets (72), Folklore Material (120), Scenic and Historic Places of Beauty (12)

There are five areas listed for Korea as Scenic Sites. These include the area of Pulguk-sa; Naemul's tomb near Kyongju; the Ponghwa area; Sokni Mountain region; and forested area of Kaya Mountain. The category of Natural Protected Resources includes rare trees, plants and flowers. Also many rare indigenous species of birds and animals are listed including the Chindo dog from Chin-do, an island off the southwest coast. Several caves are listed as well as

nature conservation areas such as Cheju Island, Hong-do, another island region and Sorak Mountain.

The category of Intangible Cultural Assets include such cultural heritage resources as drama, music, dance, craftsmanship and other cultural activities. The materials of folklore cover clothing, foods, houses, professions, beliefs, rites and events practiced through which one can visualize the general trend of life in a given period.

The magnificent heritage of Korea's antiquity became more fully known to the outside world through the *5000 Years of Korean Art* exhibition which began at the Asian Art Museum of San Francisco May 1979. Seven museums throughout the United States hosted the *5000 Years of Korean Art* over a two-year period.

Region (date: Oct. 1982)	Kukbo (NT)	Pomul (TT)
Seoul	101	161
Pusan	2	10
Taegu	0	11
Kyonggi-do	2	40
Kangwon-do	6	44
Chungchong-pukdo	8	28
Chungchong-namdo	20	57
Kyongsan-pukto	42	187
Kyongsan-namdo	8	65
Cholla-pukto	3	61
Cholla-namdo	14	69
Cheju Island	0	1

Shopping Paradise

Learning to "haggle" is an art for economic self defense, whether it be in the crowded market places or a quiet back corner of a merchant's small shop. Though shrewd in the battle of salesmanship, the merchant usually wins the score yet most often the price is reduced . . . . and you feel a pleasant sensation that you also have won . . . . The Oriental way is that neither the buyer nor the seller loses face!

Even though prices have become inflated over the last several years, Korea is still a shopper's paradise. If you have only a few days it is best to visit first the major department stores in the downtown area. They are the Lotte, Midopa, Shinsegae and Cosmos. Here the prices are fixed and the quality is good so that the newcomer can obtain an idea of price range. Then if you want to take the "bull by the horns" head to the South Gate Market (*namdaemun*) to test your ability to "haggle." Here the prices should be cheaper than any other area but be careful about the quality.

Major shopping arcades are now mostly underground in the downtown area and adjacent to the Seoul City Bus Terminal. It is more or less expected that one should "haggle" over the cost. If one confines his shopping to the arcades of the hotels one will expect to pay more as the overhead is much higher.

A secret to good "haggling" is to keep your emotions hidden and don't demonstrate an immediate interest in the item for which you are looking. Price a few articles to obtain a feel for what is happening in your rapport with the merchant. Two strikes will be lost if you hurry, as most foreign tourists do — take your time! Remember to leave your jewelry and furs at the hotel for your style of dress will determine for the merchant his starting price. Look rich and the price will be high — and maybe too much so for your pocketbook. Don't

be afraid to start low in your bartering — as this is not a sign of cheapness, only a quality of shrewd good sense and appreciated aggressiveness.

Silk and silk brocades are two of Korea's best bargains but you must be certain that the silk is not mixed with synthetics for the price should then be considerably less. But don't overlook the synthetics for textiles are one of the country's leading exports to foreign nations.

Much of the raw silk that is exported to Thailand goes into the Thai silk, famous throughout southeast Asia. The silk center of Seoul is the East Gate Market where a maze of alleys covers huge blocks of the city with thousands of small stalls selling colorful material. The abundance of silk, cottons and various synthetics is so great that one will experience difficulty in making a choice.

Though prices have risen over the last few years, the amethyst and smoky topaz are still considered good bargains as these minerals are mined in Korea. Also don't forget to consider Korea's white jade. This jewelry is considerably cheaper than Chinese green jade and makes excellent gifts.

Jewelry stores are found all over Seoul, in arcades and department stores. Again care must be taken in choosing quality pieces. Gold items in Korea have long been popular as the quality is good but the price by weight is usually higher

124

than in the U.S. The Korean gold has a more yellow luster.

Deep within Namdaemun Market is found one of the largest cluster of stalls selling a glittering array of jade, topaz, amethyst and gold. Jade beads will range from $1.00 to ten dollars. A wide variety of carved jade items range from turtles to butterflies and masks to "long life" Chinese characters. Knot tying in a macramé fashion has a long tradition in Korea and the jade pendants used in this elaborate art are more expensive.

Ginseng in its various forms is another product in great demand by foreigners, especially from other Asian countries. The ginseng root grown in Korea is considered the best in the world and brings a high price on the world market. The production of ginseng is government controlled. For a foreigner wishing to sample ginseng, the tea in powdered form is recommended, though you will find it has a distinct earth flavor and some sugar is recommended.

Bargains on sweaters and other clothing articles can be found. Purchased at less than half price, these same items are exported to the U.S. for sale in many of the larger chain stores with well known labels placed on them.

Especially popular are the beaded sweaters which bring high prices in the export markets. Korean tourists to Hong Kong frequently buy these beaded sweaters, not realizing that they originally came from Korea. Custom made shoes, handbags and men's suits are rated high on the list as bargain items in Korea. Eel skin purses for women are high priority items for the shopping tourist.

Most of the antique stores in Seoul are located in one part of town called Insa-dong (Mary's Alley) though there are a growing number of stores in Itaewon. Here can be found Buddhist sculptured art, Yi and Koryo ceramics, old chests and other types of household paraphernalia from Korea's long past. Compared to Western prices, items can be purchased at reasonable cost. Ancient Oriental paintings as well as contempory

are displayed side by side. Prices have skyrocketed over the last few years due to greatly increased tourist trade, especially from Japan, but for those who know the market good buys in antiques are still frequently found. An area off of Chonggye-chon east of East Gate is Seoul's wholesale center for Korean antiques. The price range is wide open and little English is spoken in this area.

As a word of warning, antiques are subject to government regulation and the current policy should be thoroughly explored before attempting to take an item of great value and age out of the country. Good Korean chests many with the original brass fittings, are in constant demand among foreigners. Many new chests are being made in imitation of the old style. This is also true of the Koryo celadon and Yi ceramics. Kilns near Seoul turn out great amounts of rather good ceramics which imitate the earlier treasures now found in the country's museums. These modern reproductions of chests and ceramics are often worth buying. The merchants are reasonably honest in telling you if the article is genuine or a reproduction. Generally speaking the shops in Itaewon are cheaper.

Lacquerware has historically been a well developed handicraft. Whether it is only a tray or a gigantic wardrobe chest, the smooth red or black lacquer finish glistening in the light attracts all who appreciate beauty. Often elaborate designs using small carved pieces of "mother of pearl" are placed into the lacquered surface. This work has to be all hand done, thus is tedious and time consuming. Enamelware in the Orient also has an ancient history while in Korea the art is still practiced. Again the enamel work is all hand done. Jewelry items in brilliant baked enamel are quite popular.

Good Korean brass is becoming difficult to find but is strongly desired by foreigners. There is considerable brassware on the market, but today the quality of the new brass is inferior, thinner and less durable. Old Korean bell brass has a high resonating tone

Along the streets of Itaewon ▷

when struck, clear as a bell, and re-sounding for many seconds. The item is usually simple such as a rice or soup bowl and always sold by weight. The quality bell brass was all made during pre-war years. Shops selling Buddhist paraphernalia are located along Chong-no. Among the best finds are drums, brass cymbals, bells, shaman equipment, temple and funeral decor and lanterns.

A visit to the nation's busiest street is to wander into the shopping region of Myong-dong. Here is the throbbing heart of Seoul where on a cool summer evening crowds jostle and jampack the restaurants, entertainment houses and brightly displayed shops. In an area of little more than half an acre 500,000 persons consisting mostly of young people, daily push their way through the narrow streets. Usually 5,000 are foreign tourists. Land price in Myong-dong is the highest in the Republic. Tailor and dressmaking shops are plentiful and the work is often good and reliable as the cost of labor is still low. Stores usually stay open late into the evening.

After all your shopping you may well find yourself back in the department stores again. The wide variety of articles found in the four department stores are difficult to elaborate on fully.

The department stores have art galleries which provide various exhibitions throughout the year. Also there is an area where folklore items and art pieces are available. Just to see the folk article collection is worth the visit.

Opened in 1982 is Korea's Handicraft Center located between the Lotte First Avenue and the Chosun Hotel. For seeing the folk art of Korea this is truly the best place to go. The prices are reasonable and the quality is maintained.

With enough time your shopping spree will be an unforgettable adventure into the mysteries of Eastern culture blended pleasingly with the West. With a sharp eye out for erratic taxi drivers the tourist is relatively safe in this city of ten million people. Your shopping should be fun and if perchance you save some *won* in your bartering you will feel an inner glow of pleasure, so enjoy yourself – and happy shopping.

The shops and stalls of Itaewon are foreigners' bargain paradise. Take your time and don't be afraid to "haggle" over the price.

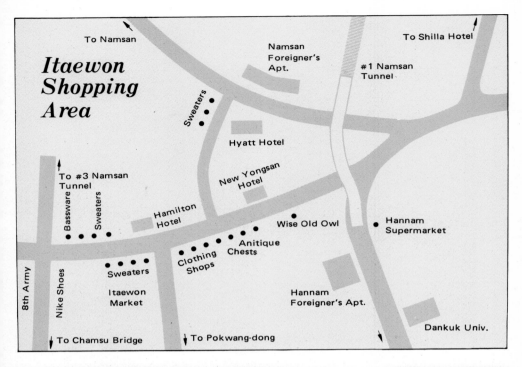

Itaewon Shopping Area

To Namsan

Namsan Foreigner's Apt.

To Shilla Hotel

#1 Namsan Tunnel

Sweaters

Hyatt Hotel

To #3 Namsan Tunnel

Basswware

Sweaters

New Yongsan Hotel

Hamilton Hotel

Wise Old Owl

Hannam Supermarket

Clothing Shops

Anitique Chests

8th Army

Nike Shoes

Sweaters

Itaewon Market

Hannam Foreigner's Apt.

Dankuk Univ.

To Chamsu Bridge

To Pokwang-dong

Chapter III.
Tours Beyond the Capital

Five Major Cities Outside Seoul
(Pusan, Taegu, Inchon, Kwangju,
    Taejon)
Cheju-do, the Citrus Island
Honoring Admiral Yi Sun-shin
Wooded Wonderland of Sorak-san
Kyongju, Legacy of Silla Culture
Paekche's Puyo and Kongju
Along the Southern Coast

Autumn scene south of Kimchon, North Kyongsang

Five Major Cities Outside Seoul

Though Seoul is THE CITY of Korea with a population of ten million people, the center of government, culture and art, a visit to the five other largest cities on the peninsula will offer a different perspective of Korea beyond the great Seoul City gates. These cities starting with the largest are: Pusan, the southern port; Taegu, the southern apple capital; Inchon, Seoul's port city; Kwangju, the Cholla region's metropolis; and Taejon, Korea's center city.

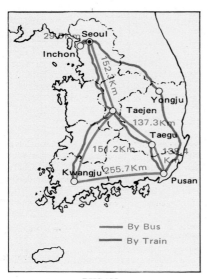

PUSAN

Pusan, like Seoul, is administratively a "special city" because of its size and has status equal to that of a province. However, Pusan cannot be really compared to Seoul, which has been the established capital city for almost six centuries. No palace grounds or majestic city gates bear witness to Korea's ancient culture in Pusan. Tall buildings are only beginning to make their appearance in this southern port city.

Pusan historically has been the gateway to Korea from Japan and the

Western world by sea. It is today Korea's second largest city, boasting a population over three million. As the city lies on the southern tip of the peninsula Pusan enjoys somewhat milder weather than the capital. Taking advantage of this and the coastal location several popular bathing beaches have developed in the suburbs such as Haeundae which is the most famous.

The harbor is well protected with a range of hills to the northwest and sentinel-like island on the south. The name of *Pusan* dates from the Koryo period and refers to peaks rising to 2,500 feet behind the port city which were thought to resemble the rim of a cauldron. The physical setting is not unattractive and if it were not for the barren conditions of the hills, could be likened to that of Hong Kong.

In 1876 Pusan was formally opened for trade by the Japanese and in 1904 the Japanese started construction of a railway north to transport troops to fight the Russians. During the next decade the Japanese undertook major development projects in Pusan to build wharves and modernize the eastern port. The south and east harbor are separated by Yong-do, an island of hilly ridges which almost completely hides the city from the sea travelers entering the port.

Until 1969, Pusan was South Korea's principal port and the harbor space is still far larger than that of Inchon while the tide range is only three feet compared to

◁ *Winnowing grain in T'ap Valley near Kyongju, North Kyongsang*

Inchon's nineteen foot tides (second highest in the world). Pusan is now behind both Inchon and Ulsan in tonnage of imports but still dominates the export trade with more than half of all overseas shipments passing through its port.

Though a commercial and industrial city Pusan has also maintained its reputation as a tourist center for the south. Tongnae is especially noted for its natural hot spring baths and there are now several tourist hotels meeting international standards. There are also the beaches at Haeundae and Songdo with pleasant public parks overlooking the bay. During the summer season it is estimated that over eight million people visit the beaches.

Near the entrance to the Seoul-Pusan Expressway is the ancient Silla temple of Pomo-sa which now has a paved road for entering the area. Situated on a secluded pine-forested mountain slope Pomo Temple is one of the three greatest temples in this southern province (the others are Haein-sa and Tongdo-sa). The eminent Silla monk, Wonhyo Taesa, is reputed to have lived at Pomo-sa. The precincts of this temple are an enchanting fairyland of natural beauty which attract crowds of visitors in any season.

Boat rides through the harbor and faster travel by ferry or hydrofoil ships to Cheju Island or along the picturesque south coast to Chungmu, Namhae-do or Yosu will provide some of the rarest beach and island scenery to be found on a peninsula noted for coastal beauty.

On a more somber note there is the U.N. cemetery located in the outskirts of Pusan in the direction of Haeundae. It is the only one of its kind in the world where the war dead from sixteen Korean War allies rest in honored serenity. These men from foreign countries offered their lives during the Korean conflict in common defense of the Korean peninsula against communist aggression.

In the late 1960s Pusan seemed remote from Seoul but now with hourly flights from Kimpo, more frequent bus service traversing the expressway, and direct telephone dialing these two major cities of Korea have been drawn closer together. In addition daily air flights link Pusan with Japan. The ferry across to Shimonoseki and Fukuoka in southern Japan provides a relaxed way to travel. In 1982 over 38,500 foreigners entered Korea through Pusan. The city a decade ago may have appeared to be at the end of the Korean peninsula but is now playing a vital role in its contacts with the outside world.

TAEGU

Taegu, with a population of more than two million people as the third largest city in the Republic, is located in the heart of North Kyongsang-do. By air flight from Seoul it takes 45 minutes or 3½ hours by expressway bus. It was on this city's outskirts that the communist drive into southern Korea was halted at the Naktong River, so Taegu never experienced the ravages of war. Prior to the Korean War its population was above 200,000. Refugees swarmed into Taegu during the conflict, causing chronic squalor from which it was difficult to recover.

Historically Taegu has been the "great market" for the entire southern region, and is especially noted for medicinal herbs. When the first Westerners arrived in the last decade of the 19th century they found the people extremely conservative. The city was once walled with traditional gates and the Western missionaries were finally permitted to eventually buy a potter's field outside the high stone wall. This cemetery was to become the site of the present compound and hospital of the Presbyterian mission. During this period the Western apple was introduced by an American missionary, James E. Adams, who discovered that these fruit trees grew quite well in the soil of the Taegu basin. Now Taegu has become the center of Korea's apple industry which is famous throughout the Orient.

Although the geographic vicinity of Taegu possesses natural mountain beauty, the city itself is somewhat drab in appearance similar to most highly industrial cities. With the exception of Ulsan, which was especially developed

Imitation brick pagoda on Pingsan Temple site near Uisong, North Kyongsang ▷

as a petrochemical center, Taegu is the most industrialized of South Korean cities, though most of the industries are small. Over thirty-five per cent of all the employed population is engaged in some manufacturing, primarily textiles, the major industry for the city.

Taegu is the only Korean metropolis completely removed from the coast; thus it regards itself as a true interior city. Situated in a large basin with surrounding peaks over 3,500 feet, the city slopes northward toward the Kumho River which joins the Naktong west of Taegu. In the summer, Taegu is the hottest city in the nation and is also considered to be the coldest in winter. City planners have broadened streets and established parks, while a new railway station has been constructed to the east, the direction the city is moving.

In addition to industries Taegu is also an agricultural market center for the central Naktong River basin. The West Gate Market (sometimes called Presbyterian Market) is one of the oldest and largest traditional Korean markets in the country. Tourists wandering the market alleys will be amazed and fascinated by the variety of items displayed.

Taegu is also known as the "college town" of Korea. Educational tradition for this city began in the late nineteenth century when foreign missionaries moved to Taegu and soon began Western schools. Taegu became Korea's first interior town to be opened to foreign influence. These schools still exist. Now Taegu has three universities and two colleges: Kyongbuk National University, Youngnam University, Hyosong Women's University, Kyemyong Christian University and a social Education College.

Haein Temple is usually reached by passing through Taegu. A paved road has been constructed from the city to this most famous temple of the region (one hour drive). The sheer mountain cliffs with cascading streams provide some of the most spectacular woodland beauty to be found anywhere is Korea. Terraced on different levels, the temple is large and expansive. The *Tripitaka,* the oldest and most complete set of Buddhist scrip-

ture wood blocks to be found in the world, are stored at Haein-sa. The *Tripitaka* blocks as well as the two major buildings where they are stored, have been designated national treasures.

A thirty-minute drive out of Taegu City another well-known Silla temple called Tonghwa-sa is found. Located on the steep slopes of Palgong Mountain, Tonghwa-sa is found in a beautifully calm forested glen with boulder-strewn streams flowing down the valleys. This temple is the fifth most important temple in both North and South Kyongsang Provinces. Many hiking trails lead out from the temple area to small hermitages while further up the slope is a gigantic Buddha image, placidly sitting on the peak of the mountain. It can be reached only after a vigorous two hour climb.

INCHON

Inchon now has a population well over one million and is the fourth largest city in the Republic of Korea. Now a major port city for Seoul, eighteen miles away, Inchon is third in importance next to the ports of Pusan and Ulsan.

Less than seventy years ago Chemulpo (Inchon) was only a small fishing village near the mouth of the Han River. In 1866 the Korean court came to blows with the French because of the persecution of Christians in Korea which resulted in the execution of nine French priests. In 1871 American ships twice attacked this harbor to avenge the *General Sherman* incident near Pyongyang.

The signing of the Korean-American Treaty of Amity and Commerce in 1882 marked the first accepted entry of Westerners into Korea. The port was officially opened under the new name of Inchon the following year, though for some time it was still called Chemulpo.

On May 22, 1982 Korea and the United States celebrated the centennial of Korean-American relations with the signing of the treaty by Commodore Robert W. Shufeldt. This treaty signed in

Inchon City and MacArthur's statue ▷

Chemulpo was Korea's first treaty of peace, amity and commerce with a Western nation.

During the Korean War, Inchon became the site of the most spectacular amphibious landing in modern warfare which led to the recapture of Seoul by the allied forces under the command of General Douglas MacArthur. As the tides of this harbor are second highest in the world the entire assault had to be timed to split seconds. A large statue of General MacArthur overlooks the beach where he came ashore.

Inchon still sprawls up and down the low hills with as yet no downtown concentration of tall buildings to constitute the civic center. Industrial progress has been made especially in glass and plywood. Now rapid development is being made to enlarge the port. Wolmi Island has lost its distinction of being an island as its banks are being used to develop a huge tidal basin. The area enclosed may well be one of the largest locks in the world capable of admitting vessels over 50,000 tons.

The new docks are connected directly to the Seoul-Inchon Expressway.

These docks are a far cry from the first locks which were constructed by American engineers in 1906. These early locks modeled after the Panama Canal system were electrically controlled using enormous wooden blocks made of green hardwood grown only in South America. During the Korean War these half century old dockgates were damaged but in 1959 rehabilitation was undertaken by a joint U.S. Army and Korean team.

Today Inchon's cargo-handling terminals can accommodate 4.5 million tons in comparison to the maximum of 2.5 million tons in 1975. These developments are of great importance to the future economic growth of Korea which is related to the development of export industries, which also depend on imported raw materials. Congestion and costly delays in sea cargo management are now greatly relieved for Seoul.

Although Inchon is well known as a port city its greater importance as an

industrial city is less generally known. Korea's second largest iron and steel mill is located here with other important industries including flour milling, plywood, flat glass, auto parts, boat building and chinaware. Inchon continues to be the major fishing port for the metropolis of Seoul.

With many tourists during the summer the beaches of Songdo are perpetually crowded. Though not as pleasant and clean as other beaches the convenient proximity of the Inchon beaches still make this area a popular vacation retreat for Koreans near the capital during hot summer days. From Inchon, however, for those who have more time to spend on their vacations, ferries can be taken to outer islands from Inchon harbor and many beach resorts such as Mallipo further down the west coast provide for summer recreation.

KWANGJU

Kwangju is a provincial capital and fifth largest city in Korea with a population well over 500,000. In this area of South Cholla, Kwangju has become the cultural and commerical center for over four million people, boasting two universities, three newspapers and three radio stations. This entire area is remote and only just recently the Honam Expressway has linked Kwangju to the north and southern regions of Pusan.

To the east is a mountain range with the summit of Chiri-san, the Republic of Korea's highest peak on the mainland. On the slopes of Chiri Mountain are some famous temples which include Hwaom-sa. This is the part of Korea where cultural remains and historic treasures can still be seen in abundance, though often difficult to reach due to poor roads. Between Sunchon and Kwangju is another historic temple of considerable size called Songkwang-sa. Over the years many foreigners have entered Songkwang Temple to take training as Buddhist priests, and in 1982 there were a total of twenty foreign priests and ten foreign nuns studying at Songkwang-sa.

Though Kwangju has grown with many industries mostly in textiles, other factories have caused this city to expand rapidly. Kwangju has been hemmed in by distance, poor roads, and an inadequate railway in the past. Only in 1968 was a direct railway line opened between Kwangju and Pusan along the south coast.

Though tourist hotels are located in the city the effect of tourism has not really impressed this area of South Cholla and it will be some time before the government develops the Cholla regions for tourism.

In 1978 a new provincial National Museum was opened in Kwangju to house the collection of Chinese ceramics discovered in 1975 in a submerged trade ship at Shinan. Even in 1982, 14th century celadon items were being recovered by government divers. Efforts are being made to raise the cargo ship for exhibition. This is now the largest collection of Chinese celadon ceramics of the Yuan period located outside of China.

On the outskirts of Kwangju is the Mudang Mountain National Park. This area is highly recommended for a one day visit. Wonhyo Temple is in the area. In 1980 excavations were made which yielded numerous artifacts including bronze and clay figures from the Koryo and Silla periods. Another temple within the city area is Chungshimsa. An iron Viroch'ana image is listed as a treasure. The temple was founded by Priest Ch'olgam during the Silla period in the 9th century.

For the adventurous enthusiasts of Korean culture and history the countryside vicinities around Kwangju still provide fascinating historic remains found much in their original state. However, due to poor roads one must still expect to do considerable walking to reach these sites.

TAEJON

Taejon, located halfway between Seoul and Taegu, is reached in less than two hours by expressway bus. With a population of about 450,000, the city

Rural cow market, North Kyongsang ▷

is the administrative center for South Chungchong Province. Formerly known as a transportation center for routes south, Taejon is now becoming more industrialized.

At Taejon the Honam Expressway branches off to Chonju and Kwangju to the southwest. Taejon did not receive city status until 1949, but since that time its growth has been rapid. Because of the total destruction of the city during the Korean War, the streets were more orderly planned as many new buildings were built following the war years.

Taejon is located in a flat basin and is the starting point for the climb south over the Sobaek Range toward Taegu. During the construction of the Seoul-Pusan Expressway this portion of the highway over this mountainous terrain

was most difficult to complete because of the many tunnels and bridges which had to be built.

A few minutes' drive from Taejon is Yusong, one of the country's most famous hot spring resorts, located near the slopes of Kyeryong (Chicken Dragon) Mountain. Also nearby is the temple of Tonghak which provides the entrance to the various hiking routes over the Kyeryong Mountain range. Historically these mountains have been famous as the home of numerous indigenous religions and cults which still exist in certain areas. Along the slopes tradition is strong and the people are found to be living under the old customs of the country. An unmarried boy with braided hair or married men with a Korean "topknot" can still be seen in some areas around traditional Kyeryong-san.

Spring plowing

Transplanting rice seedlings

Harvesting the rice crop

Carrying thatch on jigae *after harvest*

Cheju-do, the Citrus Island

With contrasting cultures Cheju, the island of wind, rocks and women, has become the vacationland of South Korea. This is where the mystic volcanic peak of Halla rises high above the citrus orchards and the honeymoon couple gazes wistfully out to sea from a snug villa along the rocky coast.

Cheju, the largest and most famous of the 3000 islands of Korea, is approximately sixty miles from the southern mainland coast and thirty-five miles from the nearest offshore island. It has been since 1945 one of the nine provinces of the Republic of Korea with a population of 500,000 and an area of 700 square miles. Cheju has had a turbulent history and has quite a different culture from the mainland.

Cheju-do's principal peak is Mount Halla, the highest peak in the Republic of Korea (6,397 feet), and volcanic cone which was last active in 1007 A.D. At least fifteen separate lava flows have been identified which have left lava tunnels, pillars and other unusual features of quick-cooling basalt. Manjang-gul discovered in 1958 by a Cheju school teacher is the world's largest lava cave and has a known length of 13.4 kilometers. It was completely explored in 1981 and was found to reach the sea. At the summit of Halla is a large crater with a permanent lake. Using the shortest trail (Yongshil Course) a around trip hike to the summit would take about five hours.

Cheju-do has become a popular tourist resort island for visitors both foreign and Korean. The air distance from Seoul is less than 1½ hours while ferry service or air flight is available from Pusan to Cheju City, the main port of the island. This island has become a popular honeymoon destination for young married couples. Weekly there are forty flights from Cheju to Seoul, 30 to

Pusan, seven to Kwangju and four to Yosu. Also, direct flights come from Osaka, Fukuoka and Tokyo, Japan.

Cheju has had a turbulent history and the distant waves of many cultures have washed ashore, making this island in many ways both fascinating and different from the Korean culture of the mainland. It first came under government control during Koryo times in 938 and later was conquered by the Mongols, who attempted a systematic breeding of cattle and horses.

During the Yi Dynasty a Dutch ship was wrecked on the island's coast and its crew detained for thirteen years, Later one of the seaman, Hamel, published an account of the incident in Europe. This early record has been translated into English with the title of *The Dutch Come to Korea.* From this period the name of "Quelpart" came into use and even today appears on English language maps though the name was never used locally. The name "Quelpart" first appeared in a Dutch East India Company report and was taken from the name of a type of ship used in Asian trade.

After the Korean War years Cheju became a popular hideout for communists and the government had difficulty subduing numerous rebellions. Because of the island's remoteness, primitive practices and beliefs have still lingered on, thus sorcery is still relevant to the local people's way of life. Replicas of primitive stone carvings, which are now sold as tourist souvenirs, are still

◁ Coastline of Cheju Island near Sogwipo

being used as phallic symbols.

On Cheju live the *haenyo* (women of the sea), who are some of the hardiest people in the world. Working the year around they learn their diving and swimming talents at an early age. The women divers range in age from early teens to well past sixty (Though now younger girls tend to find other professions). Traditionally they wear a one piece suit of white cotton though more and more are seen in rubber wet suits with snorkels.

The divers plunge in without hesitation even in the coldest weather with a huge gourd and cord basket. Their indifference to the winter's frigid blasts and cold water is difficult to believe. The gourds are used as floats while they submerge sometimes for three or four minutes to depths of forty to sixty feet. The women divers of Cheju give the island its unique atmosphere and win constant admiration from tourists.

The vestiges of a matriarchal society are still noted as the men stay home to care for the families while the women work as divers, seeking shellfish along the coastal rocks. Typical Korean sights such as the use of the *chigye* (A-frame) are not seen on the island.

Within Cheju City is Samsong-hyol (Cave of the Three Spirits). On this site appeared three gods named Ko, Pu and Yang who are considered the island's forefathers. There is an even more romantic tale which dates back more than 2,000 years when the emperor of China sent out an expedition to search for the elixir of life to keep him perpetually young. This is known today in Korean as *pulloch'o,* one of the ten symbols of longevity.

The boats landed on this beautiful island (Cheju) to take on water (previously it is said that they landed also on Namhae Island and left a mysterious pictographic inscription which is visible today and called *ipgu*). When the search party left Cheju three men were missing. Since it was impossible to return for the lost three they selected three maidens from a native village on an island further east and instructed them to sail west to meet the men. After several days the three maidens were picked up by the lost men. They married, settled and populated the island of Cheju.

Sagul (Serpent Cave) is near Manjanggul, about forty minutes east of Cheju City. During the Yi Dynasty according to legends the natives would build an altar and sacrifice a teenage girl in the belief that disaster and poor crops would not occur if the huge serpent in this cave was appeased. When a new governor arrived on the island and learned of this custom he ordered the people to set up another altar but this time with wine and food. When the reptile appeared the governor stabbed the enormous monster with a spear. Mortally wounded, the serpent disappeared into the sea.

In western Cheju City is one of the island's most unusual rock formations. The dragon's head with open mouth is about thirty feet high and silhouetted perfectly against the ocean horizon. Legends tell that a servant of the Sea Dragon King climbed Mount Halla in search of *pulloch'o* (the elixir for longevity) but was killed by an arrow shot by a *shinson* (Mountain Spirit). The servant was buried here and his body became a petrified dragon with only the head protruding above the surface. Also if you are interested in eating raw fish this area is the cheapest and freshest place to buy it directly from the *haenyo.*

On the eastern side of the island are vast meadows suitable for grazing land which have supported Korea's leading livestock breeders through the centuries. One large 200,000 acre ranch is rated by foreigners as one of Asia's best stock farms. Imported stock has improved Korea's livestock. Now historically famous for horse breeding, Cheju still has over 17,000 ponies of Korea's total 25,000.

Of special interest to tourists are the Hallim Wool produced by the Irish Catholic Mission. Father McGlinchey imported 500 sheep from New Zealand twenty years ago and now the herd is 2,500. Woven Hallim sweaters are now famous world wide.

◁ *Volcanic cone of Ilch'ul-bong and rocky coast near Sogwipo, Cheju Island*

Sogwipo is a small town located on the southern side of the island known for its beaches, waterfalls and oranges. Good tourist hotels are found in Sogwipo, with some of them overlooking ocean cliffs. East of Sogwipo is Chongbang Waterfall which drops 75 feet directly on to the beach. Also near the city is Ch'onji Waterfall famous for its tropical beauty. Further east is another waterfall called Ch'onjae-yon near Chungmun town. This area is being developed by KNTC as a major tourist resort.

One of Cheju's most unusual rock formations is the strange needle rock a few meters off the coast west of Sogwipo. There is a sad legend of a fisherman lost at sea and his grieving wife. This view and the dragon head rock of Yongdam are the most beloved by the Cheju people.

Though difficult to reach the folk village of Songup located 35 miles from Cheju City should be included in your tour of the island. Designated as a Folklore Reservation Zone this village of 300 homes continues to maintain most of the traditional customs of the island. The thatched-roof rock homes with high lava stone walls surrounding the courtyards can still be seen. For visitors who wish to try something different, the pork *pulgogi* (barbecued meat) is quite famous in this village and can be ordered for lunch.

Near Cheju City is Moksok-won (Wood and Rock Park). For anyone who enjoys nature's uncommon beauty and comedy in both wood and stone this park is highly recommended. The many pieces belong to the private collection of Park Un-chol.

As a highlight to your "Cheju Adventure" the sunrise from the Eastern Sea viewed from the castlelike formation of Ilch'ul Peak near Songsan would be an unforgettable experience. This is Cheju's largest volcanic rock cone, surrounded on three sides by the ocean.

The mild southern climate is suitable for the production of oranges, grapefruit and tangerines so Sogwipo has become the citrus center for the entire country

Lava rock walls were built around the orchards to protect the trees from the constant winds. Traditionally Cheju oranges were used as tribute payment to the royal courts and during the occupation the Japanese introduced the tangerine. In 1965 it was discovered that a high quality orange could be successfully grafted on the roots of the native thorn bush variety. Now the orange production involves 12,000 farm families or about one sixth the farming population. Yearly production profits are valued at well over ten million dollars.

Cheju-do has long been territorially a part of Korea though its geography and cultural differences have been extreme. Historically the island was used as a place of exile for those who fell out of favor in the Korean court. Possibly because the island is still somewhat remote the fascination and contrasts of this island continue to draw the inquistive tourist to Cheju whether it is to hunt gamebirds or sightsee.

Majestic Mount Halla, regarded as one of three sacred mountains in Korea, is seen from any place on the island. However, it is often shrouded in clouds as the peak casts a romantic spell over this island of unusual folklore. The yearly average for clear visibility is only 33 days thus it is said that the goddess of Halla changes her mind twelve times a day. The slopes in spring are covered with azaleas while the autumn and winter scenery is also truly spectacular. Snow usually remains, on the slopes until late spring.

The future of the island is bright in the area of tourism and the production of oranges, beef and sea products for which the island is particularly well suited.

Present government plans call for Cheju to become a completely developed recreational region which will appeal to Korean tourists as well as foreign visitors within the next few years.

It is to be hoped that these recreational projects will be carefully planned, resulting in balanced development, so that no harm is done to the ecology or natural beauty of this unique island.

Halla Mountain in autumn and winter ▷

Cheju Island with a culture far different than on the Korean peninsula continues to attract the honeymoon couples. Songup, Cheju Island's folklore village, is a popular place for pork pulgogi *(barbacued meat).*

Cheju Island

Young and old come to visit the famous sites of Cheju Island; Dragonhead rock (left page), Wae-tol Kwae (above) and Ch'onji-yon waterfall (left) near Sogwipo

Honoring Admiral Yi Sun-shin

Korea's foremost military hero and one of the world's outstanding naval strategists, Admiral Yi Sun-shin is often compared with Sir Francis Drake and Lord Nelson of England. When the Japanese fleet defeated the Russian navy in 1905, the Japanese admiral was quoted to have said, "You may wish to compare me with Lord Nelson but do not compare me with Korea's Admiral Yi Sun-shin . . . . he is too remarkable for anyone."

Located at Asan near the hotspring resort of Onyang is the country's most impressive shrine, dedicated to one of the greatest military heroes of history. Take the Seoul-Pusan Expressway to the Chonan exit and then go on to Onyang (1½ hours from Seoul).

The shrine of Hyonch'ung-sa was first erected in 1706 and was to become a haven for Koreans seeking inspiration for the spirit of national vigilance and independence. In open defiance to Japanese oppression, the shrine was renovated in 1932 under the auspices of the *Dong-A Ilbo*, a Korean language daily newspaper in Seoul. In 1966 the President of the Republic of Korea designated Hyonch'ung-sa a national shrine to honor Admiral Yi Sun-shin. Major renovation of buildings and beautification of the grounds were again accomplished recently through government funds.

Admiral Yi Sun-shin was born on April 28, 1545 in Seoul to a humble Confucian scholar who remained poor most of his life, as he was uninterested in entering government service. The family soon moved to the small village of Asan where the young boy Sun-shin grew up. At the age of 31 he received his first appointment as a military officer. It wasn't until 1591 that he was appointed fleet commander for the eastern coast. The following year the seven-year invasion of Korea began by the Japanese armies of Hideyoshi.

As a military leader, Yi Sun-shin had a rare gift for developing strategy and a faithful respect for duty to his country. He drove his men night and day to prepare weapons, ammunition and the necessary supplies for the tragic conflict. In secret harbors off the south coast near Yosu, Namhae-do and Chungmu he perfected the almost forgotten designs of the world's first ironclad warship, the now famous "turtleboat."

When war began in 1592, the unprepared and outnumbered Korean army was driven back beyond Pyongyang within three months. Fortunately the naval operations under Admiral Yi Sun-shin saved Korea from complete collapse. The loss of every sea battle discouraged the Japanese invaders as it deprived them of a supply route to their armies in the far north. This strategy of cutting these supply lines signed the death warrant of the Japanese invasion of China through Korea.

The sea battle of Hansan Bay was indeed one of the greatest naval conflicts of the world and is referred to as the "Salamis of Korea." Though greatly outnumbered, the Korean fleet had the advantage of superior firepower and the awesome destructive capabilities of the feared ironclad "turtleboats." Out of a total of seventy-three Japanese vessels, fourteen managed to flee the site of battle.

Within several months Japan brought in many more warships to reinforce her losses, making a total of 500 warships

◁ *Painting and replica of Yi Sun-shin's turtle boat*

152

which met at the Port of Pusan. The fleet under Admiral Yi numbered 166 ships. An attack was made on Pusan port with a loss of 130 Japanese vessels. Continuing to focus on Japan's weak link, the supply route by sea stretching from Japan to northern Korea, the Admiral struck again and again, sending the Japanese fleet into pandemonium and destruction. The Japanese warships were no match for the ironclad "turtleboat."

Meanwhile the politicians in Seoul became jealous of Admiral Yi's successes, and false charges were made. He was brought back to the capital in chains. Without Yi Sun-shin's leadership the Korean navy soon regressed. Fortunately in 1597 the Admiral was vindicated and restored to his command. However, during this period under

Memorial statue to Admiral Yi Sun-shin, downtown Seoul

another commander the navy had shrunk to only twelve ships. With his small but brave flotilla he made a defense line between several southern islands. Heading for the west coast was an armada of 133 enemy ships. When the battle on September 16, 1597 was over more than thirty enemy ships had been destroyed while the rest of the Japanese fleet was forced to flee.

In an attempt to rescue General Konishi's blockaded troops near Sunchon a combined Japanese fleet of more than 500 ships came to the rescue. Informed of this Japanese maneuver in advance, Admiral Yi Sun-shin prepared to intercept the enemy armada at the narrow strait of Noryangjin. This last great battle took place during the early morning hours, costing the Japanese navy more than 200 ships.

At the peak of the fighting Admiral Yi Sun-shin was fatally wounded by a stray shot. He asked to be held up on the flagship so that his men would not know that he had been wounded. On November 19, 1598 the dramatic life of Korea's greatest hero came to an end at the age of 53. He was first buried on Kogum Island, the location of his last naval base, but in 1614 his tomb was relocated to a site near Hyonch'ung-sa in the rolling foothills of the valleys of his youth.

At the shrine of Hyonch'ung-sa remain the war diaries of Admiral Yi Sun-shin as well as other personal articles owned by him. The family home has been reconstructed and the original well still produces fresh water. The grave of his favorite son, who died early in the war, is nearby as well as a gnarled old gingko tree under which the Admiral during his youth practiced archery. A small museum maintains a replica of the "turtleboat" as well as other articles reminiscent of this period and the famed Admiral Yi Sun-shin.

A trip to Hyonch'ung-sa should also include a visit to the Onyang Folk Museum. This private collection is considered the best folk museum in the country. It is located on the road to the shrine on the outskirts of Onyang.

Wooded Wonderland of Sorak-san

As cooler temperatures come to the Korean peninsula and autumn foliage begins to turn to crimson red and golden yellow, the scenic spires guarding the valleys of Sorak Mountain beckon to Korean and foreign tourists. The Sorak range, which is part of the Diamond Mountains, is considered one of the world's most spectacular natural wonders. Since the Korean War the southern region of the Diamond Mountains' monolithic natural rock formations, cliffs and cascading streams has become accessible to the southern half of the divided country of Korea.

Sorak Mountain, located along the eastern coast north of Kangnung City, is readily reached by air, though an express bus ride offers the sightseer unsurpassed mountain beauty on the way. A new expressway which passes Wonju has been completed to Kangnung, which is the largest city on the coast near this growing resort area. Several tourist hotels are available as well as numerous cheaper inn facilities. During the tourist season it is recommended that reservations be made first through tourist agencies in Seoul.

Mount Sorak is the third highest peak in southern Korea, next to Halla-san and Chiri-san. The dense forests bordering crystal clear streams which tumble over cataracts and drop from precipices to form fleecy waterfalls, as well as awesome sawtooth cliffs spiraling into the blue skies, give this area an unparalleled popularity.

The Sorak range is divided into two regions, Inner Sorak and Outer Sorak. For adventuresome hikers the valleys of Inner Sorak near Paektam Temple are still virtually untouched by commercialization. However, Outer Sorak has been more developed. The main temple of the area, which is only a ten minute walk from the parking area, is Shinhung-sa. A temple called Hyangsong-sa was first constructed on this site in 632 by Priest Chajang during the reign of Queen Sondok of Silla.

Priest Chajang; coming from the ranks of Silla nobility, chose the way of the Buddha and isolated himself deep in the mountains for study and meditation. As a young boy his keen mind quickly grasped the rich pleasures of learning and scholarship, so he could have advanced rapidly in court politics.

The Silla ruler, realizing his abilities, constantly requested that Chajang accept an official position in the government and finally threatened him with a death penalty if he didn't obey. Chajang calmly replied, "I would rather die keeping the laws of Buddha for only one day than live for one hundred years while breaking them."

Seeing the wisdom of his answer, the wise ruler then permitted this noble-born son to continue his austere life in the Buddhist priesthood. After many renovations this temple built by Priest Chajang was again destroyed by fire in 1842 and rebuilt in 1847. At the time of this final reconstruction, the temple's name was changed to Shinhung-sa. There are now seven buildings.

On the stone stairway and retaining wall in front of the main hall are several unusual relief carvings. Two circular stone faces of ferocious devil-chasing spirits are positioned on each side of the staircase to guard Shinhung-sa from the enemies of Buddhism. Also floral designs of lotus blossoms provide good subject materials for those interested in stone

photo by Kang, Woon-gu

Outer Sorak Mountain, Kangwon Province

rubbing. Permission from the head priest of the temple can be obtained.

A large bell located on the premises is a fine example of a Yi Dynasty bell, though the quality of craftsmanship is far removed from that of earlier Silla and Koryo. Also carved wood blocks with large decorated letters of calligraphy can be shown by the priests upon request.

The calligraphy was written by King Sejo, who became a devout Buddhist after he ordered the strangling of his sixteen-year-old nephew Tanjong (6th king) on a cold November day in 1457 to secure the crown.

In trying to appease his own conscience for one of history's most cruel and tragic events and find a cure for a skin disease, King Sejo sought for solace in the Buddhist teachings. For this reason he frequently travelled the countryside visiting Buddhist temples and supporting their work. During the Yi Dynasty, except for King Sejo's reign, the teachings of Buddhism were generally unfavored in the royal court.

If there is time for only one hiking trip then the one-hour walk to scenic Kejo-am is recommended. This cave hermitage also dates to the Silla period and traditionally was founded by Priest Chajang. Two of the best-known and eminent of Silla priests, Wonhyo and Uisang, studied at this cave hermitage. In front of Kejo-am on a spacious stone slab is a huge spherical rock which is so perfectly balanced that it can be gently moved by a simple push of the hand.

The valley to the left of Shinhung-sa leads to Pison Falls where Miruk Peak rises majestically above the valley. One hears many legends of the heavenly nymphs who come to laugh and play while they bathes in the placid pools of the many glens hidden from human eyes. High among the crags of Miruk Peak is Kumgang Cave, once used by the early priests of Silla as a sacred sanctuary for meditation. Modern steps are now provided with a guard rail; however, the climb is still steep and exhausting. If you make it to the cave the view over the undulating mountain ranges is reward enough for this memorable experience.

In another valley a hike to Yuktam and Piryong Falls from the resort area takes visitors across swinging suspension bridges which will give an eerie thrill as you gaze down at the rocky streambed far below.

For the lanquid non-hiker there is now a modern cable car which begin on the valley floor and rises to a panoramic promontory of the entire valley. There is short hiking trails to other scenic locations. During the holiday season one may have to wait over an hour to take this short cablecar ride to the peak.

Along the coast between Sorak and Kangnung City is Naksan-sa, a temple founded by the Silla Priest Uisang. This coastal region is regarded as one of the eight scenic wonders in Kangwon Province. The temple buildings were rebuilt after the Korean War.

When Priest Uisang returned from his first visit to China he heard that the Kwanseum (Goddess of Mercy) had taken up her abode in a sea cave on the eastern coast. Priest Uisang went to worship and beheld the Buddha who presented a string of crystal beads to him. As he was leaving the cave the Dragon of the Eastern Sea offered him a jewel which he accepted. In this cave beneath the floor of the temple hall the sea dragon may still be heard roaring with the incoming tide. A place is provided where the floor boards can be lifted to see the foam of the tide below. The story of young Chosin, the lovesick monk, and the bizarre escapades of the Priest Wonhyo are only a few of the many legends relating to Naksan-sa.

Autumn is the time to travel. Whether it is Sorak-san or one of the many picturesque mountainous regions near Seoul you will find that the spirit and happiness of the people in this season is as bright as the fall foliage glistening from Korea's rugged peaks.

Kyongju, Legacy of Silla Culture

The legends of ancient Silla echo across the years, leaving a legacy of beauty and mystery through the Kyongju Valley where kings and queens once reigned supreme for a millennium. The resonance of their achievements and devotion to Buddha are still felt and recognized.

Kyongju Valley, the cradle of Silla culture and site of the dynasty's capital from 57 B.C. to 935 A.D., is located in a geographically secluded basin between Taegu and Pusan along the route of the Seoul-Pusan Expressway. Royal tombs, temple sites with weathered stone pagodas and Buddhist reliefs, as well as fortress ruins are scattered around the vicinity of this ancient Silla capital. Many of the unique sculptured art objects of this country's Buddhist heritage can be found well off the beaten trails and tourist haunts. Recently the government has developed the Kyongju region into an "outdoor tourist museum." The Po-mun Lake Resort, a government tourist project, recently opened with three deluxe hotels, comprising 850 rooms.

Kyongju is Korea's "culture city." In December 1979, during a UNESCO conference held in Thailand, Kyongju was selected as one of ten ancient historic cities throughout the entire world. A large-scale cultural survey will be undertaken as part of UNESCO's preservation program of the world's ten most important historic sites.

In 1975 a new branch of the National Museum was dedicated, containing some of the finest Korean treasures of the Silla period. For more detailed information about Kyongju reference should be made to the 1979 published book, *Kyongju Guide*. This publication of 420 pages contains over 600 carefully selected photographs with numerous charts and maps of the Kyongju vicinity.

Between 1973-75 several Silla tombs have been excavated under government sanction. Many gold art treasures including crowns, pendants and jewelery were brought to light. A "white horse" painting delicately designed on a birchbark saddle guard was discovered in near perfect condition in a 5th century tomb (Tumulus 155). Called the "Heavenly Horse Tomb," it opened in 1975 as a museum in Tomb Park and is now one of Kyongju's most popular attractions.

The Unified Silla period carried Korean culture to unprecedented heights. T'ang was one of the most brilliant and prosperous dynasties in all Chinese history, and Silla's close relationship with T'ang was fruitful both politically and culturally. All the houses within the city walls were roofed with tile. The estimated population of the capital was one million inhabitants, ten times the size of the present small city of Kyongju (pop. 120,000). A visit to the many ruins gives the tourist some idea of the city's magnificent scale, height of cultural attainment and superiority in art and learning during more prosperous days of Silla over one thousand years ago.

O-nung (Five Tombs): A grove of pine trees surrounding five tomb mounds is first noticed when one comes off the Seoul-Pusan Expressway. Pak Hyokkose, first king of the Silla Dynasty, his queen and three other early rulers of the Pak family are buried here, tradition indicates. Nearby is the memorial shrine of Sungdok-jon, while across the road in

◁ *Kyungju City view and Kyongju National Museum*

another grove of trees called Najong is where Pak Hyokkose first appeared from a gourd, which was carried from heaven by a white horse according to the legends. From Nam-san, a mountain nearby, this event was witnessed by six village elders who were searching for a ruler.

Kyerim (Cock Forest): In an elm woods on the outskirts of town is a shrine marking the site regarded as the sacred birthplace of Kim Alchi, ancestor of the Kim clan which held power the longest during the Silla Dynasty. Traditions say that Sok T'alhae (4th king) heard a cock crowing and upon investigation discovered a golden box hanging from a tree. When opened it was found to contain a handsome young boy. (The Chinese character for Kim is *kum* meaning gold.) The kingdom was known as Kyerim and then later was called Silla.

Ch'omsong-dae (Nearer the Stars Place): Near Panwol-song and Kyerim is probably the most well known of Korea's historic remains, the stone astronomical observatory built during the reign of Queen Sondok, (27th ruler) in 634. Listed as the country's National Treasure No. 31, this twenty-nine foot cylindrical bottle-shaped tower was constructed on a square base. It is considered the oldest observatory in the world and one of the oldest man-made structures left in Korea. In the middle is a small window which was probably reached by a ladder. Unfortunately there is no literary source whatsoever to show how this oldest astronomical observatory was operated and no comparable structure of this type has been found in the Far East.

Panwol-song (Half Moon Fortress): Now used as a resort site, this half-moon shaped earth fortress is now beautifully landscaped with large trees and grassy knoll. This area is believed to be the site of the first known palace for Silla kings established by King Sok T'alhae in the first century. A small memorial shrine is still maintained in honor of the Sok family and a stone ice house listed as a cultural treasure can also be seen.

Anap-ji (Pond of Geese and Ducks): Located near Panwol-song is a small pond which at one time was the most spacious palace garden in the kingdom where the rulers kept various species of birds and animals. Overlooking this pond is the historic Imhae-jon, reconstructed on a much smaller scale. Anap-ji was to become the site of the final surrender of Silla.

Punhwang-sa Pagoda: Listed as National Treasure No. 30, this imitation brick pagoda located on the temple grounds of Punhwang is considered, with Ch'omsong-dae, one of the two oldest structures in Korea. This massive pagoda was built in 634 during the reign of Queen Sondok. First it was thought to have had nine stories, though now only three remain. This large pagoda was constructed with thin slabs of stone which look like bricks, intending to imitate the Chinese-style brick pagoda. On four sides of the first story are doors guarded on either side by scowling deva guardians. Also on the four corners of the platform are sculptured stone lions, the traditional guards of Buddhist scripture. Near Punhwang-sa is the site of Silla's largest temple, Hwangyong-sa.

Nang-san: This small hill (348 feet high) referred to as Wolf Mountain is located in what was once the heart of the ancient capital of Silla and has been designated as Historic Site No. 163. The hill is seen at the intersection of Kyongju City and Pulguk-sa when coming off the expressway exit. At the peak is the tomb traditionally belonging to Queen Sondok, Silla's beloved ruling queen who died in 632. At the western foot of Nang-san is located the historic site of Sach'onwang-sa (Four Heavenly Kings Temple) and Mangdok-sa (Yearning for Virtue Temple). The highway to Pulguk-sa divides these two temple sites. Foundation stones, pillars and stone turtles are still seen in this area. On the eastern slope is a three-storied pagoda listed as National Treasure No. 37, located on the site of Hwangbok-sa (Imperial Blessing Temple). Stone remains include

Stone astronomical observatory (ch'omsong-dae), *Kyongju City* ▷

Posok-jong, *West Namsan, Kyongju (Historic Site No. 1)*

Punhwang Temple pagoda, 634 AD (National Treasure No. 30)

King Naemul's Tomb (Historic Site No. 188)

Underwater tomb of King Munmu (Historic Site No. 158)

a turtle, well stones and several zodiac figures carved in relief. Rare Buddhist objects were discovered in this pagoda and are now on display in the National Museum of Seoul. Also seen is the study hall for Ch'oe Ch'i-won, famed scholar of late Silla and father of Korean literature. Nearby is the site of King Munmu's cremation, called Nungji-t'ap. A small temple with several relief carvings and a pedestal can also be found on the slopes of Nang-san.

Kulbul-sa Site: Near the temple of Paegyul-sa is a large four-sided stone with many images carved in bold relief on its surface. The site is Kulbul-sa (Excavated Buddha Temple). Considered one of the masterpieces of Silla stone sculpturing, this rock is found in the foothills northeast of the city. Legends tell that when Kyongdok (35th king) approached this area he heard a strange sound coming from the ground, as if a monk was chanting a "sutra." He ordered the site excavated and found this huge rock with Buddhist images carved on four sides. A temple was built. On the west side is the Amit'a Buddha while on the east is the Yaksa Yorae or Buddha of Medicine.

Posok-jong (Abalone Stone Pavilion): Located on the slopes of Nam-san (South Mt.) near O-nung is the site which marks the final tragedy and death of Silla. Kyongae (55th king) and his queen were assassinated in 927 while in the midst of merry-making. Beautifully carved but strange-looking stone channels form a stream course which meanders in a circular fashion to outline an abalone shell. Cups of cool wine were floated on the waters in these narrow channels and if one stopped in front of someone, he had to drink. Often contests of poetry writing were held as wine cups floated within reach of a struggling scholar, desperately searching for the right verse.

Buddha Triad of Sungbang Valley: Located on the west side of Nam-san near Posok-jong is the small shrine of Sambul-sa (Three Buddha Temple) where three stone images now stand which were discovered in 1923. Though the exact date is not certain it is believed that they were carved during the Three Kingdoms Period prior to Silla unification. This triad is considered one of the oldest Buddhist remains in the country.

Sacred Nam-san (South Mountain): Though broken fragments of Buddhist images, pagodas and other numerous stone temple objects can be found in almost every valley near Kyongju, the cultural remains in the more than twenty valleys of South Mountain (Nam-san), near Kyongju are the greatest in number. The average tourist could not possibly see everything. However, to see the stone relief carvings at Ch'ilbul-am (Seven Buddha Hermitage) would be an unforgettable adventure, as these priceless art objects of religious heritage are only surpassed by the Buddhist sculpturing found in the Sokkuram. A one hour hike is necessary beyond Namsan Village.

The twin pagodas of Namsan Village, Sochul-ji and Buddha image of Pori-sa, located on the eastern slopes of Nam-san, are easier to reach. The many relief carvings found on a gigantic natural rock in T'ap Valley also provide a treasure chest of historical mystery. On the western side of Nam-san are many tombs of the Pak clan. Also Yongjang Valley and Samnung Valley offer many carved stone remains for the adventuresome hiker. Often places are not well marked and a guide is recommended.

Tomb of Kim Yu-shin: Several Silla tombs contain zodiac animals carved in relief, but the reliefs at the tomb of General Kim Yu-shin are regarded as among the finest carved zodiac figures. Kim Yu-shin served as Silla's greatest general under King Muyol and his son Munmu in the 7th century by unifying Silla. This tomb, which by tradition belongs to Kim Yu-shin, is located a short distance west of town. The stone fence surrounding the mound was reconstructed in 1976.

Tomb of King Muyol: King Muyol (29th king) of Silla is considered one of the greatest kings of the dynasty who originated the move toward unification of Silla in the mid-seventh century. His tomb is located west of Kyongju near the old highway to Taegu. The turtle tablet located in front of this tomb mound has been designated as National Treasure No. 25. The skill and elegance of the sculpturing is difficult to match anywhere in Korea. Other royal tombs which belong to family members of King Muyol are located in a park area behind. Nearby is Soak Sowon, a Yi Dynasty Confucian study hall and a three-storied stone pagoda with relief image (T-65). Across the street is another tomb and tomb turtle belonging to Kim In-mun, second son of Muyol and brother of the unification ruler, King Munmu.

Kwoe-nung: This tomb traditionally belongs to Wonsong (38th king) and is one of seven royal tombs where the zodiac images are found carved in stone on the retaining wall. A few years ago it was believed that this tomb belonged to the Silla unification ruler Munmu (30th king) but upon the discovery of King Munmu's underwater tomb on the east coast near Kamp'o by Dr. Hwang Su-young, former director of the National Museum and President of Dongguk University, the identity of Kwoe-nung's occupant has been somewhat doubtful. Its location is easy to find beyond Pulguk-sa Station on the old Pusan highway. Kwoe-nung is one of the most elaborate of the Silla tombs, as stone military and civilian officials, as well as sculptured lions, still maintain their vigil in front of the tomb mound.

Turtle tablet (National Treasure No. 25) at tomb site of King Muyol, Kyongju

Silla Festival

Silla queen and float dramatizing the birth of Pak Hyokkose are the main attractions during this festival.

Paekche's Puyo and Kongju

Paekche culture represents a period of almost seven hundred years from the founding of the dynasty in 18 B.C. until its conquest by Silla in 660 A.D. The two national museums located in Kongju and Puyo will highlight your tour of this area of southwest Korea. Though the remains are few in number the quality and level of artistic development which dates to pre-seventh century evoke an aura of impressive antiquity.

Paekche, one of the three kingdoms which rose to power during the first century B.C., has its own unique culture and is characteristically different from that of Koguryo or Silla, though only the more serious student of Koreanology can differentiate. Originally Paekche established its capital directly south of the Han River, on the outskirts of Seoul and near the tourist attraction of South Fortress. Now nothing remains. Because of the growing strength of the Koguryo Dynasty to the north, Paekche moved its capital in 475 to the present city of Kongju in Chungchong-namdo. Once again moving further south in 538, it established its last capital in the city of Puyo along the Kum River.

It is traditionally believed that the art heritage of this kingdom was most influential in Japan and that Buddhism during its migration eastward came mostly from Paekche rather than Koguryo or Silla. However, theories vary as recent tomb excavations in Takamatsu, Japan, seem to point to stronger Koguryo influence. The Paekche religious influence was strongly felt at Horyu-ji, one of Japan's earliest temples, near the city of Nara.

To reach Puyo it is best to take the expressway to the Nonsan exit (between Taejon and Chonju). While in Nonsan it is recommended that the famed Unjin Miruk be visited. This gigantic image is located only a few miles from town at Kwanch'ok Temple. This is the largest stone Buddha image in Korea today. At Popchu-sa there is a larger concrete image, but the Unjin Miruk is considerably more aesthetic and ancient, as it dates to the Koryo period.

Puyo is a small town and the museum is located against the hill called Puso-san which dominates the Kum River. The museum's architecture is an interesting blend of traditional and modern. When it was constructed a few years ago it caused considerable controversy because of claimed Japanese influence. The stone displays in the museum yard offer more interest. Two tablet remains and a stone tub have been designated as listed treasures. Also a small replica of a Paekche tomb, similar to the ones located on the outskirts of Puyo, can be seen on the museum grounds.

Puso-san was at one time the capital's fortress, and many of the ancient pavilions have been reconstructed. One could spend over two hours meandering the many trails and enjoying the panoramic views of the river. Samch'ung-sa enshrines the memorial tablets for the loyal supporters of the last Paekche king, and each year in October a festival is held to honor these men. At the top of the hill there is the pavilion called Yongil-ru (Rising Sun Pavilion) where the king once came to watch the sun rise over his kingdom. Nearby the earthwork of the old fortress wall can be seen. There is also a shrine for the palace girls called Kungnyo-sa.

◁*Kum River near Puyo, South Chungchong*

Perhaps the most beautiful and well photographed of all pavilions is Nakhwa-am, located on a bluff overlooking the Kum River at the bend called Paekma (White Horse). Legends relate that General Su, the Chinese commander who was attacking with Silla forces, believed that he could not cross the river because of a dragon living in its depths. Using the head of a white horse as bait, the general went fishing and managed to capture and kill the dragon. As enemies swarmed into the capital the court ladies flung themselves into the water from this bluff rather than suffer the shame of submitting to atrocities of the conquering enemy armies. Thus Nakhwa-am, Rock of Falling Flowers, was so named.

Below the bluff is a small temple, Koran-sa, which takes its name from a small plant having medicinal properties that grows near the spring behind this temple. The king of Paekche always drew water from this spring.

In the center of town is a small park where there are two treasured remains which were removed from the site of the ancient Paekche temple of Chongrim-sa. An eleven-foot-high Buddha image (Treasure No. 108) is sitting on a stone pedestal. Also a five-storied pagoda (National Treasure No. 9) is seen nearby. Typically representative of Paekche style, it is one of the oldest pagodas in Korea, dating to the Three Kingdoms Period. The statue in the center of town is General Kaebaek who fought valiantly against the combined Chinese and Silla forces and died in 660.

Kongju is located north of Puyo. On the way the famous temple of Kap-sa, in the Kyeryong (Chicken Dragon) Mountain can be seen. Though somewhat off the beaten track, Kongju is a rather pleasant city. If one is to go directly to Kongju from Seoul it is advisable to leave the expressway at Chochiwon. Overnight accommodations are somewhat better than at Puyo.

Kongju served as the Paekche capital until almost the mid-sixth century. The town is dominated by the mountain of Kong-san which still has the remains of fortifications. Two rather picturesque

gates which were reconstructed during the Yi Dynasty, as well as several pavilions, provide for the people of Kongju a rather pleasant recreational area. There is also a monument honoring the Ming general who assisted in the defense of Kongju during the late 16th century Japanese invasion.

A fascinating archeological display is the remains from the excavated royal Paekche tomb of King Muryong (501-524) who was one of the last rulers to reign in the capital of Kongju. His successor moved the capital to Puyo. While accomplishing some repairs to existing Paekche burial mounds on the outskirts of town, workmen accidentally found an unknown stone wall. Authorities were called. During the summer of 1971 Dr. Kim Won-yong, one of Korea's most eminent archeologists, helped bring before the public one of Korea's greatest discoveries of the twentieth century. The tomb was found to be completely undisturbed since it was sealed in the early sixth century. Hundreds of artifacts which were uncovered are now on display in Kongju and Seoul's National Museum.

Along the Southern Coast

The South Sea coastal regions of Korea have long been popular with Korean travelers, but recently, with the completion of the Honam and Namhae expressways, these picturesque coast routes are now more accessible. The areas around Chinhae, Chungmu, Chinju and Namhae are recommended as the highlights of this scenic region.

The southern boundary of the Korean peninsula is a sunken coastline which has created an irregular pattern of bays and inlets with over 400 offshore islands. In addition to the expressway and rail service, the use of the hydrofoil between Pusan and Yosu is recommended as it stops at Chinhae, Chungmu and Namhae. Reservations for transportion and hotels can be made in Seoul through travel agencies.

Chinhae City is headquarters for Korean naval activities and should be visited during the cherry blossom season in spring. During the Japanese occupation thousands of flowering cherry trees were planted by the authorities. The flowering cherry is also indigenous to Korea and may well have been exported from the peninsula to the Japanese islands. It is also known that the cherry trees in Washington DC actually came from Korea, which was then part of the Japanese empire. A festival week in Chinhae City usually brings thousands of sightseers, both Korean and foreign. This is one of the few places in Korea where bull fighting is provided as entertainment.

Chungmu is a traditional seaport of great charm and historical interest. For someone seeking a quiet place to rest and relax for a few days, Chungmu is a particularly good choice. A tourist hotel is situated on a scenic spur of land several miles from the busy port. The many offshore islands near this port city are rich in tradition relating to Admiral Yi Sun-shin, Korea's greatest naval hero. Most of the historical remains are associated with Admiral Yi who, using the famous "turtle boats," was able to halt Japanese naval activities during the Hideyoshi invasion of 1592. The name *chung* and *mu* means loyalty and military, which comes from a posthumous title conferred on Admiral Yi in 1643.

On the peak of Nammang, a peninsula jutting into the bay, is a standing life size bronze statue of Admiral Yi considered the oldest in Korea. When comparing his sword enshrined at Chungnyol-sa and this statue, one is aware of the immense size of this man. In the center of town is Sebyonggwan (Treasure No. 293), a large review hall 115 x 60 feet which was used for military training. It dates to the early 17th century and was restored in 1963. Along the compound wall are two pillars which were once used as stockades for criminals. The person's limbs were placed through the holes in the pillars.

The shrine of Chungnyol-sa, meaning "Faithful to King and Country," was first established in 1606 and is now both a museum and shrine for Admiral Yi. In the inner shrine are an altar, table and spirit tablet. Visitors can enter by permission from the shrine custodian. The eight relics (Treasure No. 440) on display were gifts to Admiral Yi from the Chinese emperor in honor of his naval victories. They include a seven-foot commander's bugle, a 5½ foot execution sword, a ceremonial spirit-head sword (weight: 66 Lbs.), tiger head standard for delivering orders, Admiral Yi's seal and several signal flags.

The markets of Chungmu offer a wide variety of basketware. Several renowned lacquer factories are producing some of the finest furniture in Korea. Another specialty is the *kat* or traditional horsehair Korean hat which is still being made by the elderly Korean artisans.

Miruk Island is separated by a narrow strait from the mainland and connected by a bridge and a tunnel. The tunnel, used by pedestrians now, was constructed by the Japanese in 1932. Miruk Island contains two small temples in rather scenic sites, Yonghwa-sa and Kwanum-am.

While in Chungmu one must certainly visit Hansan Island, the site of Admiral Yi's headquarters and where he won his most spectacular sea victory in July 1592. Boats can be rented from the city or tourist hotel. The voyage takes about thirty minutes. The scenic forested islands scattered about in blue waters will provide unforgettable breathtaking vistas of enchantment.

Chinju can be reached by air, expressway bus or train. Though one can stay in town at modest hotels or Korean inns, it is more enjoyable to stay at Lake Chinyang, only a few miles from the city. This is a newly formed reservoir lake with many hotels located on a high knoll overlooking the water.

The historic point of interest in Chinju is the old Chinju Fortress which is situated on the cliffs of the South River. Here one can envisage the tragic tale of the patriotic *kisaeng*, for Chinju is the scene of the story of Non'gae. The sad death of the faithful Non'gae has endeared her forever to the hearts of all Koreans. During the first year of the Japanese invasion, the outnumbered Korean forces soundly defeated the Japanese armies at Chinju in October 1592. Though the commanding General Kim Shi-min lost his life, this success was one of three victories on the Korean peninsula achieved by the badly unprepared Korean armies.

The following year another assault was ordered on Chinju by a force of 60,000 Japanese under the command of General Kato. The Koreans had a force of only 10,000. Though the fortress was bravely defended the odds were too great, and when the Japanese breached the inner walls the garrison commander and his aides threw themselves to their deaths in the river.

That night as the Japanese celebrated with a victory party one of the entertainers was the beautiful 21-year-old *kisaeng* Non'gae who was overcome with grief by the death of her patron, Choe Kyong-hoe, the fortress commander. Feigning some amorous attention for one of the boisterous generals, Non'gae guided him cleverly to the edge of a rocky cliff and while holding him tightly plunged into the swirling river, drowning both of them. Now this large rock near the hall of Ch'oksok-ru where the general and Non'gae perished is called Uirang-am (Faithful Woman Rock) and contains this inscription. "Eternal as the river, may the memory of her loyalty never fade."

This castle may have existed from Silla times. However, records state that it was built in 1356 during the Koryo period and has been rebuilt several times since. The walls are over thirty feet high. Directly inside the main gate is Ch'oksok-ru, one of Korea's most magnificent structures, which unfortunately was burned during the Korean War and reconstructed in 1959. To the west is the memorial shrine for Non'gae where a modern painting of her is exhibited. Views along the wall overlooking the river will excite the photography enthusiast. Other temples, shrines and pavilions are found in the fortress park.

Namhae Island is about thirty miles from Chinju over well paved roads. Take the Namhae Expressway west to the Chin'gyo exit. The island is reached by one of the Orient's longest suspension bridges. Painted in orange, it appears as a miniature "Golden Gate" of San Francisco. The hydrofoil stops at Noryang directly below the bridge twice daily on its route between Pusan and Yosu.

Namhae is Korea's third largest island, shaped like a large hour-glass. The mountains are high and rugged while the scenery is picturesquely rural, offering many pastoral views. The road is paved to the principal town in the center of the island.

Near the port town is a small shrine which memorializes the last great battle won by Admiral Yi Sun-shin in which he lost his life. This great victory took place in the Noryang Strait just off Namhae Island. The shrine was first constructed in 1658 and later furnished with a plaque by Hyonjong (18th Yi king). Inside is an altar and on the walls are several murals which depict this famous battle. In 1969 the shrine was rebuilt and a new signboard was presented by President Park Chung-hee.

On the way to Namhae town is another shrine situated on a delightfully wooded peninsula overlooking the island-dotted waters of the bay where Admiral Yi lost his life. Former President Park Chung-hee wrote an inscription that is translated "A Great Star Falls into the Sea."

On the southern tip of the island is one of Korea's most attractive beaches situated below the rugged spires of Kum-san. A skull-shaped cave with hermitages and pagodas offers a variety of scenic beauty to the more energetic hiker. The sunrise view over the southern sea is magnificent.

On the slopes of Kum-san is to be found one of the most mysterious inscriptions in all Korea. Many claim the odd writing on stone, sometimes referred to as *ipgu*, is pre-Chinese and that similar inscriptions are found on Sakhalin Island and in far-away Norway. Some scholars think it represents a hunting scene. On the boulder-strewn hillside without a guide it would be almost impossible to find this unique inscription.

Squid drying in the sun, Ullung Island off the east coast

Drying laver near Kangjin, South Cholla

Waterwheel power is often used to grind grain, South Kyongsang

Chapter IV.
Buddhist Legacy

A Buddhist priest at prayer, Yongmun-sa,
North Kyongsang

What Is a Buddhist Temple?

Shortly after arriving in Korea most foreigners usually have an opportunity to visit a Korean Buddhist temple. It often is a famous monastery south of Seoul where many tourists daily tramp through the courtyards with cameras frequently clicking, or you might be fortunate to visit a small hermitage located high in a quiet forested glen far from the chatter and clatter of people and the city. Korea has many temples, with most of them integrated into the scenic landscape to become an integral part of this country's culture.

According to the officially accepted date, the arrival of Buddhism in Korea took place in 372 A.D. Priest Sundo, a Chinese, was welcomed by the ruler of the Koguryo Kingdom, Sosurim (17th king), in the first year of his reign. Twelve years later Marananda carried the Buddhist teachings further south to the Paekche Kingdom. Only Silla appears to have been initially hesitant to accept Buddhism, and it is believed that the religion was introduced into this south-eastern region of Korea by 424 through the efforts of Priest Ado (some say Priest Mukhoja but they may have been the same person). Priest Ado's missionary zeal was doomed to failure as the Silla people were unwilling to accept the new religion, unlike their neighbors in Koguryo and Paekche.

After the martyrdom of the official Yi Ch'a-don in 527, who prophesied that his own blood would run white as milk after his death to illustrate the truth of Buddha, the faith prospered throughout the Silla Kingdom. This event occurred during the reign of Pophung (23rd Silla king) and today there remains a tablet in the Kyongju National Museum memorializing this historic event and the miracle connected with Yi Ch'a-don's death.

The golden age of Buddhist art and sculpture glittered and waned within the eighth century. Silla succumbed to Koryo in 936 and Buddhism became a powerful, influential political faction in the royal court for the next several centuries. In 1392 the famed General Yi Sung-gye (T'aejo) wrested the throne from the corrupted monarchy to establish the Yi Dynasty. Buddhism fell into disfavor with the rising popularity of Confucianism. Many temples were destroyed, and later Japanese armies under Hideyoshi marched across the peninsula completing the destruction. Most of the temple structures that one sees today postdate 1592 as a result of this Japanese conquest.

Before entering a larger temple the visitor will pass through a gate called Sach'onwang (Four Heavenly Kings). The images found in this gate represent mythical rulers of kingdoms located in the four directional corners of the universe. They are usually depicted crushing the enemies of Buddhism beneath their feet. One of the two images on the left is holding a dragon while the other is holding a pagoda. Across the aisle one image holds a sword. Occasionally at the larger temples you might find an additional type of entry gate honoring the two Bodhisattvas called Munsu Posal and Pohyon Posal. Munsu rides a tiger while Pohyon is astride an elephant.

Before the main courtyard is reached there is usually a large study hall. Often one walks under this hall into the courtyard. The main hall of the temple

◁ Goddess of Mercy (kwanseum) *at Unhae Temple, North Kyongsang (Treasure No. 514)*

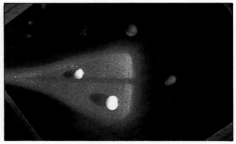

No smoking and loud talking is usually expected within the temple compound. Floral temple doors were designed with care and sari *are held as religious relics of the past. Pongjong-sa, Kumyong-sa, North Kyongsang.*

Temple guard of the Myongbu-jon at Pusok Temple, North Kyongsang

frequently carries the name Taeung-jon or Taeungbo-jon. Within the Taeung-jon is found the Buddha called the Sokkamoni or Historic Buddha.

If the main hall carries the name Kuknak-jon then the image within is always the Amit'abul, Buddha of Western Paradise. The Sokkamoni and Amit'a are the two most popular Buddha deities in Korea today. It is difficult to identify the two images, differentiated only by their hand positions.

Occasionally the Piroch'ana Buddha is found at some temples either in the main hall or a side building. It is easy to recognize this image as the index finger of one hand is held by the closed fist of the other. The Piroch'ana is the Universal Buddha made popular during the Silla period after the introduction of the Hwaom Sect.

Visitors often ask, "Why are there three Buddha images in the sanctuary?" Usually the attendants on each side are not Buddhas, but Bodhisattvas, attending the central Buddha. One might refer to

them as second rank deities as they have not as yet entered Nirvana to become Buddhas, but have passed all the qualifications. The Bodhisattvas have elected to remain behind to help poor mortals who are trying to gain Nirvana (paradise). Usually the attendants on either side of the Sokkamoni are Munsu Posal and Pohyon Posal, while the companions to the Amit'abul are Kwanseum Posal and Taesaji Posal. The Kwanseum commonly referred to as the Mercy Goddess is the most popular Bodhisattva in Korea.

There are other buildings at the larger temples. Without exception you will always find the Myongbu-jon (Judgment Hall) which contains the Bodhisattva Chijang Posal, his two attendants and ten judges who determine one's fate after death. Usually murals depicting punishment for various types of sins are prominently displayed behind the judges. One standing attendant beside Chijang Posal is holding a box which contains the keys to paradise.

Dragon-headed carp of Pokyong Temple, Kyonggi Province

188

Another building often seen is the Yongsan-jon, named for a sacred mountain in India. Within is the Sokkamoni Buddha with numerous *nahan* (disciples of Buddha) images. The total number might range from sixteen to a maximum of five hundred, and some temples have just that many each with different expressions if one takes the time to count.

Occasionally the building Palsang-jon contains large murals honoring the eight most important events in the life of Buddha. Also the Yaksa Yorae is a popular Buddha in Korea. This healing Buddha is often found somewhere within the temple vicinity, and at larger temples the Yaksa Yorae will have its own shrine. The image is easy to recognize as it always holds in its hands a small round *kusul* (medicinal capsule).

One of the most intriguing aspects of all temples is the shamanistic influence to be found in Buddhism. The shaman images may be seen in separate buildings or found together within one building or

even inside the main hall of smaller temples. Nevertheless, the shamanistic spirits are almost always present and are referred to as Samsong (Three Spirits). First is the Mountain Spirit or Sanshin which is the most popular. This spirit is usually depicted as an old bearded man with a tiger reclining at his feet. The second is Ch'ilsong (Seven Star Spirit) representing the spirit of the seven stars of the Big Dipper. The last of the three spirits is the Lone Spirit called Toksong, represented simply as a solitary old man. Often these three spirits are enshrined in small buildings located behind the main hall and further up the mountainside.

Before leaving, look for the five musical instruments traditionally used in temple worship. The bell of course is easy to notice. Some of the finest and oldest bells in the world came from Korea's temples. There is also the drum and smaller bronze gong. The fourth instrument might be more difficult to recognize as it appears to be a giant wooden fish but upon closer inspection you will find that it is hollow. This colorful carp is struck with sticks within the hollow space. To be used in the chanting of the *sutra* is the *moktak,* a wooden clacker hit by a small stick. The hollow *moktak* with a small opening is held in the left hand. Its clacking helps to keep the rhythm as the priest chants.

If your time in Seoul is limited the two temples which are recommended and easy to reach by car, yet typical of Buddhist temples in Korea, are Kyong-guk-sa in Chongnung Valley and Pongun-sa. Though it does not have a large Sach'onwang Gate, Kyongguk-sa is the most beautifully landscaped temple in the city. Pongun-sa, located south of the Han River near Yongdong Bridge, will take less then thirty minutes to reach from downtown Seoul. Pongun-sa has the best *sach'onwang* images in the Seoul area.

To learn more about the many temples in the Seoul vicinity the two volume book *Through Gates of Seoul* is recommended.

Mokt'ak *and typical temple musical instruments; drum, gong and carp*

Koryo wall painting of the Goddess of Mercy (kwanseum) at Muwi Temple, South Cholla. Main hall Kuknak-jon is National Treasure No. 13 (left page)
Temple wall painting of heavenly devas with musical instruments, Taehung Temple, South Cholla
Portrait of Priest Sa-myong, soldier monk, Taehung Temple

Wall painting of souls entering Nirvana over sea of hell, Naksan Temple, Kangwon Province (Renovation in 1979 destroyed this painting)

Nunnery of Unmun-sa, North Kyongsang

At Kolgul-am a priest offers prayer, near Kyongju

Pulguk Temple and Sokkuram

Starting with Korea's best-known temple, Pulguk-sa, and the world famous Sokkuram, seven additional temples are presented with historical background and legends. These temples are the most ancient as they all date to the Silla period and are now considered the more important temples of the country. Accessibility and natural beauty of the regions were considered in making the selection. The mountains surrounding these temples provide excellent hiking trails, often leading to small hermitages high on the slopes.

Built on a series of stone terraces ten miles from Kyongju City in the foothills of Toham Mountain, the recently renovated Pulguk-sa (Buddhist Country Temple) probably draws many more tourists than any other Buddhist temple in Korea today. Pulguk-sa is known as one of the oldest surviving monasteries in this country and according to legends was first constructed in 535 during the reign of Pophung (23rd Silla king). This king was the first to accept the teachings of Buddha and gave this religion royal sanction. A few years earlier (527) Yi Ch'a-don was martyred for espousing Buddhism and from this period the faith rapidly spread throughout the Silla Kingdom. Later in life the king stepped down from the throne and took on the garb of a Buddhist priest while his queen entered a nunnery.

Two hundred years later during the reign of Kyongdok (35th Silla king) the temple was redesigned and rebuilt by Kim Tae-song to honor his parents. The many legends surrounding the person of Kim Tae-song are fascinating to say the least. He first lived with his widowed mother in the small village of Moryang west of Kyongju (this village can still be found). He was an odd boy with a big head and flat forehead; thus, he was teased with the name of *taesong* meaning Big Fortress.

Though extremely poor, he was honest and faithful to Buddhism. The boy died early and was reincarnated into the family of the Prime Minister Kim Mun-yang. The lad's rebirth had been prophesied by a mysterious voice from heaven and when the prime minister's wife gave birth to a baby boy they found in his palm the characters for *taesong* written in gold.

As the boy grew to manhood his heart was moved by divine inspiration and he designed this marvelous memorial, Pulguk Temple, honoring his parents. The Sokkuram behind Pulguk-sa was, according to the legend, built to honor the parents of his first existence.

As we ponder about Kim Tae-song, the man who in 751 was credited with building this graceful landmark which epitomizes the spirit and soul of Silla, we may smile at the legends, but we must also stand in awe before Korea's most remarkable achievement. Pulguk-sa and its rear hermitage, the Sokkuram, symbolize the apex of architectural artistry, leaving for the world lasting footprints of ages gone by.

When we contemplate the achievements of Silla's artists we cannot but admit that they bear witness to a refined aesthetic taste. Restraint and classical beauty are unmistakable characteristics of Korean artistic development. In architectural design the total effect of Pulguk-sa is of restrained dignity and peaceful harmony. Large stones are loosely patterned together, without mortar of

◁ Sokkuram grotto of Pulguk Temple, Kyongju (National Treasure No. 24)

Stone bridge entrances to Pulguk Temple, Kyongju (National Treasures No. 22 and 23)

any kind, and have somehow outlasted the earthquakes and wars of the last twelve hundred years.

Including recent renovations completed in 1973, there have now been twenty-three reconstructions. Pulguk-sa is one tenth the size of the original temple site during Silla. However, the balance and symmetry of its former glory are still seen in walls, bridges, pillars and stone pagodas. It is no exaggeration to say that Silla was responsible for the most beautiful classical works of art in the Far East, differing both from the ornate and often distorted works of China, and from the frequently sentimental and pattern-ridden arts of Japan. This Buddhist temple still remains one of the most remarkable ancient achievements of the Far East.

At Pulguk-sa the visitor can view six of Korea's national treasures. The stone staircases and gates are the two traditional entrances to the temple grounds; one leads to the main hall (Taeung-jon) while the smaller entrance bridge leads to the Kuknak-jon or hall for the Amit'a Buddha. These bridges have been designated as National Treasures Nos. 22 and 23. In the architecture of the bridge and wall we find simplicity harmonizing with a strong artistic sense of symmetry and proportion. Since the 1973 renovation neither of these two bridges can be used by tourists.

The new roofed corridors now extend out and around the Taeung-jon and Kuknak-jon. Also connected are the Drum Pavilion and the Kyong-ru which contain the temple gong and a large wooden carp gong.

On the high terraced courtyard before the main hall are two great pagodas of Silla, one simple in construction and the other complex, complementing each other and symbolic of Buddhism's contemplation and detachment from the world.

The legendary designer and architect was the master craftsman, Asadal, who it is believed came from Paekche. The sad romantic tale of Asadal who lost his lovely young wife Asanyo near Pulguk-sa pulls at the heartstrings of the Korean people. After his wife's death Asadal left for his own country, never to return.

The genius of Asadal's craftsmanship is characterized by the calm simplicity of lines, the elegance of proportion which avoids exaggeration, and the loftiness of expression in the form of the Sokka Pagoda (National Treasure No. 21) which represents the Buddha absorbed in transcendent peace. The complexity of the Tabo Pagoda (National Treasure No. 20) symbolizes the Tabo Buddha's manifestation in a diversified universe. There are few stone monuments in the East which, without a trace of mortar, are pieced together so tastefully and with such rich variation as this pagoda.

The Tabo-t'ap or "Pagoda of Many Treasures" is unique in Korea and for that matter in all of Asia. It is Korea's best known pagoda and can be seen on ten *won* coins as well as travel posters around the world. This unique and elaborate thirty-four-foot structure reveals unsurpassed majesty and beauty. This pagoda has been held up as an example of the versatility and genius of Korean artisans.

Located within the Kuknak-jon and Piro-jon are 6.5-foot bronze images of the Amit'a and Piroch'ana Buddha. These images are two of the three bronze statues extant in Kyongju which were believed to have been produced during the eighth century within the period of Kim Tae-song. From an artistic viewpoint these images are considered to be truly classical masterpieces of sculpturing. The round shapes, lines and symmetry of the anatomy are quite apparent in spite of the new paint of recent years. Only the hand positions are different. The images are both listed as National Treasures Nos. 26 and 27.

The Piroch'ana (one hand holding the index finger of the other) Buddha is considered the oldest bronze statue of this type in Korea today. Silent in its aesthetic beauty, the Piroch'ana's robe is draped simply about him, falling from the arms in unsurpassed grace. Few Oriental artisans have attained the noble exquisite charm demonstrated by this Korean image which ranks as a classic example of the refinement of Buddhist art of Korea.

The corridors surrounding the worship halls have recently been reconstructed as were several of the buildings themselves. Often on weekends during the spring and fall the temple compound is packed with people, so much so that the temple has taken on a carnival atmosphere. Though Pulguk-sa is not typical of most Korean Buddhist temples, which still manage to maintain an aura of calm serenity, nevertheless to tour Kyongju and not visit this famed temple of Silla's "golden age" would be unthinkable.

The grotto known as *sokkuram* was built by Kim Tae-song who is also credited with building Pulguk-sa. To see the classic example of Silla stone sculpturing, a tour to the "stone cave hermitage" behind Pulguk Temple will be an unforgettably rewarding experience. One can drive the distance on a paved toll road or walk on a wide path which takes over one hour. Within a thirty-foot domed rotunda is a large stone carved Buddha image of magnificent artistry. Encircling the chamber are the ten important seven-foot disciples of Buddha in relief.

The relief image of the eleven-headed Goddess of Mercy on the center rear wall of the sanctuary will hold visitors spellbound. Considered by critics as the most beautiful sculptured figure in all Korean art, this *kwanseum posal* is slender and elegantly dressed in astonishingly realistic and fluid garments with tassels and jewelry arranged in loops, cross folds and knots.

The supple feminine form contrasts abruptly with the fear-evoking guardians positioned on either side of the entrance to the grotto. Eight heavenly *palbujong* and two scowling *inwang* threaten to strike intruding evil spirits. The *sach'on-wang* or Four Heavenly Kings are depicted firmly crushing beneath their feet demons representing the enemies of Buddhism.

Unfortunately several years ago the government decided that the Sokkuram

was in danger of damage and was closed to the general public. A glass partition was placed across the entrance so now visitors can see only a portion of the Sokkuram. Images on the rotunda wall and the Kwanseum figure on the rear wall are hidden.

The natural sense of beauty in lines and proportion depicted in baffling simplicity, this masterpiece produces an eerie magnetism for those coming to visit the Sokkuram. Here in this grotto is found a certain distinctive quality in Korean art – a real earnestness matched with dignity and grandeur, classic and idealistic naturalism, yet simple with modest and unobtrusive interpretation of form. Korea in her position between China and Japan maintained a role of assimilating and passing on to Japan the arts of China. During this period of T'ang assimilation Silla improved upon it in accordance with national characteristics and raised it to the highest classical plateau in the Far East. Korea not only accepted the tradition of her teacher but in many cases ennobled it, and in the Buddhist art of cave temple tradition, Korea has produced the world's classical example – the Sokkuram of Kyongju.

Sokka-t'ap of Pulguk Temple (National Treasure No. 21)

Tabo-t'ap of Pulguk Temple (National Treasure No. 20)

Popchu Temple

Popchu-sa, located in the rugged Sokni range east of Taejon, can be reached by a completely paved road in three hours from Seoul. A fine tourist hotel is in operation and there are numerous small inns in the vicinity, so that accommodations within the valley are more than adequate. Within the last few years this mountainous area of Sokni, meaning "escape from the vulgar," has become increasingly popular for Seoulites wishing to escape from the drag of close urbanization.

According to temple records Popchu-sa was first established in 553 during the reign of Silla's King Chinhung by one of the most famous of Korean priests, Uisang. In the early 12th century it is noted that the king gathered over 30,000 priests together to pray for the ailing National Priest Uich'on. The large iron pot on display at the temple may well have been used to feed this large gathering.

Popchu-sa has been rebuilt many times over the years. The last major renovation took place in 1906. The more recently built seventy-five-foot concrete image of the Miruk (Buddha of the Future) rises quite impressively over the temple compound. It is the largest Buddhist image in Korea.

The legends of Sejo (7th Yi Dynasty king) at Popchu-sa are probably the best known among Koreans. King Sejo was the second son of Sejong (4th king) who invented the *han'gul* (Korean alphabet). Sejong's eldest son mounted the throne but soon died leaving the crown to his eleven-year-old son, Prince Tanjong. Sejo, the boy's uncle, plotted to have the boy-king killed, setting the stage for one of the most tragic episodes in Korean history. According to legends, during the night of Tanjong's murder, the angered spirit of the boy's mother appeared to King Sejo and spat a curse on his body while prophesying that Sejo also would lose his eldest son. Tokjong, the crown prince, died within a year and Sejo developed a skin disease which proved incurable (probably leprosy). As a result

he became a devout Buddhist and searched the countryside constantly for a divine cure. Here in a mountain stream behind Popchu-sa he was cured by heavenly intervention.

A melancholy tale is told about King Sejo's only daughter Princess Uisuk. She pleaded with her father to stop all the senseless killing of the scholars loyal to Tanjong. King Sejo in a blind rage threatened to have her killed the next day. Assisted by the queen, Uisuk feigned suicide and was able to slip beyond the city walls. Fleeing into the mountainous regions of Sokni-san, the young girl happened to notice by the side of the road a young man also traveling in her direction. The youth asked if he might assist the weary travelers. Along the road their companionship grew into love and eventually they married. They built a small hut and settled down as farmers. Later two sons were born and all this time the girl continued to hide her true identity.

At last they agreed that each really should tell about his own family background without fear, and Uisuk revealed that she was actually the king's daughter. The husband immediately became gloomy and despondent. Finally he told her that he was the son of General Kim Chong-suh whose entire family had been killed by King Sejo, and only he had lived to escape. Their love for each other overcame the shock and they continued to live in harmony.

Many years later as King Sejo was passing through this area on his way to Popchu-sa, undoubtedly near the gnarled giant pine whose branches legendarily rose to permit the king to pass, he was accosted by two small boys. *"Haraboji, haraboji,"* they shouted and needless to say the surprised king stopped the procession and asked, "Who calls me grandfather?" The small youngsters ran off and the king followed them to a humble dwelling.

At the gate a woman appeared and, bowing low, asked Sejo if he recognized her. The king did not, but soon the entire story was revealed. The old king, weak with emotion, fervently asked his

Palsang-jon (National Treasure No. 55) at Popchu Temple ▷

Korea's largest Buddhist image, Miruk Posal, Popchu Temple

Lotus bud stone cistern (National Treasure No. 64)

Lion base stone lantern (National Treasure No. 5)

daughter and son-in-law to forgive his past actions and return to Seoul with him. Arrangements were made, but the next week when the palace servants arrived from Seoul to assist the family they found only the charred remains of the farmhouse.

The family had left and all efforts to find them proved futile. It is believed that deep in the valleys behind Popchu-sa the royal family found true happiness that would never have been realized in the political arena of Seoul.

Now by this same pine tree Zo Zayong has established his folk museum called Emileh. It was dedicated on Buddha's birthday, 1982. Visitors should take the time to see one of the finest Korean folk art collections in the country.

Popchu-sa boasts three national treasures and numerous other cultural assets. The five-storied P'alsang-jon (NT No. 55) which was reconstructed in 1624 during the Yi Dynasty era is a rare architectural structure for Buddhism, not only in Korea but also in China. It is often compared with a similar five-storied pagoda in Nara, Japan.

The name of the hall refers to the most important events in Buddha's life, depicted by eight paintings around the hall.

Wooden pagodas were known to have been built during the Silla period, with the most famous one located on the site of Hwangyong-sa in Kyongju. This nine-storied pagoda towered to a height of 224 teet in the center of the ancient Silla capital during the 7th century until the 13th century.

A carved lantern (NT No.5) supported by twin stone lions standing face to face is a rare example of the magnificent sculpturing of the Unified Silla period. A stone water cistern (NT No. 64) shaped like an open lotus flower is considered unique for beauty and design. It is believed that it was carved during Silla King Songdok's reign in the 8th century. This stone lotus blossom is supported by a round short stone carved like a mushroom.

Other stone lanterns and carved images are on display in the temple courtyard. Nearby are two stone pillars which once held the temple banner pole. An excellent stone carved relief image called a *ma-aebul* can be seen near the entrance to the temple.

For tourists interested in hiking, many trails are available leading to numerous hermitages and eventually the peak of Sokni-san.

Tongdo Temple

Korea's largest temple is also one of the easiest to reach. A paved road leads to a wooded valley a few miles west of the Tongdo-sa exit on the Seoul-Pusan Express way between Kyongju and Pusan. Priest Chajang, one of Silla's greatest monks, founded Tongdo-sa in 647 during the reign of Queen Sondok. The main temple consists of 35 buildings, while in the valleys behind are thirteen small hermitages affiliated with Tongdo Temple.

Priest Chajang came from the ranks of the royal Kim family and because of his keen mind was asked repeatedly by the ruler to take a responsible position at court. Chajang adamantly refused until the king finally issued an ultimatum to the priest saying, "If you do not accept this official position I offer, I will have your head severed for disobedience." Priest Chajang's reply was classical. "I would rather die keeping the commandments of Buddha for one day than live for a hundred years while breaking them," he retorted. The king upon seeing the wisdom of his reply bowed to the will of Chajang and permitted this noble aristocrat to remain a monk.

Chajang travelled to China for study and upon his return became a *taeguksa* (Great National Priest). Though this eminent priest founded many temples probably the most important was Tongdo-sa. Tongdo-sa is traditionally a Zen temple and the meaning of the temple's name implies, "To Save the

World by Mastering the Truth."

The main hall called the Taeung-jon is uniquely different, and has been designated as Treasure No. 144. There are no images within, as this hall serves as a worship sanctuary for the Kumgang-dan (Diamond Stair), which is behind and contains a bell-shaped monument within a rock fenced enclosure called the Sokka Sari-t'ap or (Sari Pagoda of Buddha). It is here according to tradition that the *sari* (calcified jewels remaining after cremation) of Buddha are enshrined which were brought from China by Priest Chajang. This elaborate tomb with many relief images is the focal point for the entire temple.

Priest Chajang. This elaborate tomb with many relief images is the focal point for the entire temple.

After one enters the gate of the Four Heavenly Kings or *sach'onwang* the drum tower is seen to the left. On the right is the hall of Kuknakpo-jon containing the Amit'a Buddha of Western Paradise. Yaksa Yorae, Kwanseum, Piroch'ana and many other deities of the Buddhist hierarchy are represented by shrines within the temple area. Also in front of the Miruk hall is a large stone bowl on a pedestal referred to as a "monk's bowl." Dating to the Silla period, this stone bowl is another treasure (No. 471) for Tongdo-sa.

Near the portrait shrine for Chajang is housed one entire set of the *Tripitaka,* copied from the oldest complete Buddhist scriptures known in the world. The original wooden blocks carved during the thirteenth century are preserved at Haein Temple.

Chajang-am, located a short distance from Tongdo-sa, has an interesting legend about a gold frog which Priest Chajang placed in a rock hole. The hole can be seen with supposedly the immortal gold frog still within. Nearby is a twelve-foot relief carving of Buddha with two standing attendants. The origin and age of this fine sculpture are unknown.

In the small hermitage of Kuknak near Tongdo-sa lived one of Korea's greatest Zen master, Priest Kyongbong. Physically towering over other men, but with eyes piercingly alert yet gentle, he continued in the tradition of Zen masters who had served throughout the centuries at Tongdo. Priest Kyongbong died in 1982 at the age of 92.

Magok Temple

If you wish to visit a truly traditional temple in the deep Korean mountains virtually untouched by modern civilization, then Magok-sa is to be recommended. The clean clear scenic beauty of mountains and water is refreshing, while the varied rock patterns, formations, and coloration in the vicinity will make your trip unforgettable. Magok-sa is large and relatively untouched by recent renovations, though this may not last if tourism reaches this area. Still remaining is the quiet meditative atmosphere seasoned by mountain charm, lulled by the musical rhythm of stream water flowing through the temple grounds and the wind rustling in the dense woods.

Take the expressway to Chonan and follow the old Taegu highway south for 18 Km on a paved road. At a junction take the road to Kongju for another 13 Km to Kwangjong-ni. From Kwangjong-ni turn right and travel an additional 19 Km to Magok-sa. From Kongju it is 25 Km to Magok-sa. There are few inns available in the temple vicinity.

Near the entrance of the temple is a side compound of buildings of which the Yongsan-jon is the main structure. Yongsan is a reference to a sacred mountain in India where the Sokkamoni (Historic Buddha) first preached the sermon of the "Lotus of True Law." Often in the Yongsan-jon is found a large congregation of disciples called *nahan.* Though difficult to count, there are traditionally five hundred. These small white figures, mostly males with a few females, are positioned in tiered rows behind the central images on the altar.

The main entrance to Magok-sa is quite traditional for a typical Korean Buddhist temple. The initial gate is the Haet'al-mun where two large guardian

Entrance to Tongdo-sa, Korea's largest temple near Pusan City

Weary farmer pauses near a cluster of pudo, *Ulsan*

deities are found positioned on either side. Near the guard on the left is Pohyon Posal astride an elephant, while on the right is the Munsu Posal riding a lion. These two Bodhisattvas, Munsu and Pohyon, are the traditional attendants of the Sokkamoni and are usually positioned on either side of the main Buddha, as seen in the Taeungbo-jon of Magok-sa.

The next gate is the Ch'onwang-mun which houses four other temple guardians called the *sach'onwang* (Four Heavenly Kings). Large and ornate, these images provide one of the best examples of these deities found in Korea today. These four deva kings are often referred to as guards of directions. The first East King on the right is holding a sword while standing next to him is the North King holding a lute.

On the left side stands the king guarding the south while holding a dragon and a *kusul*. Beside him is the West King holding a pagoda and a banner.

Magok-sa was founded by the Silla Priest Chajang during the reign of the dynasty's first queen, Sondok. Priest Chajang, coming from the aristocratic ruling Kim clan, chose to wear the monk's robe and rose to become one of Silla's greatest priests. He was responsible for the founding of many temples, including the largest in Korea today, Tong-do-sa. Magok-sa now serves as the temple headquarters for the province, with the head priest having administrative control over seventy other temples.

A story relates that Priest Chajang came to this mountain region to establish a temple which he decided to call *magok* (Flax Valley) because he felt that many good priests would come from this area to cause the rapid growth of Buddhism similar to the rapid growth of the flax plant. Flax cloth is still used to make sackcloth to be worn at funerals or to honor the ancestors.

In the center of the temple courtyard is a five-storied Koryo pagoda called Tabo-t'ap. From the eave corners of the top story small bells hang glistening in the sun and gently tinkle with the breezes. On the second story are four carved Buddhist reliefs. The bronze cap of this pagoda is most unusual. The styling is Indian. In 1974 when the Tabo-t'ap was reconstructed portions of the Diamond Sutra were discovered inside. The name *tabo* means "Many Treasures" and refers to the Tabo Yorae (the Buddha of Many Treasures) who was the Sokka Buddha's disciple.

To the left before crossing the stream is the Myongbu-jon, honoring the realm of the afterworld. Ten judges sit in judgment while the human spirit after death comes before them. One attendant is holding in its hand a small box containing the keys to paradise.

The halls behind the Tabo-t'ap are rather different in style. One is Taegwangbo-jon which houses the Piroch'ana Buddha. The image faces down the hall lengthwise. At the time of the temple's construction the geomancer prophesied that all images of this temple should face east and this is the case except for the Taeungbo-jon. The building faces south, while the Piroch'ana faces east.

The Piroch'ana is the Body of Truth Buddha which became fully developed during Silla because of Priest Uisang and the popularity of the Hwaom Sutra. This concept of the Buddhist trinity places Piroch'ana as the Buddha head of Truth while the Sokkamoni is the historical manifestation of Buddha on earth. The third body is Hwashin or the changing spirit of Buddha called Nosana.

The building behind the Taegwangbo-jon is a two-storied Taeungbo-jon housing the Sokkamoni and two attendants. The pillars reach the top of the second story. Located to one side is an eighty-foot *bodhi* tree which traditionally Buddha sat under when he received his enlightenment. Today the nuts from the *bodhi* tree are used in making the Buddhist prayer beads.

To the west of the courtyard is the Uijin-jon, housing again the Sokka Buddha and eighteen *nahan* (disciple) images. On the hillside behind the Myongbu-jon is the Sanshin-gak housing the Mountain Spirit.

Haein Temple

Considering all the temples of Korea, if you had time to visit only one Korean temple then Haein-sa should be chosen. In size it is one of the three major historic temples in Korea, but the mountainous scenery alone will awe any visitor. In 1975 the road from Taegu to Haein-sa was completely paved so that the travel time is now under one hour. A visitor can stay at the tourist hotels in Taegu or at the numerous small inns situated a fifteen-minute walk from the temple entrance.

In 802 two monks, Sunung and Ich'ong, after returning from T'ang China built a small hermitage in the Kaya mountains. Aejang's (40th king of Silla) queen became ill and the ruler looked to Buddhism for a cure. These two monks were able to do this miraculous deed. In appreciation the king ordered Haein-sa to be built and went himself to live there for a while. He stayed at the site of Wondang-am. The word *haein* means the seal or reflection of a smooth sea, which is an important symbol in the Hwaom Sect. The wisdom of Buddha and truth of the *sutra* are reflected to the people as a calm sea which is mirror-like.

The Koryo kings continued to patronize Buddhism. During this period in China the printing of the entire Buddhist scriptures was undertaken. The Koreans collected these texts and first undertook the project of carving blocks of the entire collection in the 11th century as a petition to Buddha to help expel the invading Khitans. This wood block collection was later destroyed by the Mongols. This project was undertaken in the mid-thirteenth century during King Kojong's reign.

Since its establishment the temple has been destroyed seven times, and only the buildings housing the *Tripitaka* survived the 1817 fire. There are now 250 monks in residence.

Kugwang-ru (Nine Lights Pavilion) was built in 1824 by a lay Buddhist who

The Tripitaka Koreana of Haein Temple ▷
(National Treasures No. 32 and 52)

collected funds. It is two-storied and the lower floor is used for storage. The top floor now houses an interesting museum. Also a bell, drum, bronze gong and wooden carp gong are housed at one side. These are the four traditional instruments, along with the small wooden clacker called a *moktak,* used at temples.

In the courtyard is a typical Silla three-storied pagoda built in 808. A stone lantern of the same age is placed in front. On either side are resident buildings for the priests.

On the next level is the Taejokkwang-jon or main hall built in 1818 which houses the Piroch'ana Buddha, the source of all Buddha's enlightenment according to the Hwaom Sect.

The elaborate carvings of the interior are typical of the late Yi Dynasty. The use of bright colors gives an exuberant feeling of the folk art which is so opposite to the simplicity of Japanese temple decor. A wooden canopy covers the five images on the altar. The center image is the Piroch'ana dating to 1769. On the left wall are eight paintings depicting the life of Buddha.

To the left of the main hall is the Myongbu-jon or Hall of Judgment. In the center is the Bodhisattva called Chijang Posal. Two attendants stand on either side. On each side are five judges. The penalty for sinning is portrayed by murals behind each of the ten judges. Buddhism has absorbed this Taoist concept and the kingly judges in the Myongbu-jon are seen at larger temples.

A smaller shrine called Ungjin-jon facing the main hall contains the Sokkamoni (Historic Buddha) and sixteen *nahan* (disciples). The hall of *nahan* when found at temples may contain anywhere from 16 to 500 of the more famous disciples of the Buddha.

Behind the Myongbu-jon is the shrine of three spirits in an unusual octagonal building. These spirits are often depicted in temples and consist of Sanshin (Mountain Spirit), Toksong (Lone Spirit) and Ch'ilsong (Seven Stars Spirit). These spirits are not derived from Buddhism but come from the ancient shamanistic heritage of Korea.

Behind the main hall are two long buildings which house the *Tripitaka.* These 81,258 wooden blocks engraved with scripture on both sides were completed in 1251 during the reign of Kojong (23rd Koryo king). King Kojong fled to Kanghwa Island to escape the Mongol intrusion into Korea and decided to seek the help of Buddha to expel the enemy. This gigantic project became a national undertaking. The tomb of Kojong is found on Kanghwa Island as he did not live to return to the capital.

The wood used is said to have been imported from China. For three years it was kept submerged in salt water then for another three years in fresh water. The wood was buried underground for three years and later dried in open air for three additional years. The engraving then actually took sixteen years. Every block is 9.5" x 29" and 2.5" thick. On the average there are twenty-two lines to a page and fourteen characters in each line.

This project was accomplished at Chondung-sa but during the early Yi Dynasty it was decided that the blocks should be moved to a safer place. A legend relates that nuns were recruited and each carrying one block on their heads walked the entire distance to Haein-sa. This *Tripitaka* collection is unique in the world as it is the oldest, and best preserved of all Chinese translations of the Buddhist Scriptures.

In 1488 during Songjong's (9th Yi king) reign this library was constructed and called Taejanggyong-gak. It is the oldest structure at Haein-sa. It was built so as to control temperature and level of humidity so that the blocks would be better preserved. The atmospheric condition was controlled by the window construction design.

Above the passageway after entering the entrance gate is a complete set of the printed *Tripitaka.* Two other sets are kept at Tongdo-sa and Kumsan-sa. The building is now a designated National Treasure No. 52 while the *Tripitaka* blocks are listed as National Treasure No. 32.

Haein Temple in the Kaya Mountains, South Kyongsang ▷

Songkwang Temple

Songkwang-sa (Pine Spreading Temple) is one of the three greatest monasteries in Korea, along with Tongdo-sa and Haein-sa. The temple is still considered to be the center of Son (Zen) Buddhism from the twelfth century period when Priest Pojo expanded the temple under the auspices of the Chogye sect. According to one temple record there was previously a small temple called Kilsang-sa which was established by Priest Hyerin in the final days of Silla.

During the following Koryo period, Priest Pojo and sixteen national priests resided at Songkwang-sa. The portraits of these famed Buddhist leaders are enshrined in the Kuksa-jon which has been listed as National Treasure No. 56. Two other national treasures (*kukbo*) and twelve cultural treasures (*pomul*) can also be found at Songkwang-sa. In recent years many foreign Zen adherents have come to Songkwang-sa for study under the Zen Master Kubong. During 1982 about 20 foreign priests and ten nuns lived on the premise.

Priest Pojo entered the priesthood at the age of eight and diligently studied the teachings of the Chinese Zen Master Hyenung. Priest Hyenung was the sixth generation spiritual master from Dharma, the founder of Zen. During doctrinal rivalry with his contemporaries Priest Hyenung fled to southern China. A wealthy Buddhist devotee by the name of Cho donated money to Priest Hyenung so that he might build a temple. The temple was given the name of Chogye, meaning "Valley of Cho" to honor the wealthy contributor.

Priest Pojo lived at Songkwang-sa until his death in 1210. At Pudo-am, located behind the main temple, is a large and impressive tablet dedicated to Priest Pojo. The epitaph was written by Kim Su, son of Kim Pu-shik who was the author of the *Samguk-Sagi* (History of the Three Kingdoms). The tomb monument, called a *pudo,* for Priest Pojo is located in the main temple grounds directly behind Kwanum-jon. Before Priest Pojo's death, King Huijong in 1179 changed the name of the temple to Suson meaning the "Study of Zen" and the mountain behind to Chogye. Later the name was changed to Songkwang-sa.

Two years after Priest Pojo's death the temple was greatly expanded and then again rebuilt in 1400 during the reign of the Yi Dynasty's second king. Songkwang-sa was almost completely burned during the Hideyoshi invasion in the late 16th century. Besides the Kuksa-jon, which is believed to be about 400 years old, the Hasa-dang, Yaksa-jon and Yongsan-jon are three additional buildings which have been designated by the government as cultural treasures (Nos. 263, 302 and 303).

In 1948 several edifices including the main hall (Taeung-jon) were burned by Communist guerillas in a vicious revolt in South Cholla. Only the Taeung-jon has been rebuilt. Oddly enough, within the Taeung-jon has been placed the Piroch'ana Buddha because there was no better appropriate place.

A special museum has been constructed to house the numerous Buddhist art objects preserved at Songkwang Temple. Normally the doors are kept locked but by special permission can be opened for visitors. Before the temple entrance flows a picturesque stream spanned by two bridges, Ch'imgye and Ch'ongyang. The covered entrance bridges crossing this stream are considered unique for this temple.

Songkwang-sa is remote from tourist routes and a stay of two days is recommended. Western hotel accommodations can be found in Kwangju City. The expressway to Sunchon is taken to Pongam (54 Km) while a dirt road is followed 10 Km further. Several inns are available for anyone wishing to remain overnight in the temple vicinity. On the other side of the Chogye Mountain is Sonam-sa, a temple of non-celibate priests. The expressway can be taken 20 Km further (two additional exits from Pongam) and a dirt road for another 7 Km to reach Sonam-sa. A famed rainbow bridge and twin stone pagodas are listed as cultural treasures for Sonam-sa.

Bridge entrance to Songkwang Temple near Kwangju, South Cholla ▷

Kumsan Temple

The "Gold Mountain Temple" located on the western slopes of Mount Moak is easily reached by a paved road from Chonju City, the capital of North Cholla Province. Kumsan-sa is the most impressive and expansive temple in the province, as well as one of the largest temples in Korea. It was first built by Priest Chinp'yo Yulsa in 766 during the reign of Hyegong (36th Silla king).

Chinp'yo was one of the great monks of Silla who also built Popchu-sa in Sokni-san and Tonghwa-sa near Taegu. He traveled to China after becoming a priest at the age of twelve, and after undergoing various ordeals of self-inflicted punishment for his sins he was given the commandments of purification by Chijang Posal. Returning to Korea he lived at Yongsan-sa (Pyonsan) and from the Miruk (Maitreya) received the Buddhist Book of Divination. Hearing of his fame, Kyongdok (35th king) asked Chinp'yo to come to the palace so that he might receive the esoteric doctrines of the Bodhisattva.

During the Koryo period Kumsan-sa was expanded but burned in the Japanese invasion of 1592. In the mid-seventeenth century it was reconstructed and the present structures date from this period (1635). However, there are many stone remains which date to the Silla period . . . . one national treasure and eight second-ranked (pomul) treasures.

The most impressive structure in the entire temple grounds is the Miruk-jon which rises impressively over 70 feet and contains the standing stone image of the Miruk (Buddha of the Future) with attendants standing on either side. The massive central image is well over 39 feet high. The three-storied building is so unique in Korea that it has been designated as National Treasure No. 62. A replica has become part of the architecture of the Seoul National Museum in Kyongbok Palace. Corner eave pillars are used to support the tremendous weight of the roofs.

There are eight other designated treasures also located at Kumsan-sa. A five-storied stone pagoda of Silla origin (Treasure No . 25) rises 24 feet high in the courtyard before the sari-pudo.

This unique sari-pudo or sari-t'ap (Treasure No. 26) has a large two-level platform surrounded by protective stone guards. In the center is a bell-shaped stone under which the ashes of the deceased priest were buried.

In front of the Miruk-jon is a strange hexagonal stone pagoda (Treasure No. 27) consisting of what appears to be a series of many roof stones, totaling eleven. Also near the Miruk Hall is a small square-shaped stone (Treasure No. 22) designed with lotus patterns. This early Silla carving is only about four feet high. Near the entrance of the temple is a beautifully designed lotus stone pedestal (Treasure No. 23). On the eight sides are flower patterns alternating with lion relief figures. On the top are two holes which were once used to connect a stone image to this pedestal.

A turtle with tablet stone (Treasure No. 24) was believed to be erected in the 11th century for Priest Hodok during the Koryo Period. Though the stylized dragon-shaped turtle is magnificent, the calligraphy on the stone has been badly mutilated by time and people over the many years. It is situated in a compound where there are many other pudo monuments which memorialize famous priests of Kumsan-sa.

Also near the entrance of the temple are the twin pillars (Treasure No. 28) once used to support the temple banner pole. The sculptured base stone for these pillars is unusually well preserved. Within the center of the flanking pillars is the circular hollow where a center pole once stood. At the small hermitage of Shimwon-am is a small three-storied pagoda (Treasure No. 29).

Between the fall of Silla and rise of Koryo in the 10th century, an unusual tale was told about General Kyonhwon who called himself the King of Later Paekche. He was one of three famous rebel leaders of this period who attacked the capital of Silla in Kyongju and killed the royal family at Posok-jong, which is now one of the most famous and popular tourist attractions in Kyongju.

The myth was perpetuated that Kyonhwon was fathered by an earthworm. A shy modest farmer's daughter began to receive a nightly visitor through her locked door.

The young man each morning left in a wisp of cool vapor. Though embarrassed she eventually told her parents about what had been happening almost every night. The wise parents advised her to slip a needle with thread into the man's garments if he should come again . . . . This the young maiden did the following night as the mysterious young man was about to leave her room.

The next morning she followed the trail of white thread into the garden where she found her needle piercing the back of a large earthworm. The girl conceived and gave birth to a baby boy who was named Kyonhwon. Other

legends tell that this brave general was nursed on the milk of a tigress, the reason for his tiger temperament.

As the old general saw that heaven was not favoring him against the strength of the Koryo armies he wished to surrender and live out his days in peace. Of his nine sons many objected to the thought of the old general surrendering. Several of his sons rose up in revolt and Kyonhwon was thrown into a cell at Kumsan Temple. With a body of strong Buddhist guards he had with him his favorite concubines and servants. One night while entertaining his guards he succeeded in getting them uproariously drunk and with his favorite companions slipped into the night. One wonders what happened when the jovial Buddhist priests from the night before awoke to find their host had fled.

The old fox Kyonhwon surrendered

Chijang Posal is housed in the Myongbu-jon (Judgment Hall)

to the Koryo king and convinced King T'aejo that he would help in the fight against his own sons who had turned against him. Later when his sons were captured in an ensuing battle but were spared death by the kindhearted King T'aejo, the old Tiger King of Later Paekche upon hearing the news went into a rage and died in a fit of anger.

Whether in spring or fall, Kumsan-sa is a temple with magnificent scenic beauty. There are many small inns before the temple area and most of them are comfortable. Back in Chonju are many tourist hotels for those who might desire better overnight accommodations.

Hwaom Temple

Hwaom-sa, located near Kurye in South Cholla, is now easily reached. The shortest route is from Chonju through Namwon over good roads. One can visit Kumsan-sa and the historic pleasure shrine associated with Ch'unhyang in the town of Namwon. Ch'unhyang was a *kisaeng's* daughter who left a love story of devotion and honor that can hardly be equalled in the historical pages of Korea. Ch'unhyang has been the theme of more movies, literature and dramas than any other heroine in Korea.

From Namwon there are two routes the longer one through Koksong. One can also use the expressway and exit beyond Kwangju.

On the slopes of Chiri Mountain Hwaom-sa is one of Korea's greater temples, most famous for the Hwaom Sect of Buddhism which was introduced from China by Priest Uisang. According to the temple records the site on the boundary of Silla and Paekche was first selected by an Indian monk, Yon'gi Taesa, in 544. However, Priest Uisang is the great priest who expanded the temple in 634 during the reign of Queen Sondok (27th Silla ruler). As there is little known about Priest Yon'gi, scholars wonder that he was only a legendary person. This temple, dedicated to the

Piroch'ana Buddha, the cosmic head of the Hwaom trinity, is situated high in a boat-shaped valley which points toward the rivers, indicating good geomantic values. The temple's two five-storied pagodas symbolically serve as the ship's masts. The boat is often used as a symbolic vehicle to transport Buddhist souls across devil-infested waters into the realm of Nirvana.

The first gate called Ilju-mun (single pillar) is in a direct line with the second gate dedicated to the Bodhisattva's Munsu and Pohyon, one riding a lion and the other an elephant. However, the gate dedicated to the *sach'onwang* (Four Heavenly Kings) is not directly in line with the entrance. "The way is crooked," mentions the priest. "The straight path often leads quickly to destruction. The crooked way is hard to follow. It is hard for one to enter the priesthood and follow the life of Buddha but once you have entered it is then difficult to leave. Unless you know the secrets of Hwaom it is not understandable," murmurs the priest.

There are three national treasures at Hwaom-sa. Probably the most famous is the three-storied lion *sarit'ap* (National Treasure No. 35) located on the hillside to the west. The image sitting under the pagoda is believed to be Yon'gi, the temple's founder, who is offering tea to the figure under the lantern who is probably Priest Yon'gi's mother.

Though difficult to discern, the faces of each four-foot lion portray a different expression representing the four basic life emotions of joy, anger, love and sorrow. Standing at the lantern and facing toward the pagoda the left face might be love while the right could be anger. On the back side the left could be sorrow while the right is joy. Love and sorrow are closely related emotions, while the emotions of joy and anger are more similar.

The 14-foot base is decorated with twelve relief devas playing musical instruments. The first story depicts six *inwang* (guardian) reliefs and two Bodhisattva reliefs. The entire structure is about 17 feet high.

Kakhwang-jon and lantern, Hwaom Temple (National Treasures No. 67 and 12) ▷

Below the lion pagoda is the massive two-storied Kakhwang-jon (National Treasure No. 67) with wooden pillars towering 160 feet. Before this hall is Korea's largest stone lantern (National Treasure No. 12).

This fifteen-foot lantern is believed to have been built by Priest Uisang in 670. Also in front of this hall is a square *pudo* monument (Treasure No. 300).

The temple has suffered five major devastations during its existence. Prior to the invasion by Japan in 1592 there were many stone tablets of late Silla origin completely surrounding Kakhwang-jon, which contained the entire Hwaom Sutra. Many pieces of these smashed tablets lay about the temple grounds until recently when they were gathered up to be stored in 163 boxes (14,350 pieces) beneath the main altar of Kakhwang-jon. In 1630 Hwaom-sa was rebuilt by Priest Pyogam. His memorial tablet is seen in front of the temple. However, Kakhwang-jon was only reconstructed in 1703.

An unusual legend tells that when temple authorities were considering the right person for the task the head priest had a strange dream. The following morning he called the priests together and placed before each a pot of sand. He instructed each one to dip his hand into a bowl of honey and then place that hand into the pot of sand. The entire procedure baffled and mystified all the priests. Of course each hand came out grimy with sand.

The head priest then inquired if all the temple's priests were present. He was assured they all were except for a visiting priest and several temple novices . . . "Bring them," the head priest commanded. The procedure was repeated and this time a humble Kyep'a brought his hand out clean of any sand . . . "This is the man who will build our great hall," the head priest announced.

The following night a *shinson* (spiritul being) appeared to Kyep'a and told him to go out the next morning and ask the first person he should meet to help him build the hall. But the first person was an old woman who often came to the temple to collect alms. The shocked grandmother kept insisting

that Kyep'a must have made a mistake. Kyep'a continued to ask for help. Realizing she had no resources, she decided to take her life in the firm belief that in another existence she would be able to assist this sincere priest. As the grieving Kyep'a felt responsible for the cause of her death he fled to China to escape his guilt.

Seven years passed. One day while standing with a crowd of people watching the royal procession the Emperor's daughter suddenly saw the priest and ran to him. Since birth the little girl had been unable to open her hand. Now holding out her hand to the monk she cried, "Here is my monk! Please open my hand for me!" The Chinese characters for *changguk* were written on her hand. This was the former name of the great hall of Hwaom-sa.

The Emperor's daughter was believed to be the old woman reincarnated. When the Emperor heard of the miraculous recovery of his daughter he had two million *kun* of gold delivered to Sukchong (19th king) for the purpose of rebuilding the hall. King Sukchong decided the name should be changed to honor the Chinese Emperor and so called the new building Kakhwang-jon (Awakening Emperor Hall).

In Kakhwang-jon the center image is the Sokka Buddha, the left, the Amit'a Buddha and the right, the Tabo Buddha. The Tabo Yorae is relatively unknown in Korea. The attendants from left to right are the Kwanseum, Pohyon, Munsu, and Chijok (all Bodhisattvas). Kakhwang-jon has been duplicated in the architecture of Seoul's National Museum.

In the main courtyard are two five-storied twenty-foot pagodas. The east pagoda (Treasure No. 132) called Tabobunjo-t'ap was dedicated by Priest Toson during late Silla and is simple in design with no relief carving. The west pagoda (Treasure No. 133) is more elaborately decorated with many reliefs. Twelve zodiac images appear along the lower base while eight deva images are carved into the upper base. The first story depicts the *sach'onwang* reliefs.

The Taeung-jon (Treasure No. 299) now enshrining the Piroch'ana Buddha was reconstructed in 1960 by Priest Pyogam. A calligraphy book of Sonjo (14th Yi - king) compiled by Uijang Taegun, his grandson, and a set of four lacquer bowls, a spoon and a bronze bell which were the personal effects of Sosan Taesa, a 16th century priest, are on display in this hall.

One building enshrining disciples of Buddha is called the Nahan-jon. Nearby the Myongbu-jon contains the deities of judgment and Chijang (Bodhisattva of the Underworld). In the Wondong-jon are stored a great number of wooden blocks containing carved Buddhist Sutra. Next to Wondong-jon is the Yong-jon where portraits of famous priests of Hwaom-sa are enshrined. These portraits include Priest Yon'gi and Pyogam as well as Samyong Taesa, who was the disciple of Priest Sosan, and Puhyu, who held the same rank as Sosan in southern Korea.

The temple's great drum vibrates low and somber through the valley while long shadows creep across the courtyard and priests silently file into the Taeung-jon to offer the evening service before the golden Buddha. The smoke from the kitchen fires drifts above the tiled roofs while in the clear sky a calm permeates Chiri-san.

A visit to Ch'onun-sa (Hidden Stream Temple), ten Km away, is a must. One of Korea's most photographed structures is the arched covered bridge crossing the cascading stream at the entrance to the temple. Constructed in 828 the buildings date to 1774 during the reign of Yongjo (21st Yi king). Yaksa-am is much older.

For the more adventuresome a side trip of 20 Km (over a rough road) to the site of Yon'gok-sa will reward the visitor with some of the finest Silla stone monuments to be found in any one area. There are two national treasures and four listed treasures (NT Nos. 53 and 54: T-151, 152, 153, 154). The sculpturing is most remarkable and exquisite. Founded also by Priest Yon'gi, it is strange that only Hwaom-sa and Yon'gok-sa carry the name of this shadowy figure.

Legend of the Emillie Bell

The truth about this tragic legend we will never know, yet one will always wonder. During the period of achievement and devotion to the Buddha even kings and queens are as nothing. Through the years the many known records of the scholars and historians were lost to the ages and today so little is left from which to learn, but what is briefly carved in stone or molded on the bronze surface of a temple bell . . . .

Looking at the Buddhist art achievement of Silla with its many sacred images, we are awed by their exquisite development; yet rivaling these accomplishments is the superb artistic beauty of the bronze bells which hung in the numerous temples long ago.

Some of the oldest metal objects found in Korea have been small bronze bells for animals which were found in the earliest known tombs. However, the technique of bronze bell casting reached a peak of perfection during eighth century Silla, never to be duplicated again during the more recent years of the Koryo and Yi dynasties. We have only a record of the massive bell, the largest ever cast, which hung at Hwangyong-sa (Imperial Dragon Temple), now only a temple site near Kyongju.

According to historical records this bell was cast in 754 and weighed four times more than the famed Emillie Bell now located in the Kyongju National Museum. Four hundred and ninety thousand *kun* of metal was used in the Hwangyong-sa bell, compared to one hundred and twenty thousand *kun* used in the Emillie Bell. In present day calculations for a *kun* the Hwangyong-sa bell should weigh about 240 tons while the Emillie Bell should weigh 60 tons (actually the Emillie Bell weighs about 20 tons). The Emillie Bell is eleven feet high while the same records indicate that the Hwangyong-sa bell was only one foot higher, thus indicating that probably

historical inaccuracies did occur. It is also an established fact that the *kun* measurement varied in earlier Koryo and Silla periods.

Of the Silla bells completely intact in Korea today there are only three, with the most recent one found in 1970 and now on display in the Kongju National Museum. This small 37.5-inch bell has no inscription but was probably cast during the late ninth century. The bell has two relief devas on the surface.

The other two Silla bells are registered national treasures. The Emille Bell (National Treasure No. 29) located in the Kyongju National Museum is the largest. The other Silla bell, though smaller, is the oldest known bell (National Treasure No. 36). Now kept at Sangwon-sa in Kangwon Province, it was originally located in Andong City, north of Kyongju. The 5'6" bell of Sangwon-sa was cast in 725 during the reign of Songdok (33rd king).

Another early bell located at Yongju-sa near Suwon City has been listed by the government as National Treasure No. 120. It is accepted by most scholars that this bell was cast during the early years of Koryo. This 4'9" bell, is one of the finer bells of early Korea and even though it is not ranked with the Silla bells, it is considered probably one of the earliest of Koryo bells now to be found in Korea.

Over the years many bells have been taken from Korea and even now most of the ancient bells of Korea are to be found in Japan. Bells were pirated out of Korea as early as the Koryo period. A large number of bells were taken to Japan during the war years after 1592. Actually very few bells were taken during the Japanese occupation of Korea after 1910.

Though difficult to make accurate determination, there are apparently ten to twelve large bells in South Korea of Koryo origin, while in Japan over fifty larger Koryo bells can be found in various temples and Shinto shrines throughout the country. Four or five other bells believed to be of Silla origin are also found in Japan. Within the last ten to fifteen years many smaller bells of Koryo origin have been recovered from Korean temples through the use of modern electronic metal detectors. They can be found in both museums and private collections.

The quality and artistic achievement of Korean bell making have been recognized around the world, and must be

ranked among the proudest examples of Korea's unique cultural achievements. The apex of this development was reached during the Silla era with the perfect example seen in the famed bell of Emillie. Though not the largest in the world (the twenty-foot Moscow bell is larger) it is one thousand years older and without question infinitely more beautiful and graceful. When struck, the bell's solemn strong tone reputedly will travel as far as forty miles on a clear, crisp night. Buddhist temple bells of Korea which are generally not geometrically stylized are uniquely different from either Chinese or Japanese bells in shape and design, though some Chinese characteristics were retained, such as the use of the series of nipples within an arabesque border. The quality of the Koryo and Yi dynasty bells was inferior to that of Silla. It is believed that initially large clay vessels were buried in the ground beneath the bell which was hung close to the ground. Korean bells have no clappers. When the bell was struck on the side near the rim with a wooden log hanging from a chain the sound would echo into the clay vessel. From this echo chamber the sound would be transmitted through the tube at the top of the bell.

The Emillie Bell embodies all the true characteristics of ancient Korean bronze bells. There is a lengthy inscription carved into each side of the bell as well as two sets of devas facing each other and depicted separately in a kneeling posture on a lotus flower amid vapor wisps and fleecy floating ·garments swirling into heavenly clouds. This magnificent bell has no sculptural defect whatsoever and, therefore, is matchless in the Orient.

Kyongdok (35th Silla king) commissioned artisans to cast a bell to honor the spirit of his deceased father Songdok (36th king), who died in 737. However, King Kyongdok died before its completion in 770 during the reign of Hyegong (33rd king), the grandson of King Songdok. King Hyegong had the bell hung in Pongdok-sa which had been established by King Songdok.

The question is often raised as to how such gigantic bells could be cast in these early days with such artistic beauty of design and form. So much is unknown and apparently the technique is now lost to the world. We must certainly stand in awe and respect before the master bell artisans of Silla, for their accomplishments were unequalled in later years in Korea and believed by most historians to be unmatched in the world.

One theory is expounded that wax was used in the casting of Korean bells. An inner clay mould in the shape of the bell would be made within a large pit. Lime might have been used to harden the clay, or the clay may have been left to harden in the sun.

Then a thick layer of wax would be placed over the entire mould to the desired thickness of the bell. The relief devas and other decorative patterns would be carved into this wax layer. Finally, a second layer of clay would be placed over the wax and allowed to harden sufficiently. The entire pit would then be filled in with additional dirt and clay so that only the top of the mould would be left open for pouring in the liquid metal. As the molten metal (copper and tin) was poured into the mould the wax would melt out through the bottom into the ground. This pouring of the metal would be accomplished during the continual beating of the temple drum and fervent prayers of the priests for a successful casting of the bell.

The legends of Silla are more numerous than the seeds of a pomegranate, and yet most are virtually unknown. But among all the myths of this ancient civilization the strange unrecorded Buddhist account of the casting of the Emillie Bell has travelled to the furthest corners of the world. To come to Kyongju and not see the Emillie Bell is to come to Korea and not hear the legend of this bell, a tale held close to the hearts of the Korean people.

Yet the strange fact of the matter is that nowhere in the early annals of Korea is this legend recorded. Apparently it has survived to this day by word of mouth,

◁ *Emillie Bell in Kyongju National Museum (National Treasure No. 29)*

from father to son. This is the legend that gives this bell its name yet the source, – and there must have been an origin, has remained lost – an unresolved mystery. Some point to the Middle Kingdom as the origin of this legend, as certain bells in China were known to have similar tales of human sacrifice in the casting.

The great temple of Pongdok-sa had been completed and dedicated by the royal family. Hyosong (34th king) had arrived in person to mingle with the thousands of priests arriving from all corners of the Silla kingdom. But something was missing: a bell could not be heard calling those who desired peace to come and worship. But the money had all been spent from the royal treasury, so the king suggested that donations come from Buddhist believers throughout the country. The monks of Pongdok-sa went from door to door and the people gladly donated what they could for the bell.

The giant bell was then cast, but strange to say it would not ring. Again and again they tried but always with the same results, while the bell technicians shook their heads in disbelief.

But one night the chief priest of Pongdok-sa had a strange vision in which an old *shinson* (Spirit of a Supernatural Being) accosted him. His long snow-white beard and tousled silvery hair above bushy eyebrows made an alarming fantasy in the vision of the sleeping priest. "Who are you?" he stammered.

The lips of the ancient hermit moved slowly. "You may call me the guardian deity of your silent bell. Complete submission to the will of Buddha has not been accomplished. My bell will always remain mute unless you do what I ask."

There was a long pause as the frightened priest gazed into the dark, emotionless eyes of the spirit. Finally the priest nodded and the *shinson* continued, "When your monks were collecting donations throughout the city they came upon one poor widow who offered to the temple her baby girl. This child was born in the year, month, day and hour of the dragon and the sacred bell will only ring when it is possessed with the fire-spirit of the dragon. You must recast this bell and offer this child to the fiery metal."

The priest gasped, "Surely the merciful Buddha would not . . . . . " and his voice trailed to a whisper. "A noble and glorious death indeed for a child to enter paradise, and isn't it far better to sacrifice one for the souls of many? The only course for the mute bell" . . . . The vision faded and the dazed priest awoke to the melodious deep tones of a temple bell vibrating through the still night from a bleak hillside where there was no temple.

The chief priest called the other monks together and asked if any of them remembered talking to a poor widow who had offered her child to the temple. One monk came forward and said that a girl had been offered but he thought the mother had been only jesting when she offered her daughter. She truly had nothing else to offer for the temple. "Do you think you can find the place?" asked the chief priest. The young monk nodded, but wondered as he tried to search his memory as to which part of the capital he had traversed.

Groping to recall, he wandered for several days until he finally found the woman and child, a small girl of about three. "What can I say?" thought the monk as he pretended to beg alms from behind the hedge. "I have nothing to give!" shouted the woman, but the monk continued to chant while thinking how he might approach the subject.

"Is this your beautiful daughter?" he then inquired. "She is surely four or five."

"Actually she is only three," the good woman replied. "You see, it is strange but she was born in the year, month, day and even hour of the dragon. Yes, unfortunately she will be difficult to marry," she lamented, "though you can see she is attractive."

The monk had a friendly face and pleasant nature so the two continued to chatter in the courtyard. "Several months ago another priest came to my humble cave to ask for donations for making the bell of Pongdok-sa," the woman mentioned. "Do you know if this bell has been completed?" "Yes, I only wish I was not so poor," she lamented. "All I have is my daughter and I offered her to the temple, thinking that possibly she could be of service to the Buddha. The priest refused my offer and went away empty handed."

The young monk cleared his throat, "My good lady, I am that priest . . . . . do you not remember?" The woman peered intently into the priest's face. "Yes, you do resemble him. Why do you return?" she asked.

". . . . . to accept your offer of donation for the casting of the bell," he whispered in a low voice. The woman stared as fear clouded her eyes. "I don't understand," she stammered. "The bell has been cast and rumors have reached me that it makes no sound. Why do you need my daughter?" For a moment the priest's eyes wavered. Then in a trembling voice he related the account of the strange vision received by the chief priest of Pongdok-sa.

The mother almost fainted as she pulled her child closer to her. "How can the merciful Buddha expect this of me?" she wailed. "An innocent baby, and mine, why mine?" The monk too felt like weeping but could say nothing and politely bade farewell to the distraught mother. Yet he repeatedly came to call upon the woman over the weeks and months, using every persuasive argument that he knew to convince her to donate her child for the bell.

Finally one day the mother brought the girl to the temple. The bell was melted down to be recast. As prayers for the soul of this small virgin were lifted up to the lotus paradise the infant girl was thrown into the molten metal. The sound of her tiny voice was heard echoing . . . "Emi! Emi! (Momma, Momma)" . . . . .

On the day the bell was to be tested the monks gathered about while the chief priest prepared to strike the bell. As the wooden log struck and the pealing notes sounded out loud and clear there was a gasp of astonishment while eyes dimmed with tears. The heartrending peal of the bell sounded like a child calling for its mother. "Emi . . . . Emi . . . . llie" . . . . sometimes low as in a sigh and sometimes strong and loud, but always sad . . . . a mournful tone resounding over the Silla countryside. The dragon spirit was enshrined within the soul of the bell, while the legend of the sacrifice of a child continued to be told over the centuries, recalled by the mournful tolling of the bell . . . . Emillie! . . . . Emillie!

This legend is hard to reconcile with the compassionate spirit of Buddhism, and many feel that the story is unfair to the tenets of this religion. This inscription on the two sides of the Emillie Bell leaves a far more noble thought as it reads:

"True religion lies beyond the realm of visible things while its course is nowhere seen. As a sound heard through the sky without a clue to its origin, so is religion. We hang this great bell that it may awaken our need for Buddha. So large that it will not be moved, a fitting place to inscribe the virtues of Great King Songdok whose deeds are eternal as the hills and streams while his glory is like the sun and moon. The noble and true he called to aid him in his rule. Fitting music and proper ceremonies always accompanied him. He encouraged the farmers to enjoy their toil and the merchants to exercise honesty. He had no use for much gold and other valuable jewels, while sound education and talented skills were considered treasures beyond compare. His great aim was to conduct his life in a noble manner, and for this reason people came from distant regions to seek his counsel. All revered him."

The bell of Emillie with its mystic and melodious peal leaves a bit of history etched into the pages of Buddhist art. Through the years its tone has echoed through the valleys of Korea, sweet yet sad, but distinctly clear down to the twentieth century. The vibrations and matchless tone of bronze . . . . in hearing the Emillie Bell you will not forget the legend.

Chapter V.
Cultural Allurement

Shaman ceremony conducted by a mudang

Religions of the Country

Religious liberty is a right guaranteed to all citizens of the Republic of Korea. All faiths are freely practiced, in contrast to the ruthless suppression of any religion by the communists in northern Korea. Korea's religions are Buddhism, Confucianism, Christianity, animism and several indigenous cults. Both Buddhism and Confucianism have played an important historical role in the early cultural heritage of Korea, while animism has persisted over an unknown number of centuries and is still practiced in the rural areas. Christianity and the indigenous religions have developed since the 19th century. Families often have members of different faiths living in harmony under the same roof.

SHAMANISM

Spirit or nature worship is Korea's oldest belief, the origin of which is lost in the haze of antiquity. Over the earth, man's first attempt to understand and come to terms with his environment has been expressed in a primitive spirit-religion. Called animism or shamanism, it is based on the belief that human beings are not the exclusive possessors of spirits as they also reside in natural forces and inanimate objects. The shaman is the sorceress or priest (called *mudang* in Korea)who attempts to mediate with the spirits or propitiate them in preventing natural disasters and curing illnesses. Not all of these spirits are friendly. Animism still today appeals especially to the rural people who throughout the centuries have had to struggle against hostile elements. Occasionally in the country "devil posts" can still be seen guarding each side of the trail to a mountain village, which is thus protected against the spirits of sickness and hunger.

In Korea the introduction of Western thought did not result in suppression of shamanistic practices. Neither Buddhism nor Confucianism considered itself to be in conflict with the rites of nature worship and often all three existed in harmony with each other.

In Korea most of the shamanists are women. To witness a shaman ceremony or *kut* is an unforgettable experience as usually foreigners are not invited or even particularly welcomed. Near the Inwang-san in Seoul is one enterprising center of shaman activity. Traditionally the *mudang* were not permitted to enter the capital city.

BUDDHISM

Buddhism is a highly disciplined philosophic religion stressing personal salvation through renunciation of worldly desires, thus preventing an endless cycle of reincarnations and bringing about the absorption of the soul of the enlightened into Nirvana, a paradise without want. With the spread of Buddhism from India through China to Korea many local aspects of beliefs were absorbed, thus producing an elaborate and complex hierarchy of deities, saints and guardians. This type of Buddhism called Mahayana appeared in Korea about 372 A.D. while picking up additional regional peculiarities as it became firmly established.

First arriving in the kingdom of Koguryo it later spread to Paekche and finally was brought to Silla by Priest Ado. Buddhism was to become Korea's state religion. During the Koryo period Buddhism reached its apex of power and

◁ *Buddha's birthday festivities, Chogye Temple, Seoul*

Buddha's Birthday

① *Preparing lanterns*
② *Koryo Amit'a Buddha at Samsong-am, eastern Seoul*
③ *Altar at Shinhung Temple, Seoul*

◁ *Sanshin (Mountain Spirit) at Ch'ilbul-am, Namsan, Kyongju*

▽ *Ch'ilsong (Seven Star Spirit of the Great Dipper), Chongup, North Cholla*

△ *Stone male* changgun *(spirit post) in Chongup, North Cholla*

Wooden female changgun *(spirit posts) near South Fortress, Kyonggi Province*

influence upon the Korean people. At the height of its political control over the country in the 14th century, every third son of a family became a Buddhist priest. There were more than 80,000 temples in active operation, while the religion had enormous influence on the development of Korean art, literature and culture.

At the close of Koryo in 1392 a dramatic change took place as Buddhism was replaced by Confucianism as the state religion with its greatest following among the educated and official classes. Following the decline of popularity and official patronage during the Yi Dynasty, the Buddhist movement in Korea experienced a revival during the Japanese occupation. Temples and monasteries still own large tracts of mountain and farmland, the income of which has been used for modern education, social services and spread of Buddhist teachings through mass communication techniques.

Buddhism has blended well with other religions, including animism, and today at most temples numerous examples of this fact are evident. At every temple a shrine altar is seen honoring the mountain spirit, depicted as a bearded man with a tiger crouching nearby. Derived from local animistic beliefs, the mountain spirit will receive due veneration following the ceremonies honoring the Buddha in the main hall, lest the local mountain spirits on whose land the temple stands should become angry.

Though historically there were many Buddhist sects, today there are only two major sects which can be loosely divided into the married group (T'aego Sect) and the larger celibate group (Chogye Sect). Headquarters for the celibate sect is Chogye Temple located in Anguk-dong, Seoul. Chogye represents twenty-five major temples and 1127 registered temples throughout Korea. There are 8,313 priests, 6,326 nuns and five million laymen registered with this order. The married priests are splintered into fifteen different sects with the larger group called T'aego. T'aego has administrative control over 460 minor temples. There are 2,500 priests, 300 nuns and 1½ million laymen registered with this Buddhist order. Dongguk is Korea's Buddhist university located on the slopes of Nam-san, Seoul.

Today it is believed that about one third of the population of Korea are Buddhist and two thirds of all Buddhist believers are women. (last census, Dec. 1980)

CONFUCIANISM

Confucius, the Chinese scholar and statesman who lived from 550 to 478 B.C., set up an ethical-moral system intended to govern ideally all relationships in the family, community and state. Confucianism is not a religion in the strict sense of worship of a divine power but rather it is a code of morals and conduct which has formed the standards of ethical behavior in Korean society. The philosophy holds no consideration for the supernatural (nor had Buddhism done so in its original form) but as time passed Confucius and his disciples were in effect canonized or deified by later followers.

In Korea Confucianism was accepted so eagerly and in so autocratic a form that the Chinese themselves regarded Korean adherents as more virtuous than themselves. In Korea it meant a system of education, ceremony and civil administration during the monarchy, but with its passing only the first function remained important.

Confucius taught that society was made up of five relationships, those between ruler and subject, husband and wife, father and son, elder brother and younger brother and between friends. The chief virtue was filial piety, a combination of loyalty and reverence which demanded that a son show respect to his father and perform the demands of his elders. From this belief stemmed the practice of ancestor veneration. Members of a family will always be very careful not to breach etiquette or perform any act that would bring disrespect or discredit upon their ancestors.

The spirit of the "mother earth" is placed on a funeral bier as it is carried to ▷ the grave site, Yesan

240

In 1392 Confucianism became the state religion while Buddhism was relegated to a position of lesser importance. Study halls or *sowon* were established over the countryside with Sungkyunkwan (Confucian University) in Seoul becoming the center of Confucian thought and study. Even now twice a year the ancient ceremonial rites of the Yi Dynasty are conducted at the main memorial shrine with traditional music, while visitors are permitted to witness the service with all its color and pageantry.

Today in modern Korea the tight family system is fragmenting and the previously ingrained Confucian concepts are becoming less influential. However, the stability and individual security encouraged by Confucianism, despite its tendency toward conservatism, has much to recommend it.

Though the Confucian teaching has disappeared as a basis for government administration, Koreans have not really discarded the customs, thought patterns and habits derived from the Confucian

tradition. Social stability, respect for learning and reverence for age are still practiced. This Confucian heritage is still in many ways very much evident in society and perhaps its better aspects should be cultivated and preserved.

CHRISTIANITY

The first Western Christian clergy, it is believed, came to Korea in 1592 when a Jesuit priest accompanied a Japanese invasion force in the area of Pusan. As he was to minister to Japanese soldiers his influence on Koreans was non-existent. In 1785 a Jesuit named Peter Grammont crossed the northern border secretly and began baptizing believers. Ten years later James Chou, a Chinese, became the first foreign priest to enter Korea and reside in Seoul, but due to repression of Christianity he was executed. The faith persisted and in 1836 the first Western resident missionary, a French Catholic priest named Pierre Maubant, entered Korea in disguise

(some say as a mourner) followed by others, though there was still a strict ban on the religion.

Despite the ban, converts increased in number and by 1853 there were possibly over 20,000 Christians. In 1866 severe persecution began by order of the *taewongun* regent, of the boy king. Nine out of twelve French priests living in Korea were executed along the banks of the Han River (near the present-day Martyr's Church) while three escaped to China.

The initial Protestant Western contact with Korea was in 1832 when a German Protestant missionary to China, the Rev. Carl A.F. Gutzlaff, aboard the British ship *Lord Amherst,* landed along the Korean coast. He was serving as an interpreter to investigate the possibilities of opening trade relations with Korea. The ship anchored about a month during which time Gutzlaff passed out Bibles and other literature.

In 1866 during the great persecution of Christians an American merchant ship, the *General Sherman,* sailed up the Taedong River toward Pyongyang. It was burned and sunk with the loss of its entire crew. Also aboard the ship was Robert J. Thomas, a Scotch missionary to China who, as the story is told tried to present a Bible to the man who executed him on the banks of the river outside the city of Pyongyang.

On May 22, 1882 a diplomatic Treaty of Amity and Commerce was signed between Korea and the US known also as the "Shufeldt Treaty." Protection was now provided for the missionaries. (In 1982 the centennial celebration was held in Korea and the US). Various Protestant denominations began sending ministers, medical missionaries and educators. The missionaries found a deep need among young Koreans for modern education as a tool that would lead to social reform. Missionaries quickly became identified with progressive movements and introduced the ideals of democracy. After the Japanese annexation missionaries encouraged the resistance movement as much as their own restricted activities permitted under close Japanese surveillance.

With appeal directed toward intellectuals and national leaders, Christianity achieved and maintained a degree of influence much greater than its actual membership indicated. As of 1981 there were well over seven million Protestants (one out of every five Koreans) and 1.3 million Catholics. There are over 23,500 Christian churches. Churches are conspicuously present all over the countryside while Seoul City is often called the "city of churches" because from any vantage point numerous steeple spires can be seen on almost every hill.

Due to restrictions on the Christian movement in the north, many Christians fled south during the days following liberation. Before the war the greater concentration of Korean Christians was in the north. One of the largest church congregations in the world with a membership of more than 20,000 is the Yongnak Church, established by refugee Christians fleeing south from communist terror in the north.

Koreans have not forgotton the aid and comfort given to them by missionaries in their darkest hours during Japanese annexation and the Korean War. Though Korea is not predominantly a Christian nation, it has been a nation where the leadership and ideals during the 20th century have been drawn to a large extent from the Christian church.

INDIGENOUS RELIGIONS

During the chaotic last years of the 19th century, many native religious movements emerged calling for social reform, usually through the divine intervention of a savior. Many were short lived but a few had significant historic roles to play and some survive today. The most important of the new religions is the *tonghak* or Eastern Learning movement (as opposed to Catholicism called *sohak* or Western Learning), established around 1862 by a rural scholar's son near Kyongju, Ch'oe Chae-u, who was executed in Taegu for heresy and subversion two years later. The move-

◁ *Catholic Church in Umsong, North Chungchong*

242

ment persisted under other leaders, sparking several armed rebellions with the 1894 outburst comparable to the Boxer Rebellion in China. The revolt was quelled with great loss of life. Tonghak changed its name to Chondogyo in the 20th century and became primarily a religious movement rather than a political force. Its adherents still number around a million and a half.

Other new religions include Taejong-gyo, which seems to be a revival of an ancient creed based on Korea's legendary founder, Tan'gun. About two dozen additional cults are active and sizable enough to matter. Some of these are heresies of Christianity, Buddhism and Confucianism, or a blend of all three.

The Unification Church led by Reverend Moon has recently become a powerful religious force. Moon, a declared reincarnation of Christ, is Korean by birth, and his heresy has spread in the United States. The church tentacles of control with vast sums of money involved have reached into many aspects of society in both the US and Korea.

ISLAM

The Islamic religion was introduced to Korea in 1950 when Turkish troops arrived to participate in the Korean War. In 1966 the Federation of Korean Islamic Churches was established and the first mosque was built in Itaewon, Seoul. Two additional mosques have been built in Kwangju and Pusan. There are an estimated 20,000 converts.

Traditional funeral procession along a country road and honoring the spirit of the deceased at the grave site, Ichon, Kyonggi Province (right page)
Confucian ritual honoring ancestors of Yi T'aejo, Chonju City (below)

Pageantry of Holiday Festivals

Holiday festivals are an important feature of Korean life. Many are of a religious nature, but some commemorate national events of ancient and modern times. Often the festivals associated with holidays are great celebrations filled with pageantry, merrymaking and colorful rites. Don't forget your camera!

Korea is a photographer's dream. Traditional rural villages, the beauty of the countryside, colorful dress of the people and the many ancient palaces, shrines and temples make fine subject material on the top of your list for picture taking.

Korea officially follows the Gregorian calendar, the calendar used in Western countries, but many of Korea's holidays originated centuries ago and are based on the ancient lunar calendar of the Orient. The Lunar New Year usually falls during the end of January or first part of February by the Gregorian calendar.

Korea's traditional festival days may still be celebrated in the old ways in the countryside. Modern urban Koreans vary in their manner of observance. Some will follow customs out of habit or nostalgia, while others simply use the free day for family or social gatherings, catching a movie or having a night out on the town.

January 1, New Year's Day:

The first three days of the Gregorian New Year are recognized and celebrated officially by the Korean government. However, many Koreans still traditionally observe the Lunar New Year. Members of the family get up early, don their best clothes while the younger generation bow to their parents and grandparents as a reaffirmation of family ties. Traditionally, women would prepare special dishes for this annual celebration for the family ancestors. For the wealthy

families there is a special shrine, while others conduct the ceremony in their living rooms. The younger generation wearing brightly colored garments call on their elders for the *sebae* (low bow with forehead touching the floor), while small pieces of food or money are given to the children.

The host entertains adults with rice wine called *sul*, soup and meat. Though the New Year's food at each home varies according to the economic condition, the *ttokkuk* or rice dumpling soup is universal from street vendor to the millionaire. The *ttok* or glutinous rice is often eaten by itself. It is steamed and pounded until it is like dough, then cut into small pieces. To have a New Year's celebration without great quantities of *ttok* is unthinkable.

Traditionally the *yut* game is quite popular during this season. Four oblong wooden sticks, flat on one side and rounded on the other, are thrown to see how they fall, which determines the number of moves to be made on the game board. Girls often play see-saw but traditionally stand up on the board. In the olden days of the dynasty girls were not permitted to wander outside of the home courtyard. In curiosity the girls adopted the see-saw game to gain fleeting glimpses of the passing outside world over the garden wall. Kite flying, especially among the boys during the New Year season, is also traditionally a favorite pastime. Teams of boys might have contests with kite strings coated with powdered glass as they try to cut loose each other's kites.

◁ *Kite flying and sledding are favorite winter games for children*

Brightly colored hanbok *worn during* ▷
the Lunar New Year

Sol (1st day of 1st lunar month)

The Lunar New Year is still one of the biggest holidays of the year though the government does not officially recognize it as a legal holiday. People still dress in their traditional *hanbok,* take a rest from work for three days, and families gather to observe the ancestral ceremonies. There is usually a feast and younger members make New Year's greetings to their elders. This tradition though weaker in the cities is still traditionally strong in the countryside.

Tongshin-Je (15th day of 1st lunar month):

Though now seldom celebrated except in the rural regions, this day was originally set aside for a community festival in order to pray to the local shaman spirits for good crops. The festival is actually a fertility rite.

In the evening a variety of traditional games takes place under the full moon. Tug-of-war, stone fights and other mock fights with torches might take place between neighboring villages. Traditionally the winner will be blessed with a bumper crop, it is believed. Such games perhaps started to determine priority in use of water from a common source.

March 1, Samil or Independence Day:

Celebrated as a National Holiday, Koreans observe the anniversary of the March 1, 1919 Independence movement against Japanese colonial rule. On this day the Proclamation of Independence which was signed by thirty-three Korean patriots is read at Pagoda Park in Seoul. The word *Sam-il* means the third month and first day.

Hanshik (105th day of the lunar year):

Koreans on this day prepare wine, fruit, cakes and vegetables to take to the graves of their ancestors where they are placed with due ceremony. Cold Food Day or *hanshik* is more often called "Grave Visiting Day," and in rural regions where numerous graves are found the hills will be covered with people of all ages in traditional dress. Though it is usually treated as a picnic day, still the cry of *aigo!* from weeping mourners may be heard echoing across the valleys. The grave site is repaired, the area weeded and possibly a tree or two might be planted nearby on this day. On "Cold Food Day" in olden times people refrained from making a fire.

April 5, Arbor Day:

Trees are planted over the countryside as part of the Republic of Korea's reforestation program on this day. School age children and groups of adults are noticed in all parts of the country planting shrubbery and trees.

248

Buddha's Birthday (8th day of 4th lunar month):

This day of celebration is known as the "Feast of the Lanterns" commemorating the birthday of Buddha. In 1975 this day was designated as a national holiday by the Korean government. This is one of the most colorful of festival days. Elaborate and solemn rituals are held at many Buddhist temples across the entire country while lanterns are carried in a parade through the city streets. The main temple of Chogye-sa in downtown Seoul is always a popular place for tourists on this day.

Traditionally in the country districts tall lantern posts were erected before the home with pheasant feathers, pine branches and colored silk cloth at the top. Children made dolls of rice straw to be hung from the lantern poles to dance in the wind. The lanterns traditionally were made in many shapes with Buddhist symbols painted on them and inscribed with characters for long life, blessing, or peace.

May 5, Children's Day:

Originally celebrated in both Japan and Korea as "boys' day" this particular holiday in spring has become increasingly popular for families to take their children on excursions. To further strengthen the family institution the Korean government in 1975 made Children's Day a national holiday. The various parks and children's centers throughout the country are packed with excited and colorfully dressed children. The spirit of this gala occasion is catching even for the elderly grandparents who are seen with their active grandchildren.

Tano Day (5th day of 5th lunar month):

Tano rates as one of the three great celebration days of the lunar year, in conjunction with the New Year and Chusok Day. Summer food is offered at the household shrine of the ancestors. It is known also as "swing day" since girls dressed in their prettiest clothes

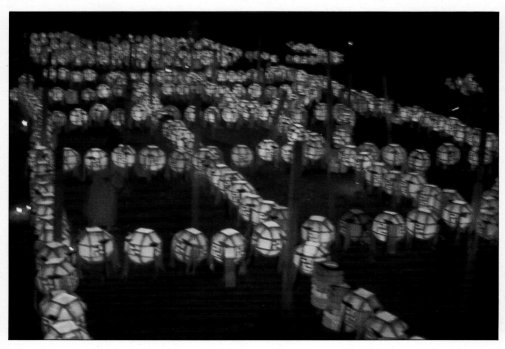

often compete in swinging matches. They first wash their hair in water boiled with iris and make ornamental hairpins of iris roots carved with characters of "long life" or "blessing." Long ropes are hung from the branches of the tallest village trees. Secluded in their homes during the winter months, women can now come out to the mountain slopes in colorful dress to fly back and forth on the high swings like spring swallows. Their full skirts like multicolored butterflies flit through the heavens. An ancient poet describes the sight:

> Not in heaven nor on earth
> But in the middle sky
> Blue hills and green waters
> Seem to swing to and fro.
> You come as falling flowers,
> You go as skimming swallows.

Special events for this day traditionally may include wrestling matches for men in which the winner receives a bull as a prize.

June 6, Memorial Day:

On this day the nation pays tribute to the war dead and memorial services are held at the National Cemetery in Seoul. Memorial Day is a legally recognized Korean holiday.

June 15, Farmers' Day:

Though not a legal holiday this day is set aside to honor the farmers. Throughout the country, the exciting colorful dances accompanied by traditional music played by centuries-old instruments are featured in the celebration. This period is the agricultural work season. Farmers from different villages organize bands whose members join together for mutual aid on their farms. Going to the fields early in the morning and returning home late, the procession is led by a flag bearer of the village with the *changgo* drum, flutes, and gongs being played. As the farmers transplant the rice seedlings or weed the fields the boisterous band accompanies the work with dances and songs.

July 17, Constitution Day:

Celebrated as a legal national holiday, Constitution Day commemorates the proclamation of the Constitution of the Republic of Korea on July 17, 1948. Ceremonies are usually held in Seoul's capitol plaza and all major cities.

August 15, Liberation Day:

This national holiday commemorates the acceptance by Japan of the Allied terms of surrender in 1945, thereby freeing Korea from thirty-six years of Japanese domination. Also marking the formal proclamation of the Republic of Korea in 1948, military parades and ceremonies throughout the country highlight this day's activities.

Ch'ilsok (7th day of 7th lunar month):

According to tradition on this night the unmarried girls must bow to the heavenly love-stars, the Herdboy and the Weaver, while praying for improvement in sewing. Also the young scholar over his wine cup writes poems to the two love-stars. Legends tell that long ago a young princess on the east side of the Milky Way always sat at her loom day and night until the king, her father, took pity on her and married her to the handsome herdboy in the western skies. But after her marriage she neglected her weaving so the king grew angry and brought her back home. He permitted her to cross the Milky Way once a year on the seventh night of the seventh month; thus forever the two love-stars could see each other across the stream but were unable to meet because there was no bridge. On this one night all the magpies on earth would fly to heaven to form a bridge spanning the Milky Way so that the love-stars might meet. If rain fell that night the drops were tears of joy and if they fell the next morning, the tears were for farewell.

◁ *Buddha's birthday celebration, Seoul*

Chusok (15th day of 8th lunar month):

Chusok is one of the great national holidays of the year and is referred to as Korean Thanksgiving Day. This is the day of the full moon and harvest festival. People visit family tombs and make food offerings. The traditional dress is usually worn, especially by the women, and in the past archery contests were held by the men. In the country the farmers are merry with food and wine as they play the native musical instruments and dance in the village streets. In the evening the young people go out to the hills to view the full moon, each trying to catch the first glimpse as the round moon peeks over the crest of the hills. Rice cake called *ttok* filled with sweets or bean paste are made in abundance for the celebration of this day of thanksgiving.

October 1, Armed Forces Day:

This national holiday is marked with many colorful military programs. Military parades, aerial acrobatics and honor guard ceremonies are held around the reviewing plaza at Yoi-do, an island in the Han River.

October 3, National Foundation Day:

This national holiday is also called Tan'gun Day as it commemorates the day when the ancestral founder of the Korean nation, Tan'gun, established his Kingdom of Choson in 2333 B.C. Tan'gun emerged from the shadowy prehistoric past near the Ever-White Mountain (*Paektu-san*) in northern Korea and established his capital at Pyongyang, making this city one of the oldest cities in the world. Tan'gun arrived at Mani Mountain on Kangwha Island near Seoul to worship. The remains of a stone altar are still seen. On this day crowds of people meet at this mountain to climb the arduous trail to the peak. Usually a flaming torch is brought from the peak by runners to Seoul to begin the athletic activities of this day in the capital city.

October 9, Han'gul Day:

This national holiday celebrates the anniversary of the promulgation of *han'gul,* the national written language of Korea, invented by King Sejong in the mid-15th century. The Korean alphabet is considered one of the most amazing inventions of ancient history and is still used as the written language of Korea with few alterations. Elaborate memorial ceremonies with Yi Dynasty court dances are performed at the tomb site of King Sejong (1418-1450).

The Tenth Month for Kimjang:

During this month of October one frequently hears the phrase, "Have you finished *kimjang?*" This is the month that the *kimchi,* considered the national dish of Korea and an indispensable subsidiary food for Koreans, is prepared to last for the winter months. Every Korean household is busy in this preparation and the women take great care to make the *kimchi* tasty.

December 25, Christmas Day:

Christmas is observed as a national holiday in Korea as it is in the Western countries.

Other Korean Festivities:

If one stays longer in Korea he might be fortunate enough to witness or participate in other types of celebrations. The most important events in the life of any Korean are the 100 day ceremony, 1st birthday and the 60th birthday. After birth the mother is given a diet of seaweed soup and rice. Across the gate of the house a straw rope is tied for 21 days. If the baby is a boy pieces of charcoal and red pepper are fastened to the rope. If the baby is a girl pieces of charcoal and pine sprigs are hung on the straw rope. No visitors are allowed for three weeks.

On the 100th day after birth a banquet is held and there is a great celebration.Guests and friends are invited. An appropriate gift is a gold ring. On the child's 1st birthday another large banquet is prepared and the baby is placed in the seat of honor. Certain items such as noodles, money, books, yarn or brush are placed before him. These symbolic items are considered an indication of the child's future. The adults enjoy waiting to see which item the child will pick. When the ceremony is over relatives and acquaintances are invited to enjoy the food, and presents are bestowed. In Korea the boy rather than the girl is pampered with more ceremony and expense.

At sixty a person reaches his *hwan'gap* and traditionally is considered to have completed his cycle of active life. This occasion is marked by many family festivities and a large feast. Though occasionally traditional funerals and marriages are seen these days they are simplified, partly due to the government austerity campaign. Such ceremonies were often ruinously expensive.

In Korea there is still the feeling that an unmarried adult is still a child regardless of age. Traditionally the boy's hair was permitted to grow in a long braid until his marriage, at which time it was cut and made into a topknot under his horsehair hat (worn only by a married man). Young girls would braid their hair but after marriage would wear it in a bun with a hairpin at the nape of their neck. Marriages even today are arranged by matchmakers and even modern girl prefer this method as long as they can have the final veto power. Though marriages are usually conducted in marriage halls, where the photo taking following the ceremony is four times longer, still many families continue the traditional ceremony with close relatives in a smaller room afterwards. At this time they will be dressed in traditional marriage garb.

Another celebration which still is continuing and popular is the *ham* ceremony. A *ham* box (a small wooden chest) is delivered by the groom to the bride's home before the wedding. There is considerable goodnatured teasing and demands for payment before the box can be actually brought into the house and given to the family.

Twice a year at the spring and fall equinox the ancient Confucian ceremonial rites honoring history's Korean and Chinese sages are still held in the main Confucian Shrine on the grounds of Sungkyunkwan (Confucian university). One may see the traditional stone chimes and bells as well as other unfamiliar instruments which are played only on several occasions each year. As the ceremony is colorful and picturesque visitors should bring their cameras.

Traditional Yi Dynasty ceremonies honoring the spirits of the rulers of the dynasty are presently held once a year at Chongmyo, the ancestral shrine in Seoul. Also in summer a memorial ceremony is held at the tomb of Yi T'aejo, the founding king of the Yi Dynasty (Tonggu-nung). Visitors are permitted to attend and rare scenes of Korea's colorful past are reenacted very faithfully in their original manner.

In the autumn the Silla Culture Festival in Kyongju, usually lasting three days, has now become one of the most exciting and elaborate Korean festivals of the year. Here the complete spectrum of parades, dances, competitive sports and drama can be viewed in all their splendor among the ancient relics of the former capital of Silla.

In the spring a cherry blossom festival is held each year in the port city of Chinhae, west of Pusan. People flock to this small town to see the flowering trees and the many activities of this gala occasion.

Other festivals that are held annually are the mask dance drama of Hahoi Village near Andong, the Yangju mask dances north of Seoul and numerous other festivals honoring great sages and heroes of the past. The Korean government is making an effort to promote this type of cultural tradition for Korean people as well as for the foreign community.

Graceful Flow of Traditional Dress

Korean clothing is distinctive and unique to Korea, and not uncommonly found in present daily use. Though the younger generation finds Western clothing more practical and comfortable in offices, the women often return to the traditional dress, especially on special occasions. The graceful flow of the "chima-chogori" charms the foreigners who come to Korea and witness this blend of the traditional and modern.

Probably more commonly than in any other Oriental country, the national dress of Korea continues to be worn. As one travels through the countryside one cannot fail to notice, against a backdrop of freshly transplanted pale-green rice seedlings, people moving along narrow paths... the women with their full pastel skirts billowing gracefully in the breeze.... like butterflies floating near the earth. In the villages the dignified grandfathers are seen in flowing white or pale-blue *turumagi* and wearing high wide-brimmed horse-hair hats. A small silvery wisp of a beard punctuates his dignity as a scholarly Confucian.

Today considerable color is noted in the traditional dress of the women. In the past white clothing was common. Since it was very difficult to keep clean, one wonders why white clothing was worn. Traditionally white was the color for mourning, and when royalty died the mourning period usually lasted three years. During the latter part of the Yi Dynasty there were so many deaths in the royal family that for the Koreans the white attire became habitual.

Especially for women not well endowed with good figures there were few problems as the long flowing skirt would gracefully cover waist, hips, and legs. The origin of Korean clothing comes from China but now in China the dress design has radically changed, and older patterns continue to be preserved in Korea.

Korea greatly admired the T'ang Dynasty and during the Silla era copied the Chinese patterns. However, the *chima* (skirt) and *chogori* (blouse) came into use during the 15th century. The traditional clothing for both men and women is called *hanbok*. The man's blouse or shirt is also called *chogori* and the voluminous trousers are called *paji*. Korean clothing has always been cut loosely for comfort. Usually in the winter several layers of underwear are worn. Buttons or hooks are not used in the *hanbok*, but long cloth strings or straps.

At weddings the bride and groom wore special clothes and also mourning clothes are quite different. Mourning clothing was made from coarse hemp material and differs according to sex, marital status and relationship to the deceased.

The *kat* (hat) has always been an important adjunct to the Korean male. Traditionally these hats were made from the hair of the horse's tail, though bamboo was occasionally used. Underneath the hat was worn the traditional topknot. A man could wear a hat covering his topknot only after marriage. An unmarried man wore his hair in a long braid and without a hat. The width of the brim varied according to fashion as lengths of skirts vary today.

There is an inner hat and outer hat. It is meant to be worn inside the home as well.

Even in the millennium before the

birth of Christ the wearing of hats was recorded on the Korean peninsula. One ruler decreed that all should wear ceramic hats. The individual who did not have the rim of his ceramic hat chipped and broken was considered the most even-tempered, and thus stood in a better position to receive a higher government post.

Koreans have always taken great pride in appearing in freshly laundered clothing though the conditions are still primitive for washing and ironing. Every stream near a village has its small groups of chattering washer women. Laundry sticks are used to beat out the dirt and with the constant scrubbing of clothing on rocks it is amazing how Korean fabrics manage to survive. The traditional wooden ironing sticks have given way to flatirons, but one can still occasionally hear the rhythmic beat of the two sticks behind rice-papered doorways.

In Korea today tourists are able to buy the Korean national dress ready made, easily found in the arcades and department stores. The east and south gate markets are a must for traditional shopping.

When foreigners wear the *hanbok* they often feel self conscious and awkward....indeed with some justification, for a Westerner seems ill suited, with different body proportions. However, the foreigner will continue to admire Korean dress wherever it is seen, whether on the streets of Seoul or along the rural village paths of the picturesque countryside of this nation.

Beauty of Dance and Music

Korea has mistakenly been considered only a bridge for Chinese culture to cross and settle in the art repository of Japan. Now it is known that much of this cultural transmigration such as dance and music did not always originate in China. In many cases the origin was Korea itself . . . . then it moved westward and eastward. The Korean dance . . . . portraying symmetrical beauty and exotic motion . . . . creates for spectators an inner spiritual awareness which expresses irrepressible joy. The exuberant folk dances portray the extrovert nature of the Koreans and are closest to the roots of the people, while the austerities of the court and religious dances add worthy dimensions of discipline and elegance . . . . a perfect balance of the dance spectrum. Western ballet seemingly seeks overt beauty of form through rigid control of techniques while the Korean dance attempts covert aestheticism of the inner spirit. The qualities that once gave Korean dance its greatness and uniqueness are now passing into oblivion.

The origin of Korean dance, as in many cultures, evolved from shamanistic religious ceremonies over 3,000 years ago and was closely linked to the agricultural cycle of the tribes. The shaman priest was the composer, musician and dancer.

Later during the Silla Dynasty the famed *hwarang* (flower youths) carried on the shamanistic tradition of song and dance. The *hwarang* was a unique society of young men associated with a fearless warrior class, a type of knighthood. Korea's earliest records compiled in 1145 mention that the *hwarang* were chosen from nobility for their beauty to be arrayed in cosmetics and fine clothes. Of high moral standards, they entertained one another with singing, music and dancing among the hills and streams. Good ministers, kings and generals as well as priests rose from their ranks. The origin for some of Korea's dances was laid down by the Silla *hwarang*. Possibly lesser in degree was the influence of Paekche and Koguryo.

During the Koryo Dynasty Buddhism became the national religion, replacing the folk religion. Considerable court music and dance were imported from China for Buddhist rituals. The mask

dance which first appeared in the writings of the famed scholar Ch'oe Ch'i-won in late Silla was more fully developed in the Koryo court. Also the Silla lyrics called the *hyangga* which were meant to be used in song and dance were passed on into records of the Koryo Dynasty. Many of these shamanistic poems, such as the famed Ch'oyong Dance, are believed to be the oldest of the court dances, and to have potent powers against diseases.

The masked dances are believed to be Central Asian in origin and initially used with Buddhist ceremonies. The lion, unknown to Korea, usually devoured those who transgressed the precepts of Buddha but later, during the Yi Dynasty when the mask drama dance came under folk influence, the satire was of Buddhism with the lion devouring the decadent priests.

A most important feature of Korean dance during the Koryo period was the *kisaeng* institution. They were a selected professional group of women, similar to girl entertainers of the T'ang Dynasty in China. The origin may well have gone back to the pre-unification period of Silla when an institution called *wonhwa*

◁ The folk ritual fan dance, Korea House, Seoul

(original flowers) was established by the king. The *wonhwa* predates the *hwarang* and consisted of women of good moral character who sang and danced for the Silla nation. Though undoubtedly shamanistic in character they may well have been the first recorded court entertainers. Due to jealous friction among the leaders the *wonhwa* was disbanded.

The *kisaeng* were chosen for their charm and beauty, trained from childhood, and knew how to sing, dance and play many musical instruments. Becoming the companions of artists and scholars as well as rulers of the nation the *kisaeng* became the most highly educated women of the country. The *kisaeng* experienced great social freedom and were one of the most privileged groups in a highly restrictive society. They were not prostitutes; thus it is difficult to draw an exact analogy from Western culture for the *kisaeng* institution. As the *kisaeng* culture passed from Korea to Japan it developed into the well-known and popular institution called *geisha,* meaning accomplished person.

The *kisaeng* entertainment was initiated by the court and was firmly established during the Koryo Dynasty. It remained under the patronage and protection of the crown.

The *kisaeng* dances range from the allegorical and semi-religious to stylized forms with emphasis on rhythm and grace. With the fall of the dynasty *kisaeng* were driven from the palaces and became the diversion of high-ranking Koreans and Japanese. The reputation of the *kisaeng* collapsed and the best they could hope for was to become the concubines of wealthy businessmen or government officials.

The most favorable climate for dance and music was the Yi Dynasty. The fourth ruler was King Sejong, who gave himself over to the development of dance and music as well as science and literature. Music and dance were classified, and the system of performances was standardized, while costumes of court musicians and dancers were systematized. His son, King Sejo, followed in the musical steps of his father with the

Changguch'um *(Hourglass Drum Dance)*

development of a theory of musical notation.

King Sejong's grandson commissioned Sung Hyon to compile the most comprehensive book ever written on music and dance in Korea. So precise is the content that it may be used even today as a reference in recreating dances that have fallen into disuse. In 1759 during the reign of King Yongjo (21st ruler) the first book of dance scores was compiled.

With Japan's annexation of Korea in 1910 the royal patronage of the dances came to an end. Also the Korean folk dances which had been flowering among the common people in the Yi Dynasty now entered into gradual decline during the occupation period as modern Western dance was introduced into Korea by the Japanese.

In the 20th century the last great dance master was Han Sung-jun who stood alone and unexcelled in the field of traditional Korean folk dance. Before his death in 1938 he was rewarded by the Japanese who could not overlook the merit of his achievement. Han Sung-

jun's most talented student Choe Sung-hee dealt Korean dance its most devastating blow. She went to Japan for further study and was enthusiastically received. She was called "queen of Korean dance" by the Japanese, though her dance performances were not popular in Korea.

As time passed Korean dance became more Westernized by the talented Choe Sung-hee and her students. Today, except for the *kisaeng* tradition and a few remaining court dancers, a whole generation has grown up on a misconception of Korean dance form. Little concerted effort is made by any dancer to restore or preserve the traditional dance and music. A grand-daughter of Han Sung-jun may be cited for her superior efforts as well as Kim Cheung-hung for his knowledge of court music and dance. Most artists of today receive greater satisfaction from their own creations rather than trying to preserve the legacy of Korean dance.

The traditional dance of Korea can be divided into three major forms: the

Pukch'um *(Drum Dance)*

260

Court Dance, the Religious Dance and the Folk Dance. The form of the Court Dance varies considerably and is divided into two areas now called *hyang-ak* (native Korean) and *t'ang-ak* (Chinese origin). Many court forms have been discontinued and lost to the general public due to the collapse of the dynasty. Traditionally most of the court dances were performed exclusively by men. If the dancers were females they could be the royal *kisaeng*.

Epitomizing the poetry and grace of human motion in all her dazzling attire, the court *kisaeng* is truly an impressive and striking figure in Korea's cultural heritage. The dress often worn consisted of a bright green frock decorated with rich and radiant floral patterns over a crimson base. A wide waistband also partially covered the breasts so as to flatten them as much as possible. A puritanical result of a pro-Confucian culture, the breast-flattening apparel of the female dress was purposely designed to control that portion of the female figure most likely to arouse sexual stimulation.

The full loose-fitting wide skirt was often bright red with an equally vibrant yellow blouse. The hands were covered by long rainbow-colored sleeves and on the dancer's head was a small, gaily decorated crown which shimmered with every slight movement. Through the smooth glossy black hair of the *kisaeng* drawn tightly up in a bun at the nape of the neck was stuck a large golden hairpin, often studded with precious stones. From the hairpin hung two very large red ribbons with gold floral designs.

Today the unique *kisaeng* in her regal resplendent attire has become symbolic of something that was intimately and inimitably Korean in all its grace, originality and nobility. The *kisaeng* image has found its place in tourist posters and many leading commercial advertisements. Korean people though eager to modernize and accept international conformity find it difficult to erase this particular symbol along with the many traditions that are buried and forgotten.

There are three categories of Religious Dance: the Buddhist, Confucian and Shaman ritual dances. The Buddhist ceremonial dances which probably entered from China with the Buddhist teachings have now been thoroughly Koreanized. The dances are used as supplication to Buddha so that departed souls may more easily enter Nirvana (paradise). Today the dances are usually performed by the married sect of priests during special ceremonies.

Though the austere Confucian Dance originated first in China it is only in Korea that this solemn and stately dance ceremony can still be seen in its most authentic form. To honor Confucius the ceremony is performed twice yearly on the campus of Sungkyungkwan University in the spring and fall. Also the Confucian ritual dance can be seen at Chongmyo, the Royal Ancestral Shrine, where the spirit tablets of the Yi Dynasty kings and their wives are enshrined. These dances now open to the public were traditionally performed only by men.

The ceremony called *ilmu* is divided into civil and military dances. The dancer carries a type of flute and stick bearing pheasant feathers on a wooden dragon head. A dragon-head shield is struck with a wooden hatchet, giving off a resounding "clack" during the ceremony. Cups of wine are offered to the spirits within the shrine.

Incorporating the ritual of Buddhism and Confucianism, the influence of shamanism has prevailed from Korea's earliest history and has had a most significant role in Korean dance. Nearly all practicing shamans today are women called *mudang*, while the ceremony itself is called a *kut*. The traditional aspects are passed on from mother to daughter and most *mudang* or sorceresses lack any formal education. A shaman may be called upon because of tragedy such as illness and death, or for a happy occasion such as a birthday or building dedication. A *mudang* can also be a medium for communicating with departed souls of relatives.

Unlike other religious dance ceremonies, the shaman ritual richly in-

corporates humor and satire or lengthy narratives, using occasional vulgarity and scatological remarks. In the ceremony a pig's head is often impaled on a trident. The mystical and supernatural is always an element in the *mudang kut.* However, the charm and humorous characteristics of the shaman ritual clearly relate this type of religious dance to the folk style.

Tourist performances of the shaman dance usually lack artistic merit because of major alteration. Authentic *mudang* ceremonies though still prevalent are difficult to locate and almost impossible to photograph without prior arrangements. The *mudang* prefers privacy for her paying customers.

The Folk Dance contains the elements of what is truly traditional Korean and to understand this one must comprehend the meaning of *mut* and *hung* . . . . irrepressible joy pouring from within outward from a deep sense of beauty . . . . the feeling of exhilaration to a point of giddiness. In addition to this understanding is the appreciation of the dancer's movements which precede the importance of rhythm and meter.

In court music the rhythm and meter are strictly adhered to because of the restrictive bonds of Confucianism, while the native dance is improvisatory in nature and free in spirit. This precedence of the dancer's movement over rhythm is most pronounced in the famous Farmer's Dance where the dancer becomes a "roving musician" creating his own rhythms. His disregard for basic meter and theme is difficult for Westerners to accept and appreciate. Even Koreans who are educated in Western classical music find it difficult to place Korean folk rhythms into Western notation.

Unfortunately, among Korea's younger generation there is little evidence of creativity. Instead of improvising the folk dance it has become highly stylized. Many are concerned about the future of true Korean traditional dance. Many of Korea's elite, believing that the traditional dance is primitive and culturally

backward, wish to inject a fresh spirit of new ideas . . . . and this would be indeed unfortunate.

Of the many folk dances still performed, probably the Farmer's Dance is the most popular and without any doubt the oldest existing dance in Korea. Influenced deeply by shamanism, the dance was traditionally employed to exorcise unwanted spirits or supplicate good spirits. The small gong and *changgo* (hourglass drum) are used as the tempo increases and dancers whirl in a spinning motion. The *changgo* used in many of the dances is Korea's most popular instrument. Shaped like an hour-glass, the two headed drum is fastened to the dancer's shoulders and waist. Sliding belts regulate the tone of the drum heads. Cow skin is used on one side and horse skin on the other. A bamboo stick, wooden mallet or the hand may be used in creating a highly syncopated rhythm which accompanies the dancer's motion.

The mask folk dance drama once holding royal favor was driven from the courts by lack of Confucian patronage during the Yi Dynasty and became the drama of the masses in the rural countryside. The mask drama developed themes of bitter satire against the ruling Confucian class and the Buddhist priests. The mask dance also is closely linked with shamanism. Originally the performers of the mask dances were always men but now women are used in performances. Considering the caliber of the audience the mask dance dramas were heavy with obscenity and vulgarity.

Some of the more common themes deal with reprobate monks who seduce young girls or the amusing triangular affair of the *yangban* (aristocrat), his concubine and first wife. Little importance is attached to the musical accompaniment. Again the dancer's movement, which is broad and rough in form, is the most important. The quick jerking movements of shoulder, torso and head with high forward steps cause the grotesque mask to appear even more comical to the appreciative spectators.

In the 16th century the Buddhist Drum Dance took on new folk apprecia-

The p'ansori *performance with a drummer (top) and* kayagum *play* (bottom) *at the*▷
Korea House, Seoul.

tion when the mysterious and bewitchingly beautiful *kisaeng* by the name of Hwang Chin-i vowed that there was no man oblivious to her charms. A poet, songwriter, dancer and musician, she had many men but loved few and took special delight in seeking out those who had vowed a life of celibacy.

Legends tell of one journey into the Diamond Mountains to a lonely hermitage where a famous monk lived in celibate meditation. Dressed in the robes of a monk she commenced the drum dance in a most seductive manner. Upon the final beat, she removed her monk's robe to reveal all her feminine beauty to the poor monk who was by then deliriously overcome by desire. The Buddhist Drum Dance became a folk version of Hwang Chin-i's adventure and is still popular. An outgrowth of this is the wildly gyrating Nine Drum Dance which is now considered Korea's youngest and most lively folk dance.

Probably the dance that more perfectly illustrates the genuine tradition of Korean dance art is the *salp'uli*. The *mut* and *hung* elements are more apparent in this dance than any other. As the name means "exorcise the devil" it is believed that this dance is also shaman in origin. Only a scarf and small hand drum are used and the dance tells no story. As the dance progresses the inner exotic feeling is overwhelming, conveying a joyousness and abandoned thrill of ecstasy. One feels the presence of a gay enchantress, bewitchingly beautiful, with whom the sensual delights are boundless.

The casual Western listener who encounters Korean music for the first time is apt to come to the conclusion that it is being played out of tune. Among the many scales used around the world the Western tempered scale, in which an octave comprises 12 half tones, is one of the most recent to appear. A determined listener will find himself getting used to the five and seven note scales found in Asian music. Korean music is more susceptible to subtle manipulations with vocal and instrumental techniques.

There are fifty traditional instruments still extant that were used in Korean court and folk music but most of them are used infrequently today. These musical instruments are classified according to the eight basic materials of which they are made: metal, stone, silk, bamboo, gourd, clay, leather and wood. Following are the more important musical instruments.

Probably the most popular and well-known Korean instrument is the *changgo* or hourglass-shaped drum. This drum has two heads which are struck with the hand on the left and thin stick on the right. Often this drum is carried by a dancer. Another popular instrument is the *kayagum,* a 12-string zither. Originating in Kaya during the Three Kingdoms period, the *kayagum* was the progenitor of the Japanese *koto*. This instrument is plucked with the fingers.

The *haegum* is a two-string fiddle with the bow hairs drawn between the strings. Originating from central Asia, the tone of the *haegum* is harsh and nasal. The *taegum* is Korea's largest flute made of bamboo. Two and a half feet long, it has six finger holes and one large hole covered by a vibrating membrane when blown. As its pitch is fixed, the rest of the orchestra will tune to the *taegum.*

The *p'iri* is a small cylindrical bamboo pipe having eight finger holes and uses a double reed, making it a true oboe. The *tanso* of Korean origin is a vertical flute. The *saenghwang* or mouth organ has 17 slender pipes leading into a gourd base. The *pip'a* or lute can have four or five strings. The *komungo* is a six-string zither originating from the 7th century Koguryo period. It is played with a plectrum held in the right hand. The *pak* is a fan-shaped clapper used to begin and end ensemble music.

The *p'yon'gyong* are stone chimes consisting of 16 jade-like, L-shaped stones of differing length and thickness. To complement the stone chimes are the *p'yonjong* (bronze bells). Sixteen bells are hung in two rows on a wooden standard to be struck with a hammer made of horn. The chimes and bells were always used with Confucian rites.

At the yearly ceremony at Chongmyo and the Confucian university the bells and stone chimes can still be observed.

Gongs and drums of various sizes are used with all types of Korean music but are most popular in religious and folk music. They are found in every Buddhist temple and used at every shaman ritual. The performers in the farmers' band music play them vigorously while dancing. Horns and harps also belong to Korea's repertoire of musical instruments.

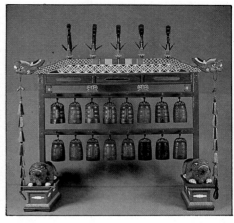

ching
(gong)

puk (drum)

saenghwang
(mouth organ)

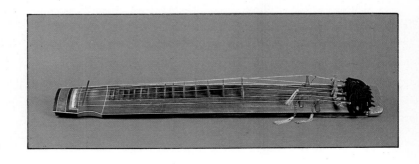

Mask Dance Drama

The evolution of the mask dance drama is seen through concepts of Korean folk art and its relationship to early spiritual beliefs. Though primarily religious, the mask dances served as a vent for the many grievances of the common people against the prevailing social restrictions enforced upon them by the nobility.

The Korean mask dance drama as it developed during the final days of the Yi Dynasty can be divided into three major categories and ten different mask dance styles still extant. The first category is the mask dance drama that was performed in conjunction with village shaman ritualistic festivals called *sonang-jae*.

These include the *pyolshin* ritual drama of Hahoe Village in North Kyongsang Province near Andong City and the Kwanno mask dance drama of Kangnung in Kangwon Province. The latter is a Tano Festival event held on the fifth day of May by the lunar calendar. This play was lost about 75 years ago along with masks and performers. However, in 1966 this ritual was revived based on recollection of elders living in the area who had previously seen this play.

The *sonang-jae* festivals were believed to be also held at Pyongsan Village near Hahoe and Chugok Village of Yongyang district of this same province. Only the masks of Hahoe and Pyongsan remain.

The second and largest category consists of the *sandae* type which might be considered the core of Korean mask dance drama which flourished until the middle of the Yi Dynasty under government sponsorship. The name *sandae* comes from the government office responsible for their activities during royal patronage (also called *sandae-togam*).

The *pyol-sandae* drama which comes from Yangju and the *sandae* drama of Songp'a are the most representative of the Seoul area. The Pongsan and Kang-

nyong mask dance dramas come from Hwanghae Province in northern Korea. In South Kyongsang Province are found the "Five Actors Play," *ogwang-dae* of Kosong and Tongyong and the "Field Play" (*yayu*) of Suyong and Tongnae. Along with these six types of *sandae* drama is the puppet drama entitled *kkoktu-gakshi* because the content is very much the same.

The subjects dealt with in the ten various mask dances known today are strikingly homogeneous in theme. The most common themes usually include the satirizing of an apostate monk who is desiring sex; ridiculing the shortcomings of the *yangban* (nobility) or poking fun at the domestic tribulations of a husband-wife-concubine relationship.

Similar to the folk literature of the Yi Dynasty period, the mask dance drama was a manifestation of the spirit of protest in the hearts of the common folk against the ruling class and formal morality.

The mask should not be considered simply as an art object for one cannot fully appreciate its quality when it is not in use. Its true merit is best appreciated when the mask is placed on the face of an actor in actual motion during the drama.

When a mask is not in use we might consider it as in a coma. The more skillful the actor, the livelier and more animated the mask becomes. The true portrayal in the performance of a mask dance lies in the skillful use of the mask

◁ *Preparing for a mask dance performance, Seoul*

itself. It is surprising how a fixed expression on a mask can have a fantastic range of expressions such as feelings of joy and sorrow.

With his mask on the actor is no longer a human being for now he can transform himself into a supernatural deity. A dead man can become a living man with a mask and at the same time he is a medium between this world and the next. The contradiction of being able to be human and superhuman at the same time is the magic formula of a mask. A mask can serve both sexes and occasionally does. This unique quality of the mask was perpetuated to endow Korean mask drama with a special charm and unique impression.

The beauty of any mask is related to the mysterious qualities of the supernatural which remain closely related to man and his early primitive beliefs. Modern man today may look upon the mask as only an ornate art-craft object, while disregarding its prime functional powers.

The most common materials used in making Korean masks are wood, gourd and papier-mâché, however, other materials are often added for necessary effect such as cloth, wool, leather, fur, clay and bamboo. Before the development of plastics the gourd called *pagaji,* which was commonly found throughout the countryside, was in popular use for masks.

In earlier periods the *kiak* masks were made of paulownia wood. Though elm, pine and camphor were sometimes used, the alder wood was the most common as it is a soft reddish wood and was also popular for cabinet making.

Generally we find that the colors used on masks are symbolic and represent the five shamanistic directions; blue as east; red as south; white as west; black as north and yellow as center. In the symbolic fertility aspect the colors of masks may also represent the four seasons. When the old monk, wearing a black mask (winter), is defeated by the prodigal Ch'wibari, wearing a red mask (summer), the battle of the seasons is portrayed.

Usually the Korean mask covers the entire face, while a piece of black cloth is attached to the back so that the entire head may be covered. Though there are a few excellent early masks still extant it is unfortunate that the identities of the master mask makers are unknown. Preserving the style of the master artisan was not a tradition in Korea as it was in Japan.

Unfortunately in Korea the mask drama never rose above the status of folk entertainment: thus the mask artisans as well as the dancers were considered lowest on the social scale with little nobility compensation or support. In Japan the mask drama received higher social recognition and support from the feudal lords.

An additional difficulty relating to the preservation of masks was the Korean custom of burning masks after each performance. Though the Hahoe and Pyongsan masks were exceptions, usually the masks were regarded as being contaminated with the spirits during the course of the drama and had to be burned. Hahoe and Pyongsan masks were regarded as sacred and pure which probably contributed to their survival as Korea's oldest masks.

Usually throughout the Orient where the mask dance drama developed it is noted that greater emphasis is placed on the music and dance rather than the speech. This is also true in Korea. The dance and music elements are more refined and developed while the plot is weak or non-existent. The main purpose is to entertain the spectators with dance and music. The gesture styles of the actors rather than their speech predominate in the mask dance drama.

The mask dance drama is always accompanied by music. The flute, *ch'anggo* (hour-glass drum), cymbals, *haegum* (two-string fiddle) and *chottae* (bamboo flute) are the major Korean instruments used in the drama accompaniment.

Traditionally the mask dance was not performed on a stage but was conducted in the open fields or hillside. The drama would continue throughout the night. In some areas such as Hahoe the drama was conducted in the center of the village. Some mask dance dramas were performed on several occasions each year yet others may not be used for over ten years. There is no regulated starting time but usually the dance begins in the evening.

Common themes are the promotion of virtue using strong satire and humor, while vice is objectionable. Antipathy is shown toward the depraved Buddhist monks while disgust is expressed for the privileged ruling class.

Shaman offering for masks

Pyolshin *ritual drama of Hahoe Village*

Korean Ceramics

Ceramics as well as other arts of Korea have often been mistakenly considered as only a cultural by-path or inferior imitations of Chinese patterns. Certainly the major influence on Korean arts has come from Korea's productive neighbor to the west, yet it is equally significant that especially in the ceramic art, Korea has constantly developed its own forms which are unmistakeably Korean in character. Most scholars and art connoisseurs agree that among Korea's artistic endeavors over the centuries ceramics are the outstanding product.

From the standpoint of understanding Korean ceramics it is important to know that one is dealing with an entirely different set of motivations on the part of Korean potters. Historically Westerners have been more familiar with Chinese ceramics and often subconsciously compare Korean pottery to a Chinese system of quality standard. Often because of this pro-Chinese bias perfection is not seen in the Chinese sense, but Chinese standards of perfection are not applicable to Korean ceramic art.

Though glazes were beautifully perfect the Korean potters would often complete pots, especially during the Yi Dynasty, with uneven effects and not brand them rejects. Korean pottery manufacturing appears baffling, even irrational, but it is this precise characteristic, this non-Chinese unaffected informality, that gives rare virtue to Korean wares as a highly developed art form which truly portrays this country's tradition. Some authorities believe that the Korean pottery industry attained heights during the Koryo period that may well have been unsurpassed even by the Chinese. Today their secrets are apparently lost.

It is strange to realize that Koryo celadon was almost completely unknown before 1910 when excavated examples came to light in great number. During the 12th century the production of

Koryo celadon cup and stand

superior pottery, uniquely Korean, reached its highest level of achievement. However, with the very earliest types of pottery from the Three Kingdoms period, Korea's debt to China must be recognized.

Fortunately the rich clay still found on the Korean peninsula was of the best quality. Over the years pottery manufacturing was in the hands of certain families or controlled by temples which operated large kilns. The potters were ranked low socially, even beneath other artisans. Certain individual potters occasionally rose by royal favor. In the latter part of the 16th century the conquering Japanese armies moved whole villages of potters to Japan from which the foundation for the vast Japanese ceramic industry was begun. Even today many of the potters on the southern island of Kyushu are of Korean ancestry.

When we look back over Korean history, marked frequently by devastation, it seems something of a miracle that anything so fragile as ceramics could survive. Fortunately the tradition of placing funerary gifts for the dead in tombs has preserved for us numerous fine pottery pieces. Even within the last several years as excavations continue on pre-unification Silla tombs in Kyongju new ceramic art objects are coming to light. Because of these warring conditions in Paekche and Koguryo much less remains today.

Silla ceramics dominate the scene for the first millennium, and it is fortunate that the capital (Kyongju) did not become a battleground when the dynasty changed to Koryo in the 10th century. With countless tombs around Kyongju the area has been likened to a vast graveyard.

Silla pots are a type of stoneware which has been baked at a high temperature to give a clear ring on the body when struck. The color is usually dark gray while varying occasionally towards black. Brownish tones sometimes resulting from oxidation and kiln ash are often noted on the surface. The decoration of Silla ceramics usually incised into the body tends to be restrained, though generally early Silla pottery is freer in originality and may carry more shamanist characteristics.

By the late 6th century changes appeared because of the sobering influence of Buddhism. The free and sometimes wilder forms were replaced by calmer and more cautious patterns and shapes. Generally Silla pottery can be described as unassuming, sturdy, and straightforward, while exhibiting a pleasing spontaneous ingenuity.

During the Koryo Dynasty an increased degree of receptivity toward greater Chinese influence, including Buddhism, gave significant impetus to the ceramic development in Korea. It is now known that the major influence came from the Yueh potters of China located south of the Shantung Peninsula and inland from the port of Ningpo. The influence of the high-fired greenish blue or olive glazed celadon was revolutionary in terms of beauty and appeal. Celadon now epitomizes to the rest of the world one specific Korean cultural achievement.

When considering the term *celadon* care must be taken. Most Westerners consider the term synonymous with the even-toned rich green colors associated with the Sung Dynasty pottery of China. Celadon is actually an iron-bearing glaze capable of an infinite range of coloration depending on the atmospheric condition of the kiln when fired. In a reducing atmosphere the colors tend to be green or bluish in tone, but if oxygen has been admitted the result might be olive color or even brown.

Korean celadon can be seen in a very wide range of various color tones. The most characteristic shade of the finer Korean celadon pieces is gray-green or as some say, "kingfisher-colored." The glaze tends to be more thinly applied than in Chinese celadon; thus the clay shows through the transparent glaze emphasizing the gray tone.

Though some kiln sites were developed around the capital of Songdo (Kaesong) and Kanghwa Island, the main celadon industry blossomed in southwest Korea, now the Cholla provinces. The Korean coastal area south of Kangjin is considered the center of the celadon production during the Koryo period. Koryo kiln sites have been excavated and in one case rebuilt for tourist interest. Hundreds of potsherd can still be found in the valley area.

The full development of Korean celadon can be divided into three periods. The betraying influences of Sung China characterize the first period, from the late tenth to the mid-twelfth century. The evolution of a more original Korean style in which the decorative use of inlay designs became prevalent exemplifies the second period for the next 150 years. It is interesting to note that Korean potters invented the inlay technique prior to its development in China. Due to the Mongol invasion of Korea the third period is marked by falling quality in both potter's technique and glaze control.

Initially there was restraint, but soon there was a noticeable tendency to increase the scale of the design. By the end of the 13th century the Korean potters had become obsessed with inlaid patterns which resulted in a more baroque style. This was the century that saw the Mongol invasion which disrupted political life as well as the cultural aspirations of the nation. The court was forced to flee to Kanghwa Island. The ceramic industry was paralyzed and finally died, taking with it the secrets of making the lustrous range of bluegreen glazes.

With the beginning of the Yi Dynasty in 1392 there was a greater concern for ethical conduct and human relations than with mystical concepts of an afterlife. Confucianism replaced Buddhism and had less need of the ceramic arts. Yi ceramics differ radically from typical Koryo.

In contrast, Yi porcelain, characterized by heavy potting and apparent slipshod technique, may seem rather coarse and humble. But during the 15th century this is what the Japanese tea masters admired, taking many potters captive. These potters gave birth to the vast ceramic industry of Japan. Yi pots had a new straightforward stolid masculinity in contrast to the refined, courtly and even feminine elegance of the Koryo pottery of the past dynasty.

Yi ceramics can be broadly placed into two categories: white porcelain and stoneware known as *punch'ong*. This stoneware met the requirements of the masses and is considered a true expression of the Korean folk art. The glaze was often iron-bearing and is considered a type of celadon. The white Yi porcelain pots also had the same characteristics of *punch'ong* pottery such as heaviness, and apparent rough style, yet a superior class of white porcelain was produced in some quantity for use

Yi Dynasty punch'ong

in the court and for ceremonial purposes. Tonal colors of gray, green and even blue were evident.

Because of the Chinese ceramists it was unavoidable that Korean potters also experimented with an underglaze design painted in cobalt-blue. In the early years of the Yi Dynasty the material was difficult to come by, as it came through China from the Middle East. However, in the 15th century a native supply, though of poor quality, was discovered in Korea. The blue was usually too dark and rather muddy in color.

Today ceramic collectors are grateful that the cobalt was not easily obtainable; thus Korean potters often turned to iron brown and copper-red to achieve their decorative designs. The result was typical of true Korean esthetics, swiftly accomplished in an assured manner but still producing a casual appearance. The copper through oxidation was usually green, but when really successfully controlled the tonal red was more pure and warm. It is in this very aspect of the handling of the decorations applied to the pot forms that Yi potters identify with the tradition of Korean ceramics guided by instinct and unpretentious assurance. This is Korea's unique accomplishment.

①

②

③

④

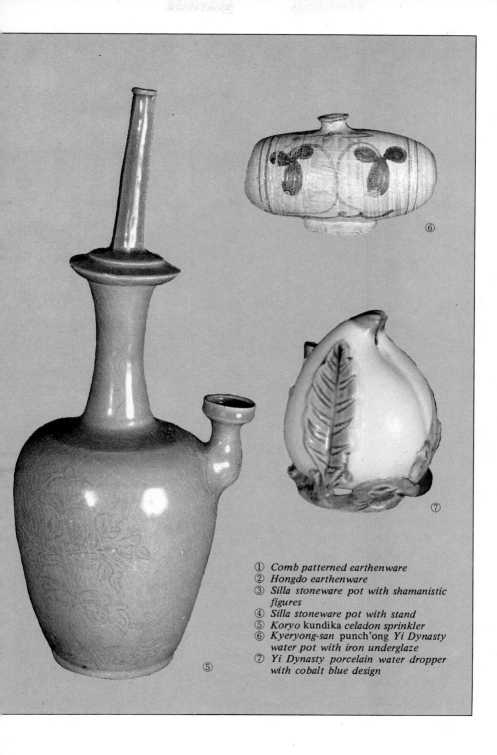

① Comb patterned earthenware
② Hongdo earthenware
③ Silla stoneware pot with shamanistic figures
④ Silla stoneware pot with stand
⑤ Koryo kundika *celadon sprinkler*
⑥ Kyeryong-san punch'ong *Yi Dynasty water pot with iron underglaze*
⑦ Yi Dynasty porcelain water dropper with cobalt blue design

Craftmanship of Korean Art

Through the craft art media Korea's indigenous art styles are clearly recognized as humorous, down-to-earth, animated and satirical as well as sentimental and recurrently original over the years. Throughout the centuries tradition shows the deft directness of Korean art, mixing some fantasy with straightforward good sense and a religious reverence that acts as much in appreciation for the elements of nature as well as deities. The craftsmanship of the sculptors, architects, metal and wood workers is demonstrated through the art Korea has in its vast repository.

SCULPTURE

As in ancient Chinese as well as Japanese art forms, the mainstream of Korean art is Buddhist from the fourth century to modern times. First introduced in 372, Buddhism gradually spread over the entire Korean peninsula, while generating a turning point in the development of fine arts. Buddhism so flourished that one ancient historian wrote that temples near the Silla capital were like "stars in the heavens" while pagodas were erected in such numbers as "geese flying south in the sky."

Especially in Paekche, known as a country of monks and nuns from which Buddhism moved into Japan, the faith was even more popular than in the kingdoms of Silla and Koguryo. The development of Korean Buddhist art was further accelerated by Silla unification of the peninsula in the 7th century.

This historical event created a force that inspired a noble renaissance of religious art called the "golden age" which spanned two centuries. During this period the Silla capital had a population of over one million inhabitants and was the fourth largest city in the world. This era paralleled the great culture of T'ang China.

A Buddhist temple was built with the objects of worship at the center.

The halls, enshrining the sculptured images and pagodas with their carved figures, occupied the main part of the temple compound. Sincere effort toward technical refinement, physical beauty and grandeur was made in the sculpturing of stone images and temple monuments. Today Buddhist art objects occupy the greatest portion of art monuments and relics still extant.

Korean Buddhist sculpture can be grouped historically into categories of gilt-bronze and stone. Early examples of wooden or clay images are practically nonexistent. All extant Buddhist images, whether in stone or gilt bronze, do not date earlier than the 6th century. Though there are many gilt bronze or pure gold artifacts, probably the most important are the meditating Maitreyas (NT-78 & 83) displayed in the National Museum.

As granite is most plentiful in Korea, sculpture was often done in stone. The stone and gilt bronze sculpture of the Koryo and Yi periods was mundane compared to the "golden age" of Silla which culminated in the 8th century. Probably the most outstanding stone sculpture found anywhere in Asia is the Buddhist grotto called *sokkuram* behind Pulguk Temple near Kyongju City. The Sokkuram Grotto was built by Kim Tae-song who is also credited with building Pulguk Temple in 751.

One can drive the distance from

◁ *Pagoda of Mujang Temple (Treasure No. 126), Kyongju*

Pulguk-sa or walk on a wide footpath which takes over one hour. Unfortunately now most tourists are not permitted to enter the grotto but can only view it through a glass window. As many of the 37 sculptured masterpieces cannot be seen on the rotunda wall from the entrance, one's appreciation is dimmed.

Within the thirty-foot domed rotunda is a large stone carved Buddha image (3.5m high) of magnificent artistry. Encircling the chamber are the ten important disciples of Buddha and four Bodhisattvas. The ten disciples have shaven heads and lean ascetic faces with long noses characteristic of Indo-Europeans.

The relief image of the eleven-headed Goddess of Mercy on the center rear wall of the sanctuary will hold visitors spellbound. Considered by critics as the most beautiful sculptured figure in all Korean art, this *kwanseum posal* is slender and elegantly dressed in astonishingly realistic and fluid garments with tassels and jewelry arranged in loops, cross-folds and knots.

The supple feminine form contrasts sharply with the fear-evoking guardians positioned on either side of the entrance to the grotto. Eight heavenly *palbujong* and two scowling *inwang* threaten to strike intruding evil spirits. The *sach'onwang* or Four Heavenly Kings are depicted firmly crushing beneath their feet demons representing the enemies of Buddhism.

While the natural sense of beauty in line and proportion is depicted in baffling simplicity, this masterpiece produces an eerie magnetism for those coming to visit the Sokkuram Grotto. Here in this grotto is found a certain distinctive quality in Korean art. A real earnestness matched with dignity and grandeur are demonstrated with classic and idealistic naturalism, yet there is simplicity with modest and unobtrusive interpretation of form.

Korea in her position between China and Japan maintained a role of assimilating and passing on to Japan the arts of China. During this period of T'ang assimilation, Silla improved upon China in accordance with national characteristics and raised such Buddhist art to the highest plateau in the Far East. Korea not only accepted the tradition of her teacher but in many cases ennobled it, and in the Buddhist art of cave temple tradition, Korea has produced the world's classic example, the Sokkuram Grotto of Kyongju.

ARCHITECTURE

Early stone structures of religious significance are relatively abundant in Korea. Dolmens are extant from several millenniums while stone tablets with inscriptions date back to the 6th century. Stone pagodas are found in abundance at Buddhist temples and temple sites. The architectural skill of pagoda construction is unique to Korea. Because of their massive size these pagodas are often not found in museums but at the many temple sites throughout the country.

With the dynamic spread of Buddhism, the pagoda became an essential feature of each temple to house relics of Buddha or ashes and *sarira* of famous priests. The earliest Korean pagodas were probably wooden structures in Chinese T'ang style, but these gave way in the early 7th century to stone pagodas, as stone was a common building material in Korea. Several sites of these vanished wooden pagodas are well-known near the Kyongju area.

From the Three Kingdoms period there remain only two examples from Paekche. The oldest stone pagoda is preserved at the site of Miruk-sa at Iksan (NT-11). Built in the style of earlier wooden pagodas, six of the original seven stories still remain. Also the five-storied pagoda at Puyo (NT-9) is a rare example of Paekche architecture.

From the Three Kingdoms period of Silla only one pagoda (NT-30) remains today, and is seen at Punhwang Temple on the outskirts of Kyongju. It was designed and constructed with small pieces of cut stone shaped like bricks. The brick architectural concept came from T'ang China and was adapted

◁*Sokkamoni Buddha of Pomun Temple, eastern Seoul*

during Silla and later Koryo periods, since brick was not a common building material in Korea. This pagoda was designed to imitate the earlier wooden styles. Three stories of seven remain. The idea of using brick architecturally continued to fascinate the architects of Silla and to a lesser degree those of Koryo.

During the Unified Silla period architects with superb creativity combined characteristics of the earlier Silla pagodas. The typical pagoda is usually three or five storied and constructed on a double pedestal. Each story is successively smaller and narrower than the preceding one, with a decorative finial topping the last story. The roof stones are almost always curved and often have turned-up corners. Step-like supporting stones under the eaves of each roof maintain a striking Chinese influence by simulating bricks.

Other variations of pagoda construction occurred such as the Tabo-t'ap at Pulguk-sa, Korea's most unique and celebrated pagoda, and the lion base pagoda at Hwaom-sa. Another architectural structure, and a type of pagoda as the term in Korean of *t'ap* is also used, is the temple tomb monument or stupa called *pudo*. When a priest died his cremated remains with other Buddhist relics would be enshrined in a stone structure near the temple. Often next to the *pudo* monument would be a stone tablet memorializing the priest.

One of the earliest known stupas is the *pudo* for Priest Yom-go (NT-104) who died in 844. The lantern-style structure with tile-like roof has eight lions carved in relief on the base. During the Koryo period the *pudo* became more bell-shaped in style.

The basic architectural features of the temple pagoda which emerged after Silla unification continued through the Koryo and Yi periods. From the 9th century the height of the pagodas became less, while elaborate decorative designs began to appear on the surface, though the basic form was retained. Many diverse patterns and Buddhist figures were carved in relief as the pagoda degenerated into an ornamental object of the temple instead of a symbol of reverence.

Probably the only well-known example of secular architectural remains from the Silla period is the stone observatory in Kyongju called *ch'omsongdae* (NT-31). This bottle-shaped structure is the oldest extant observatory in the Far East. It was constructed during the reign of Queen Sondok (27th Silla ruler) in the early 7th century.

Pulguk-sa near Kyongju City, the most famous temple in Korea, can give some impression of the architectural skills of the artisans of Silla. Two unique stone bridge stairways, pagodas, retaining walls, cisterns, banner pillars and foundation stones are some of the architectural remains from 8th century Silla.

No wooden structure is extant earlier than late Koryo. Historical records describe a 70 meter high wooden pagoda at Hwangyong Temple, built in the 7th century. A replica of Korea's only wooden pagoda is seen at Seoul's National Museum. This pagoda, located at Popchu-sa, is only several hundred years old.

The historical development of Koryo architecture is divided into two major periods. The first was the era of continuation of Silla styles with more varied forms and patterns. During the second period (13-14th centuries) the effort to innovate new styles was intensified. Often architecture was rough and crude in details which might have been caused by the general political instability. Some wooden temple structures still survive from the Koryo period, notably at Pusok-sa, Pongjong-sa and Sudok-sa.

In the realm of architecture of the Yi Dynasty, Seoul is the center of a vast array of structures which often pleasingly contrast with the modern development of the capital. The Yi period is divided into two eras with the Hideyoshi War of 1592 marking the division. The architectural pattern of the first 200 years had a more sturdy appearance as structures were huge in scale.

Building Hwangyong-sa pagoda mural, Academy of Korean Studies ▷

The architecture of the second period became more awkward in appearance with greater stress on gaudy and sumptuous decoration. The contour of roof lines began to change, which may have developed through Chinese influence. One of the finest examples of early Yi design is Seoul's South Gate (NT-1) called *sungnye-mun* (Exalted Ceremony Gate). The last complete renovation took place in 1962.

The gracefully curved lines of the double eaves and protruding round beams give this imposing structure a spacious natural beauty as 22 wooden pillars support the superstructure. The complicated bracket system, unique to Korean architecture, supports the tremendous weight of the imposing wide flaring roofs revealing a calm simplicity.

The *chapsang* (clay figures) on the roof ridges, originating in China, were designed to ward off evil and prevent fires. Today five of the city's nine gates remain and have been reconstructed. Most of the magnificent Yi Dynasty buildings still extant in Seoul are located in the palaces and royal gardens. Naksonjae built in 1846 and *piwon* (Secret Garden) behind Ch'angdok Palace still preserve the unique style of Korean architectural harmony with nature.

Though under the influence of Chinese geomantic principles, architectural designs for public and private buildings differ from China due to Korea's desire for environmental harmony. In Korea there appeared more freedom and flexibility in town planning. Free choice of style was optional with the builder who was less hampered by official regulations.

Four factors shaped traditional Korean architecture: religion, available materials, Korea's natural landscape and the Koreans' aesthetic propensity for simplicity. With gently sloping roof lines and sturdy undecorated pillars, Korean architectural art is characterized by simplicity, harmony and practical utility.

Though construction design was free, there was a common and fundamental design in building a structure through astrology and geomancy called *ch'onmun*. Careful consideration was made of these aspects before and during construction.

METALCRAFT

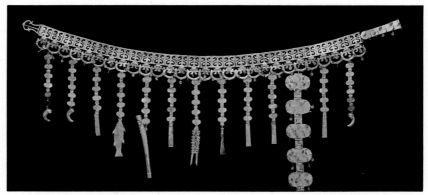

Gold girdle of Silla period

During the beginning of the first millennium BC a bronze culture began to appear on the peninsula. Bronze daggers, spades, axes, pots, mirrors and bells have been found. From about 300 BC to the Christian era bronze objects increased in quality as well as quantity all over Korea. The high standard of casting and graphic design achieved in bronze mirrors which have been discovered is striking. In technical standard and beauty they can be compared favorably with some of the best bronze pieces of China during this same period.

Some of the oldest metal objects discovered in Korea have been small bronze animal bells. The sound of the bells must have represented a mystic power for welcoming deities or dispelling evil spirits. Some of these early bells may have been ornaments worn or used by shamans. However, the technique of bronze bell casting reached its peak in 8th century Silla, never to be duplicated during the Koryo and Yi dynasties.

Unfortunately the technique used in casting temple bells during the Silla period has been lost and only three extant bells remain in Korea (several more exist in Japan). Their superior quality speaks for the tremendous advances made in Korean metalcraft during the Silla era. The largest and best example is the 11-foot "Emillie Bell" cast in honor of Songdok (33rd king) in 770. The oldest extant bell cast in 725 is now located near Woljong Temple in Kangwon Province.

The quality and artistic development of Korean bell making has world-wide recognition and must be ranked among the proudest achievements of Korea's priceless cultural legacy. Though there are many Koryo and Yi Dynasty bells, their quality is considered inferior to that of Silla.

Over the years ten gold crowns have been unearthed from Silla's royal tombs near Kyongju, which are fairly similar. The 1971 excavation of Muryong's tomb (Paekche king - died 523) near Kongju yielded an abundance of burial objects. The gold crown was more Buddhist in design than the shamanistic Silla crowns. In addition, thousands of metalcraft ornaments were recovered including belts, earrings, bracelets, rings and necklaces. Also found were gold, gilt and bronze utensils and metalcraft settings for jade, glass and crystal jewelery.

Unfortunately few specimens of metalcraft art have survived from the Koryo or Yi periods. Perhaps the most representative of Koryo's artistic taste is the *kundika* bronze bottle with silver inlay (NT-92) displayed in the National Museum.

WOODCRAFT

Prior to the 15th century Buddhism dominated this form of creative art. However, very little remains. One of the greatest undertakings during the Koryo Dynasty was the production of the entire *tripitaka* (Buddhist Scriptures) on a set of 81,258 wood blocks at Kanghwa Island. Today these blocks are considered to be the most complete and oldest set of Buddhist scriptures in the world.

Kojong (23rd Koryo king) fled to Kanghwa Island to escape the Mongol intrusion into Korea and decided to seek the help of Buddha to expel the enemy. Thus this gigantic project became a national undertaking and was completed in 1251. The wood used is said to have been imported from China and seasoned for 12 years. For three years the wood was submerged in salt water and then for another three years in fresh water. The wood was then buried underground for three more years before being dried in the open air for three additional years.

The engraving actually took sixteen years. Every block is 9.5" by 29" and 2.5" thick. On the average there are 22 lines to a block page and 14 characters in each line. All these Chinese characters had to be carved in reverse on the wood block.

During the early part of the Yi period the entire *tripitaka* was moved to Haein Temple. In 1488 two buildings were built to house the *tripitaka*. The open sides were architecturally designed so as to control temperature and level of humidity in an effort to better preserve the blocks. The buildings are designated as National Treasure No. 52 and the *tripitaka* blocks as National Treasure No. 32.

Artisans of the Yi Dynasty achieved remarkable results in wood and bamboo styles of furniture suitable for the Confucian Korean home. The craft is characterized by simple and sensitive designs portraying compact styles for practicality. Beautiful brass (both white and yellow) or wrought iron were used as fittings. Lacquerware with mother-of-

Sutra container, Yongmun-sa, North ▷
Kyongsang

pearl and ox-horn inlay was also used as well as high contrast wood such as persimmon for inlay techniques.

Korea has a multitude of patterns which are clearly different from the patterns of China or Japan. Art scholars have only recently begun to collect, study, analyze and classify them. Careful selection and meticulous handling of materials were the true mark of the Yi craftsmen. Other woods commonly used are elm, pine, pear, gingko, mountain ash, paulownia, cherry, oak and bamboo. Old furniture as a folk art is hard to find and rapidly becoming collector's items.

Woodblocks used for printing

Korean Art with Brush

Located between China and Japan, Korea was destined to have cultural ties with its neighbors. However, neighborly influences were quickly absorbed and Korea emerged early in history as a highly creative art force in Asia. Until recently the unique arts of Korea have been relatively unknown to the Western world. Artisans were on intimate terms with nature and familiar sights were often incorporated into Korean art forms. Shamanistic beliefs blended well with Buddhism and Confucianism, which intensified the Korean's strong link with nature. Indigenous aspects have kept Korea's artistic vision focused on its rich and ancient legacy.

A major contribution to Korean art is in the field of painting. Paintings on tomb walls from the Three Kingdoms period, prior to the 7th century, are some of Asia's oldest extant art. In 1973 the first of Silla's tomb art was discovered, a flying horse painted on a birchbark saddleguard. The world's oldest Buddhist painting (755) decorates the case which once held the oldest handwritten *sutra,* a portion of the Hwaom (Zen) Scriptures. This painting is in the private collection of Lee Byung-chul and can be seen at the Hoam Museum.

There are few paintings that have survived from the Koryo period and most of these paintings have Buddhist themes. Kongmin, one of the last kings of Koryo, is considered one of the dynasty's better painters, though only one painting, a hunting scene attributed to him, has survived.

When the Yi Dynasty began in 1392, Confucianism was adopted as the state religion. A cultural movement erupted which led to remarkable changes and advances in most fields of art, giving to Korea once again a distinctive culture compared to previous eras. This change can best be seen in the development of Yi Dynasty paintings.

While Yi paintings contained influences from China, most used indigenous techniques more than earlier Korean art.

Due to Confucianism a great demand arose for portraits of rulers, national figures, nobles and even deceased persons for purposes of veneration. Therefore, most paintings lacked vitality but were characterized by a simple and humble beauty.

Painters were often government sponsored. A few artists and members of the intelligentsia painted as a hobby, yet in most cases they worked in an aristocratic setting and catered to the tastes of the nobility. In general the fine arts of the Yi period were not so colorful compared to the earlier eras, for the fervor for creativity was restrained by Confucian formalism.

Generally speaking, the paintings of the Yi Dynasty can be classified into two periods separated by the devastating Japanese Hideyoshi Wars of the 1590s. The first period was dominated by the Northern School which was influenced by the Chinese arts of the Sung and Mongol cultures. Though few of his paintings are extant, Ahn Kyon is Korea's most outstanding painter of this period. One of Ahn's most prominent masterpieces called "Red Cliffs" is preserved in Seoul's National Museum.

Another ranking courtier talented in painting, poetry and calligraphy was the renowned Kang Hui-an (1419-1466). Though he considered painting only a hobby, his high-minded and peculiar

◁ *Portrait of Yi Chae (painter unknown), Seoul National Museum*

蕩晩眈龍不
得白鷗
飛ゝ
浪花ゝ前
蕙園

style of straightforward strokes is well portrayed in his "Contemplating the Water."

Madame Shin Saim-dang (1512-1559) was the greatest female painter of the entire Yi period. As her favorite themes were flowers, grass, fruits and insects found in rural scenes, she is often considered the progenitor of the genre paintings which emerged in the 18th century.

From the mid-16th century through the Japanese invasion many noted painters were to be found. The brothers Yi Chong-gun and Yi Chong-sik drew landscapes which were marvelously unique and untainted by mundane Confucian bureaucracy. Hwang Chip-jung and Oh Myong-yong were famous for their paintings of grapes and plums, while Yi Chong was the Yi Dynasty's most renowned bamboo painter.

The second period following the Hideyoshi Wars is characterized by the Southern School when the Ch'ing Dynasty was in firm control of China. The best landscape painter was Chong Son (1676-1769) who discarded Chinese styles and created unique new themes based on Korean scenes. He was particularly fond of the Diamond Mountains and scenic sites around Seoul. Another master of landscape art was Yi In-mun (1745-1821) who won the reputation of choosing nature as his teacher.

Ch'oe Puk was an eccentric painter fond of drinking, whose themes were rich in local color. Shim Sa-jong (1707-1770) who studied under Chong Son displayed superb technique in drawing flowers, grass and insects. His style resembles that of Ch'oe Puk. Also in this class of great painters was Yun Tu-so who was especially proficient in portraiture.

During the early 19th century genre paintings came into great vogue and probably the greatest of the genre painters were Kim Hong-do and Shin Yun-bok. Kim Hong-do's revolutionary contribution lies in his challenge to his narrowminded contemporaries. Shin Yun-bok (left) was a very enthusiastic feminist who brought women into his unique genre paintings and opened a new world in the history of Yi Dynasty art. The genre paintings furnished detailed aspects of customs and manners of society as well as portraying an indigenous element of Korean art.

Though early Yi artists were heavily influenced by Chinese masters, later painters emerged to develop a style independent of China with their unmatched talent and spirit. Because of their epochal achievements, artists such as Kim Hong-do and Shin Yun-bok have become a source of national pride.

FOLK ART PAINTINGS (MINHWA)

The whole range of *minhwa* (folk paintings) has yet to be assembled, analysed and researched, yet these are uniquely Korean and inseparably attached to the actual lives of the people. Unconventional and unorthodox, the folk art paintings of Korea date to ancient times. More approachable than the formal and orthodox paintings described previously, *minhwa* serve as charming avenues to approach Korean culture, since they are popular creations for practical use and produced for everyday life by a people with traditional tastes.

Serious or amusing, imaginary or real, this folk art depicts deep religious convictions or themes of life's realities. *Minhwa* are Korea's functional paintings as opposed to the pure or academic painting, though there is overlapping. Folk paintings are usually divided into four groups according to the purpose of the painting: memorial, religious, record keeping and household.

Some of them were executed by expert hands such as those of professional court painters and others by utter amateurs. Bearing no signatures, these anonymous creations were made to serve in the lives of the Korean people without conscious labels.

Colorful and vivid, the compositions are free and unbound by Confucian restraint, and utilize techniques that are often impressionistic. Usually the

◁ *Paintings by Shin Yun-bok, 19th century*

Folk art (minhwa) *from Zo Zayong's collection*

underlying spirit that permeates the folk art is religious and man's relationship to his environment as found in Buddhism, Taoism, shamanism and even Confucianism.

Korean folk paintings previously have been bypassed in art histories for several reasons. First, they have never been collected or studied systematically. Second, the Confucian scholars scorned the colorful folk motifs that did not reflect Confucian ethics. Third, the custom was followed to burn or bury old paintings when replaced by fresh new ones. Unfortunately Korea's native artistic expressions were ignored while literati works with heavy Chinese influence were considered the mainstream of Korea's art history.

CALLIGRAPHY

An art form in Korea, as it is in China and Japan, calligraphy or brush writing is regarded as more noble than pictorial painting. Historically, calligraphy has exerted strong influence on the cultural and social life of the Koreans and even today is a respected art form.

As Confucian scholarship flourished during the Yi period, calligraphy became a ·driving force in the academic world. Whoever wrote good poetry in excellent calligraphic style had the best chances for promotion. Confucian learning became the key to the development of Yi Dynasty arts, just as Buddhism nurtured the arts of the Koryo period.

The history of Korean calligraphy is as old as the introduction of Chinese characters to the peninsula. The oldest known inscription is from the early 5th century, the tombstone of King Kwang-gae-t'o of Koguryo. Calligraphic styles also are extant from the Paekche period.

Five 6th century inscribed monuments erected by Chin-hung (24th Silla king) are now important cultural assets (two are located in northern Korea). Inscriptions exist from the renowned Silla scholar, Ch'oe Ch'i-won.

Many notable calligraphers are known from the Koryo period, with Chang So-

yol's style being the most famous. Han Ho (1543-1605) is considered the greatest calligrapher of the Yi Dynasty, whose brushwork is often compared with China's eminent scholars Wang Hsi-chih and Yen Chen-ching. Kim Ku (1488-1534) another great calligrapher from the early Yi period created his own style called *insu,* which was admired for its forceful strokes.

Yang Sa-on (1517-1548) developed a unique mastery of form comparable to the great masters of T'ang China. In the writing of large characters he was second to none. Kim Chong-hui (1786-1856) was the most eminent scholar among the late Yi Dynasty literati painters. His penname was Ch'u-sa, and later this name was used for his distinctive style of calligraphy called *ch'usa-che.* His calligraphy brought about a renaissance in this unique Oriental art form.

After World War II Korean calligraphy suffered a period of decline but experienced a comeback after 1960. It is now regaining its importance as Korea's most revered art form. Requiring so few materials (brush, paper and ink), calligraphy continues to have a unique appeal for Koreans in its demand for spiritual attainment. Powerful characters, reflecting harmony and refined simplicity, transcend mere skill and technique.

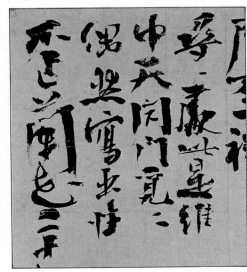

The ch'usa *calligraphy style* ▷

Han'gul, Phonetic Alphabet

"Han'gul" is a phonetic system of writing devised and used exclusively for the written Korean language. It is a combination of twenty-four extremely simple symbols, which in combination can represent almost any conceivable sound. Even the sigh of the wind, chirp of birds, and barking of dogs can be exactly described by the "han'gul" phonetic system.

As it is a purely Korean invention the Korean people can rightly be proud of the *han'gul* which is one of the most remarkable alphabets in the world. Among the many thousand types of writing developed by man, this alphabet is outstanding in that while others were the result of a gradual process of evolution, this was developed at one period during the reign of King Sejong on a specific date. Today it remains in practically the same form as its beginning, with eleven vowels and seventeen consonants.

Until comparatively recent times in all countries writing was an accomplishment of the elite, intellectual class of people. In the East owing to the complexity of Chinese characters the art of reading and writing remained exclusively for the privileged scholars.

King Sejong, fourth ruler of the Yi Dynasty, completed his work and introduced the system known as *han'gul* to the court on December 25, 1443, while emphasizing as his objectives the desire to meet the needs of the common people by providing them with a means of expressing their thoughts in writing and the hope of propagating a truly national culture. Acclaimed as a political as well as a literary achievement, the *han'gul* could be used by all classes of people.

There is a great difference between the Korean and the Chinese languages, so historically few adequate letters could be used by the Korean people in writing their language and expressing their thoughts. From early Silla (682) a system called *idu* was developed by the famous Confucian scholar, Sol Ch'ong. Though used in government business over the centuries *idu* was too complicated and inconvenient for the Koreans to use freely in expressing their own ideas and thoughts because Chinese characters still were involved in it.

King Sejong was 47 years old when the *han'gul* was completed. Annals

vowels / consonants	ㅏ	ㅑ	ㅓ	ㅕ	ㅗ	ㅛ	ㅜ	ㅠ	ㅡ	ㅣ
ㄱ	가	갸	거	겨	고	교	구	규	그	기
ㄴ	나	냐	너	녀	노	뇨	누	뉴	느	니
ㄷ	다	댜	더	뎌	도	됴	두	듀	드	디
ㄹ	라	랴	러	려	로	료	루	류	르	리
ㅁ	마	먀	머	며	모	묘	무	뮤	므	미
ㅂ	바	뱌	버	벼	보	뵤	부	뷰	브	비
ㅅ	사	샤	서	셔	소	쇼	수	슈	스	시
ㅇ	아	야	어	여	오	요	우	유	으	이
ㅈ	자	쟈	저	져	조	죠	주	쥬	즈	지
ㅊ	차	챠	처	쳐	초	쵸	추	츄	츠	치
ㅋ	카	캬	커	켜	코	쿄	쿠	큐	크	키
ㅌ	타	탸	터	텨	토	툐	투	튜	트	티
ㅍ	파	퍄	퍼	펴	포	표	푸	퓨	프	피
ㅎ	하	햐	허	혀	호	효	후	휴	흐	히

record that the king had to go to the hot springs for medical treatment of his eyes so he handed over the work of the government to officials. However, he did not give up his study of the *han'gul* development.

Many scholars of that day were diametrically opposed to the *han'gul,* claiming that it only "dragged the Chinese classics in the dust." Many reasons were given for this defiance. In the first place, it violated the principle of maintaining friendly relations with China to invent and use letters which did not exist in China. It was looked upon as a novelty for literary amusement which would only cause hindrance to study and government administration. Though not by authoritarian demands which he could have made, King Sejong was determined to popularize the *han'gul* among the people and encourage its use in their daily lives. Poems, Buddhist verses and even scriptures were translated into *han'gul* and published. Later important Chinese classics were also translated into Korean *han'gul.*

Intricate and simple, but scholarly and effective, *han'gul* has remained virtually unchanged for five hundred years. Because of the Confucian opposition the use of *han'gul* was relegated to lesser importance. As a result of the efforts of the first Christian missionaries to Korea, *han'gul* was brought out of disuse to become the common written language.

A special stage was reached in the history of writing by the invention of the *han'gul* on which the Korean people may pride themselves as their best intellectual product. King Sejong was a ruler who had done many great things but the *han'gul* invention was the greatest of all, not only as a noteworthy contribution in the Orient but as an impressive alphabetic system for the world.

At the time of its promulgation, *han'gul* consisted of 17 consonants and 11 vowel symbols. In 1933 it was standardized with 14 consonants and 10 simple vowels. (also 11 compound vowels)

Statue of King Sejong, Toksu Palace

Zodiac Cycle of Life

From Seoul to Peking, Asians have always followed the influential dictates of the Eastern twelve zodiac animals from the day of one's birth to the day of death. A man's vocation or a woman's marriage as well as many other important decisions of life are influenced by the geomancer's interpretation of the zodiac by the month, day, hour and even minute.

Sheep zodiac at Silla King Kyongdok's Tomb

In the Orient the zodiac represents a twelve-year cycle with each year dominated by an animal, one of them imaginary: rat, cow, tiger, rabbit, dragon, snake, horse, sheep, monkey, chicken, dog and pig. Each animal reigns for one (lunar) year in this fixed order with the rat first and pig last. Five twelve-year cycles complete what is called the *yukgap* and is considered the complete span of life on earth. When one reaches age sixty he celebrates the *hwan'gap,* the most important event of his entire life.

The attainment of this birthday is a very happy event, calling for special celebrations. Usually a big family reunion is held and the honored guest is beautifully attired while presents are given .

The legend is told that when Buddha died there was considerable sorrow in the world. People and animals sped to his deathbed but of the animal species only these twelve were represented. The clever rat obtained the honor of being first through trickery. Being small he rode all the way on the head of the powerful cow. Upon reaching the bedside he leaped to the ground before Buddha first. The twelve animals who came were honored by being selected to symbolize the character portrayal of each year. Today, according to Korean belief, a person born in any given year will inevitably have the characteristic traits of the representative animal.

THE YEAR OF THE RAT: 1888, 1900, 1912, 1924, 1936, 1948, 1960, 1972, 1984. Energetic and ambitious, honest and charming but quick to anger, penny pinching toward others, love of gossip, persevering, a poor leader and big spender, timid and humble, promise of wealth.

THE YEAR OF THE COW: 1889, 1901, 1913, 1925, 1937, 1949, 1961, 1973, 1985. Patient and easy going with a gift for inspiring confidence, often narrow minded and stubborn, a terror when angered but strong and dexterous, the quiet powerful type.

THE YEAR OF THE TIGER: 1890, 1902, 1914, 1926, 1938, 1950, 1962, 1974, 1986. Women are headstrong and obstinate. Men are favored, straight and true with many friends, wary of strangers, fighting spirit and deep sensitive thinkers, stubbornly courageous, troublesome tempers, not decision makers.

THE YEAR OF THE RABBIT: 1891, 1903, 1915, 1927, 1939, 1951, 1963, 1975, 1987. A born gambler, easy to befriend but melancholic much of the time, quick to show affection and receive it from others, placid and virtuous, considerable talent but not showy, not a go-getter, lacks curiosity.

THE YEAR OF THE DRAGON: 1892, 1904, 1916, 1928, 1940, 1952, 1964, 1976, 1988. A leader of men, honest, sensitive within but worrisome, fastidious and verbose, can be excitable, outwardly stubborn, short tempered, but with faults is still beloved by others.

THE YEAR OF THE SNAKE: 1893, 1905, 1917, 1929, 1941, 1953, 1965, 1977, 1989. Extremely attractive and demonstrates great wisdom, also vain and often self-centered, passionate, determined but sometimes antagonistic, will make money, deep and quiet personality, often too much heart.

THE YEAR OF THE HORSE: 1894, 1906, 1918, 1930, 1942, 1954, 1966, 1978, 1990. Hotblooded in action and quick in everything he does, able to use money well, also can flatter and get what he wants, welldressed and showy, always seems to be a winner, cheerful, popular, and stubborn.

THE YEAR OF THE SHEEP: 1895, 1907, 1919, 1931, 1943, 1955, 1967, 1979, 1991. Talents will always bring in money, easily stimulated to pity, very charitable, elegant in action and appearance, passionate in everything, best at the arts but a poor salesman.

THE YEAR OF THE MONKEY: 1896, 1908, 1920, 1932, 1944, 1956, 1968, 1980, 1992. A good and clever politician, possesses a thirst for knowledge, talented, passionate, self-willed, a big thinker and big doer, clever inventiveness, flexible but little stick-to-itiveness.

THE YEAR OF THE CHICKEN: 1897, 1909, 1921, 1933, 1945, 1957, 1969, 1981, 1993. Never will bore people but somewhat a loner, likes to think deeply into problems but shortsighted and tactless, big dreams but little action, ambitious and brave, idealistic and sometimes disliked.

THE YEAR OF THE DOG: 1898, 1910, 1922, 1934, 1946, 1958, 1970, 1982, 1994. Pillar of the community characterized by devotion and honesty but also as stubborn as they come, oblivious to the value of money but is never in want, poor at small talk and often a fault finder.

THE YEAR OF THE PIG: 1899, 1911, 1923, 1935, 1947, 1959, 1971, 1983, 1995. Remarkable integrity, shy but short-tempered, single-minded and affectionate, always kind to loved ones, dedicated and courageous, honest but sometimes impulsive, often a victim of the unscrupulous.

Noteworthy Inventions by Koreans

The Koreans can boast of a long and impressive list of many inventions, most of which date back many centuries, including a unique alphabet, the art of printing and publishing, the first ironclad warship and other scientific firsts.

The art of printing and publishing books is among the oldest of Korean achievements. Stored at the temple of Haein near Taegu is the world's oldest and most comprehensive collection of Buddhist scriptures known to exist called the *Tripitaka,* consisting of 81,258 large wooden printing blocks. Each block contains two pages of the text. This work was begun on Kanghwa Island at Chondung Temple near Seoul in 1237, taking sixteen years to complete.

Printing of books illustrates a fascinating aspect of the true inherent genius of the Korean people. Though the first movable type made from clay was originally developed during the Sung Dynasty in China in the 11th century, this new idea was not put into mass production, as the Chinese preferred woodcut printing to type printing. However, in Korea the demand for large quantities of printed books was limited; thus type printing became more popular than the carved block style.

At any rate it can safely be said that movable type made of some kind of metal was an original Korean invention which first occurred probably in the latter part of the 12th century or early 13th century, placing this invention about two hundred years earlier than the Gutenberg type in Germany. The date of this invention of movable metal type is given as 1232, the year that the royal court of Koryo was forced to flee to Kanghwa Island because of the Mongol invasion. It is recorded that the scholar and minister Yi Kyu-bo before his death in 1241 had twenty-eight copies of a book printed on Kanghwa Island using cast type.

It appears that the government publication office did not utilize cast metal types until 1403 when T'aejong (2nd Yi Dynasty king) ordered the work to be done. The king was quoted as saying, "In order to have a good government, we must read widely. Since Korea is far to the east of China, books are seldom obtained. To reprint books, block printing is too laborious, and even after being engraved the blocks are easily broken. It is hard to print all the books we need. I therefore intend to cast movable types with bronze so that whenever we come to get new books we can reprint them. If we succeed, it would do a great service to the nation."

In the 15th century, about three hundred years before the French began work on the first European encyclopedia, a 112-volume encyclopedia, the first produced anywhere, was published by Korean scholars. A copy of this historic work is in the Library of Congress, Washington, D.C.

Koreans invented a spinning wheel and various astronomical instruments in the 14th century. During the 15th century came instruments for surveying and a water clock that indicated the times of day, seasons, and hours for the rising and setting of the sun and moon. The remains of this clock may be seen on the grounds of the Toksu Palace in Seoul. There were ice houses in Korea as far back as the first century. Koreans spanned the Imjin River with a suspension bridge one hundred years before

Rain gauge (left) and sun clock (right) ▷

this type of bridge was built in the West. Today, one of the Orient's longest suspension bridges is located at Namhae Island.

Korea's most important historic structural remains is a bottle-shaped astronomical observatory located in the ancient Silla capital of Kyongju. Built in 634 during the reign of Queen Sondok, this unique twenty-nine-foot structure is considered the oldest existing observatory in the Far East. For well over two thousand years in Korea the movements of stars and known planets were carefully studied and charted. Sun and moon eclipses were predicted as well as the course of comets which came within view of the Silla astronomers.

The keeping of records of rainfall is of fairly recent origin even in the most advanced Western nations. But in Korea these records have been kept for nearly four hundred years. In 1442 King Sejong had a bronze instrument made for measuring precipitation. In 1770 another king had these instruments installed on the palace grounds and at key points in all Korean provinces. Officials have maintained records of rainfall from that time on. Korea has the oldest and most continuous record of rainfall in the world which is a valuable source of meteorological information.

Though Koreans are not known as a seafaring people, nevertheless, when Japan attempted several invasions of Korea in 1592 the Korean Admiral Yi Sun-shin built the world's first ironclad warship and with these vessels shaped like turtles he was able to soundly defeat the Japanese armada.

Admiral Yi is the most famous of Korean heroes and one of the world's outstanding naval strategists. His life is more fully discussed in another chapter. An elaborate shrine called Hyonch'ung-sa near Onyang which honors Admiral Yi has become tourist attractions.

The Feminine Tradition

One of the continuing mysteries of Korea is its women . . . . beautiful in the classic sense, charming, delightful and possessing the ability to put a guest at ease in any social circumstances. Shrewd in the business world, Korean women are now aware of their potential and also cognizant of their threatening impact on a historically male-dominated society. With grace and poise the Korean women weave through the maze of modernization with their heads held high, for they know they have contributed to Korea's precious freedom.

As one stands in the heart of Myong-dong or recently developed Yong-dong watching the young girls, laughing and chattering as they stroll along the heart of Korea's shopping centers, a mecca of shops which stay open late into the evenings, it is hard to imagine the life of women less than one century ago. Now carefree, vivacious and independent in contrast to the Confucianist's rigid ideals of the closing years of the Yi Dynasty, the Korean women stand as living proof of this country's rapid modernization.

Customs dictated that a girl's duty was to marry and provide as many sons as possible. Having no children was a cause for divorce and one of the seven sins of women according to the Confucian teachings. Marriages were always arranged by a go-between and even today this custom is surprisingly prevalent in the Westernized communities of Korea. Now the son or daughter usually has a voice in determining the partner selected by the parents.

Often a young son was married at the early age of 9 to 12 while the bride might be ten years his senior. Many comedy dramas depict the humorous relationship of the first night. Always good for laughs is the scene of the bride carrying her young husband piggy-back to the new home.

An intriguing story is often told which well illustrates the rigid Confucian patterns of the filial devotion of a wife to the other members of the family. One day a youthful nineteen-year-old wife was returning home with her ten-year-old husband and elderly father-in-law when a sudden torrential rain caused a flash flood in the riverbed they were crossing. As the water was rising too fast for the old man and her young husband to flee to safety, the wife realized that she could save only herself and possibly carry one but could not come back to save both. She had to decide quickly whom she should rescue and still fulfill her obligations to family and society.

Was she to save her young husband, as the father was old and had already lived a good life? He had passed his sixtieth birthday [*hwangap*]. Or should she carry the old father-in-law and let her husband drown knowing she could never remarry? This is the dilemma that baffles most Westerners unfamiliar with the Confucian codes of behavior.

Carrying the old father-in-law on her back the young wife dashed to safety while her young husband was lost in the deluge. After making certain that the old man was safe the grieving wife then leaped to her death in the same waters that took her husband's life. Thus all her obligations were met.

In the upper-class society during the Yi Dynasty young women were restricted from activities outside of the home. The Korean custom of see-sawing while standing on a wide board was an

◁ Korean ladies on their way out, Toksu Palace, Seoul

attempt on the part of young girls to catch glimpses of life beyond the compound wall. If male visitors should come to the house politeness required that they should ignore the presence of women in the household. One would never inquire about the health of his host's wife. Certain male relatives might go to the wife's room but only by invitation and accompanied by her husband.

As the great bell on Chongno was heard throughout the city at sundown Seoul's gates would close, but this was also a signal that men must retire from the streets to permit the women to leave the home and visit friends, provided they had permission from their husbands. The only males allowed on the streets during the night hours were the blind or those filling prescriptions at the nearest drug store. Many upper class women knew Seoul only by night when they wended their way through the dim streets lighted by a small lantern carried by a woman servant.

In the nineteenth century there were few occupations open to women of the upper class. Their world was basically confined within the compound wall. Middle-class women did not observe such strict seclusion and often appeared on the streets during the day . . . . though their faces were always partially concealed by the *chan'got* which was an outer garment thrown over the head. The sleeves hung empty down each side while the front was held closely together by a snap to hide as much of the face as possible.

Middle-class women were often shop proprietors, innkeepers, cooks, hand-maidens and even concubines of the upper class. Though considered very respectable the middle-class woman had more to say about family matters and decisions pertaining to family activities. She also had firmer control of the estate if the husband died.

Possibly the one most consuming chores was to keep the men's clothes glistening white and clean. Traditionally clothing had to be taken apart at the seams, soaked in lye water and rolled up for pounding. After washing and drying, the clothes were ironed by a process of beating them with round wooden sticks until they were pressed. The clothing would then be resewn. Though seldom heard now one of "Old Korea's" most characteristic village sounds was the rhythmic clacking of the ironing sticks late into the night. The beating would impart a smooth glossy sheen unobtainable by any other method. Later charcoal irons were used in pressing.

Women in the lower class could certainly move about freely and had little concern about covering their faces. They had no rights and no one was obligated to respect them. This class was by far the greater in number as it included the vast rural population of Korea's farming communities. This class also served as slaves in the cities. Shamans (*mudang*) and fortunetellers were of this class of women. The *kisaeng* were also in this low class but usually lived a life of ease and had more freedom of movement depending on their sponsor. A *kisaeng* might move to middle-class society if a wealthy aristocrat took her into his home as a concubine. Though it is speculation that women during the earlier Silla period had greater freedoms and privileges in society, nevertheless, during the last 500 years of the Yi Dynasty, women had almost no rights. The Yi Dynasty woman did not look for domestic happiness or the sharing of interests with her husband. As a wife she accepted the fact that her husband would live a life apart from hers and that his pleasures came from his male friends and the *kisaeng*. She was expected not to resent her seclusion, which had been customary for over five hundred years for the purpose of protecting women. A Korean woman was not envious of the freedoms that she saw exemplified by the Western women in the early 20th century. She wondered if receiving these liberties she might place her own obligation in peril; obedience to father before marriage, to husband after marriage and to son after husband's death.

Formal education for women began with the founding of Ewha Girls' School by the Methodist missionary Mary Scranton in 1885 and was the first step in changing the role of women. The first student was a concubine of a government official who wanted her to learn English so that she could become an interpreter to the queen, thus raising his own status in the court. Encouragement by the various patriotic organizations formed to liberate Korea from Japan gave impetus to the rising status of women.

After liberation in 1945 the women found themselves in a chaotic period with little direction or goals. In 1948 when the Republic of Korea was officially formed women were finally liberated from the old bonds of a traditional Confucian past. Though quite different from other nations, the liberation of women in Korea came without demands on their part or bloodshed. This may have been a liability because, for the vast majority of women, their freedom had little meaning. Education became compulsory for elementary age girls, whereas prior to 1945 less than 50% of the female population entered primary schools.

Before the Korean War women generally depended on men for their economic support but the sudden stark reality of the conflict left countless widows or wives separated from their husbands. Korean women were forced into the position of becoming economically supportive of the family and slowly became more financially independent. Today it will surprise one to know how many companies are actually controlled by a woman behind the scenes.

President Syngman Rhee who had been educated in the United States had a high regard for and awareness of women's potential. Women served in government positions as cabinet members. Dr. Kim Hwal-ran (Helen Kim) was sent as an official delegate to the United Nations. Helen Kim served as Ewha Womans University President for 22 years. She retired in 1961. Louise Yim (Yim Young-shin) served as Korea's first Minister of Commerce. She also established Chung-Ang University and served as President until her retirement. Mary Lee served as representative in Congress. Esther Park began the work of the YWCA. Dr. Kim Ok-gil served as President of Ewha Womans University and was appointed as Minister of Education in 1979. In 1982 Kim Chung-rye was apointed as Minister of Health and Welfare. Park Sun-chon served as leader of the opposition party and was a long standing woman representative in the National Assembly. Korea's first woman lawyer, Dr. Lee Tai-young, received the Magsaysay Award in 1976. Lee Sook-Chong is a member of the National Assembly and president of the National Council of Women of Korea. Park Kyong-ri is Korea's outstanding novelist who completed an eight-volume work entitled *The Land*. The list of achievements of Korean women continues impressively.

But often the question is raised as to what foreigners think of Korean women in this modern era . . . . . a delicate subject that could cause considerable embarrassment. Often because of the language barrier most foreigners come in contact with only a limited group of Korean women . . . . the more semi-Westernized or possibly more educated urban women living in the cosmopolitan areas. The vast sphere of the timeless rural country women is almost impenetrable to the average foreigner and probably to most Korean city dwellers.

Of course any foreigner who becomes a resident for any length of time will have a maid. Though without a doubt not a Seoul National or Ewha graduate, nevertheless these women will invariably be industrious, cheerful and patient with the foreigner's strange Western customs.

Now the new generation of young women graduating from colleges and universities across the country are finding themselves in a crossfire of cultural ideals and expectations. Often they are bewildered as to what is really expected of them in a country of two worlds . . . . the traditions of the Orient and fashionable measurement of Westernization

which must include a college degree with a reasonably good command of English.

Educated girls are not out desperately looking for husbands but often are finding their jobs and social contacts much more satisfying. The fear of being an "old miss" is still prevalent, yet they would rather wait as long as possible. Marriage often means giving up the job and being restricted to the home while the husband continues to enjoy his associations and an active "around the town" life.

The desire to go abroad is still great, though often women are ill prepared and gain little through educational endeavors in Western countries. Often when they return they are more alienated from their own culture, while many do not wish to come back at all. A distorted concept of Western mores has resulted in lower morality among both young men and women. Often lives are ruined as a result.

A recent phenomenon in the changing status of women which may have tragic effects on the family structure is that better educated middle aged women who now have more leisure time are experimenting in extramarital affairs in much the same fashion that their husbands have been permitted by tradition to do. This may well be a dangerous search for equality.

The strong women leaders of the freedom marches of the past are new retiring from active influence. The pioneer educators, doctors, lawyers and others of the first generation of professionally educated Korean women are turning the leadership over to another generation of more mellowed educated women. Patience is inherent in both the Buddhist and Confucian tradition and termed a characteristic of Korea's heritage.

In the meantime the average foreigner is far from being impervious to the charms and beauty of attractive Korean women, sometimes beguiling but gracious and ambitious in their desires, yet nevertheless, acutely aware of the needs of their mates who are led to think that each is a king.

Unexplored Beauty for Art Lovers

Still one of the best kept secrets of Korea is its arts and antiques both in quality and availability. Though prices have gone up over the last few years, good antiques can still be purchased at reasonable prices. If you are delighted by the traditional folk arts or even modern works, an hour's stroll through some of Seoul's districts of shops and galleries will provide many pleasant surprises. Remember there are many replicas and excellent works of reproduction.

Tourists who have recently arrived in the country will soon discover that Seoul is an art and antique haven. If you are interested in the traditional folk arts of Korea or only wish to join the world of the struggling artists then a leisurely stroll through the back alleys of Insa-dong and Anguk-dong (known to foreigners as Mary's Alley) will give you a keen sense of art appreciation.

A great number of antique stores have recently opened below the Itaewon residential area south of Nam-san. The abundance of various articles will amaze the average tourist. Ceramics of all types, some newly made imitations as well as true celadon, *punch'ong* and Silla ware can also be found. Normally the store proprietors will inform you of the authenticity of the item. As many antiques are prohibited from being taken from the country it is wise to inquire.

Most foreigners are inclined to consider only the cheaper items in a store without being informed as to the reason. To buy cheaply is not the best way to approach the problem of collecting antiques. Knowledge of the subject is vital for amateur collectors, and books in English are available for those interested in doing their homework.

Prices have a wide variation and it is often difficult to determine if a price is reasonable or not. Koreans themselves have recently become very interested in their own cultural heritage. The more recent wealthy industrial class tend to buy indiscriminately with little regard to cost, as they are proud that they are able to pay such a high cost.

The Japanese tourist industry has also caused antique prices to soar especially for pottery. If the Japanese understands the value, he is willing to pay any price, knowing it will double in value in Japan if he wishes to resell it. This is also true for new pottery which has a known name value of a potter.

Western understanding of Korean pottery is limited, so the average Westerner is baffled as to why a particular pottery piece might cost so much. Resale value, except possibly for celadon, in the Western world is limited. The cheapest pottery is still the Silla stoneware which is about 1500 years old. Silla stoneware and Koryo celadon are still being discovered at tomb sites through illegal excavations. The technique is primitive and often pieces are broken during the excavation.

Good *punch'ong* (Mishima) pottery from the early Yi period which is true Korean folk art pottery is now very expensive, as well as the more recent Yi porcelain with cobalt blue, iron or copper underglaze. This again is due primarily to Japanese tourist demands for this type of pottery to be used in their tea ceremony tradition which originally came from Korea.

It is standard procedure for store owners and buyers to haggle over the price of articles. Making contact with

certain store owners whom you like to frequently discuss various aspects of antiques will not only develop rapport but give a feeling for item value and worth. Often in reconditioning old chests new wood is used to replace the panels. New chests are frequently made with the old wood and metal fittings of several badly broken chests. Many chests may look old to the inexperienced eye but are actually newly made with traditional form and design. Medicine chests with many small drawers have become most popular in the foreign community.

In ceramics there is often considerable imitating of the traditional design of the Koryo celadon and many good pieces have high prices. Several kiln sites near Ichon twenty miles south of Seoul are producing high quality pottery.

Considering the folk arts one might try first to see the exhibits at the Shinsegae and Midopa department stores to obtain an idea of the price range and purpose of the item. Then wander among the shops with this knowledge, as often in a small sidestreet any tourist is fair game in the world of antiques.

Paintings run the same spectrum of old to new and often prices of new works are higher, but in any case if you wish to have framing done in Korea the quality is good and relatively inexpensive.

Again the Itaewon area is recommended for framing of your paintings. Large panels with glass and double framing will cost from 20-30 US dollars. Small painting can be framed for under $10.00. Prices are always negotiable.

A book store called the *Wise Old Owl* is located in the heart of Itaewon east of the New Yongsan Hotel. Here the widest variety of books on Korea in English can be obtained. Also the *Wise Old Owl* is the only store in Seoul which sells replicas of Silla pottery produced by Yu Hyo-Ung who has his kiln in Kyongju. He is the only potter licensed by the government to reproduce Silla type ware. (Tel: 794-4994).

There are numerous art galleries in addition to the government exhibition halls in the Toksu Palace, and Kyongbok Palace. Near the east gate of Kyongbok

Palace are several galleries of high standard and pleasing decor . . . Also in the "Mary's Alley" area and along the street opposite the entrance to Chogye Temple are many other galleries. North from the entrance of Chogye Temple is the well known Fine Arts Hall. There are galleries in several of the hotels as well as the Shinsegae, Midopa and Lotte department stores.

During one year in Seoul alone over 150 art exhibitions are held. Information on dates is usually given in both the Korea Herald and Korea Times. Certainly for those interested in the creative arts there is no lack of available material. Now many Korean artists have travelled abroad and many of their exhibitions are evident in Seoul's galleries. The capital city continues to be the center for art lovers from around the world who come to visit Korea.

Korean chest displayed at the Grand Hotel, Cheju Island

◁ Gift Shop at Korea House, Seoul

1988 Olympics and Sports

The Korean sports movement glimpsed a bright new future on September 30, 1981, when Seoul successfully won its bid to host the 1988 Summer Olympic Games, thus becoming the second Asian nation to have the Olympics, following Japan. Koreans are keenly competitive in all areas of sport activities which have developed rapidly with economic prosperity. The policy of keeping athletics unrelated to political objectives has enabled sports to develop in a wholesome manner.

In the field of team sports the most popular in Korea are soccer, baseball, table tennis, volleyball and basketball. Century-old skills are often demonstrated in *taekwondo*, archery, *paduk*, or the popular card game of *hwat'u*. The game of *yut* is still popular among Koreans. The Western games of golf and more recently tennis have swept the country with particular enthusiasm.

In 1936 Son Ki-jong was the first Korean to be a gold medalist in the marathon event at the World Olympics, though Korea at that time was under Japanese occupation. In the 1976 Olympic Games at Montreal, Korea gained its first gold medalist, Yang Chong-mo, who won in the free-style featherweight wrestling. A total of six medals were won in *yudo*, volleyball and wrestling. Korea ranked 19th out of 100 participating nations.

Introduced by the British in 1882, soccer is still the most popular game in Korea. Korea has remained the kingpin in Asian soccer. In 1979 Korea won the gold medal in the 10th World Collegiate Football Games held in Mexico City. A few Korean stars have joined foreign pro-teams in Europe such as Cha Bum-gun and Ho Chong-mu.

Introduced by the YMCA in 1906, baseball has become Korea's most popular high school sport in terms of number of spectators. College baseball is a close second in popularity. At present there are eleven semiprofessional

teams and a professional baseball league has been established. In 1980 the Korean team was co-winner with Japan in the 26th World Baseball Championship Series held in Tokyo. In 1981 Korea won the World Baseball Games held in Santa Clara.

Volleyball was first introduced into Korea in 1917. In the Fifth Asian Games of 1966 both men's and women's teams won second place. A Korean female team captured a bronze medal in the Montreal Olympics in 1976 and in 1977 won the First World Junior Volleyball Championships in Brazil. In 1980 Korea hosted the First Asian Junior Volleyball Championships and won the gold medal for both boys' and girls' teams.

Basketball was introduced to Korea before the turn of the century by an American named Killet. In 1967 Korea placed second in the World Women's Basketball Championship held in Czecho-slovakia and fourth in Brazil in 1971. Also in 1979 Korea hosted the championship in Seoul and won the silver medal with the US winning the gold. In 1982 the men's team won a gold medal and the women's team a silver in the Asian Games.

Though tennis was introduced to Korea over forty-five years ago it was not until 1971 that the first tennis court was opened to the public. Since then this sport has mushroomed. Korean women players have won gold medals

◁ Sports day held in Seoul City Stadium

in the 1974 and 1978 Asian Games. In the 1982 Asian Games held in India Korea won four gold medals in tennis: men's doubles, women's doubles and mixed doubles.

As in all Asian countries there is great enthusiasm for table tennis since it was first introduced to Korea in the 1920s. In 1973 Ailesa Lee won the women's singles and second in team events at the World Table Tennis Championships in Yugoslavia. Since then China has remained the strongest though Korean teams always advance to the finals. In 1981 Korean paddlers harvested one silver and two bronze medals, having been beaten narrowly by China.

Until 1969 the level of enthusiasm for swimming in Korea was very low. Since Korean swimmers gained three gold medals in the 1970 Asian Games there has been rapid development. The season for outdoor swimming is limited and there are not many indoor pools. Probably the biggest surprise in the 1982 Asian Games in New Delhi was when a 14- year-old Korean girl won three gold medals, beating out a Japanese favorite.

Archery in Korea dates back to pre-history. In 1978 archery came into prominence when a high school girl, Kim Jin-ho, won the gold medal in the Asian Games and then in 1979 went on to the 30th World Archery Champion-ships in Berlin to win five out of six gold medals. Two gold medals were won in the 1982 Asian Games.

Boxing is one of Korea's most popular sports. Kim Ki-su won Korea's first world boxing title by gaining the Junior middle-weight crown in 1966. Since then ten Korean professional boxers have gained world titles. Among all Korean athletes, Korean boxers have obtained more medals in Olympic Games. In the Asian Games more than half of the boxing championships have been won by Koreans. Hong Su-hwan is the only Korean to win world titles in two classes; bantamweight in 1974 and junior featherweight in 1977. As of January 1983 Korea holds no world titles.

It is well known that the sport of yudo (Japanese judo) is extremely popular in Korea. It is an indigenous sport which was introduced by Korea to Japan. In Seoul a Yudo College has been established and Koreans in the 1976 Montreal Olympics garnered one silver and two bronze medals.

Wrestling became popular following the Montreal Olympics when Korea won gold and bronze medals. Also in the 1964 Tokyo Olympics Chang Ch'ang-son won a silver medal and later a gold metal in the World Championship Games of 1966.

Owing to Korea's large standing army, shooting has become a popular sport. Korea was the first Asian nation in 42 years to host the World Shooting Championships in 1978. This Seoul tournament at the Taenung International Shooting Range saw the electronic scoring system used for the first time. During the 1st Asian Ladies and Junior Shooting Championships held in 1977, Korean sharpshooters won 36 of the 37 gold medals that were offered.

In 1977 the Korean sports world scored another great triumph with the successful scaling of Mt. Everest. The 18-member team made Korea the 8th nation to attain the summit. Since then Korean mountaineering interest has skyrocketed.

On May 6, 1982 five women alpinist sponsored by Sunkyong Corp. became the first female team to conquer Lamjung peak (6986 meters) in the Himalayas. Korea became the fourth country after USA, Japan and Poland to send a women's team to the Himalayas.

Recently in track and field Korea has shown great promise, Korea has also sponsored several marathon runs and in the 1982 Asian Games gained three gold, three silver and four bronze. The gold wins were in the men's 200 meter race. men's long jump and marathon.

The ambitious idea of hosting the 1988 Olympics was first conceived in 1971 when Korea began construction of massive sports facilities in the Chamshil area of Seoul. The International Olympic Committee (IOC) held its meeting in Baden-Baden, West Germany and gave

Seoul the privilege in a 52 to 27 vote over the Japanese city of Nagoya. Becoming the second Asian nation to host the Olympics, Seoul's success in the bid was solid proof of its international athletic recognition.

Korean sports leaders have repeatedly emphasized the government's policy that the Seoul Olympics will not be political but open to all IOC member countries. Sports are important in the development of physical fitness as well as the promotion of friendship and goodwill among all nations.

In the Asian Games held in Bangkok in 1978 Korea earned 18 gold, 20 silver and 31 bronze medals to become third rank, behind Japan and the People's Republic of China. In the 1982 Asian Games held in New Delhi Korea again took third place with 28 gold, 28 silver and 37 bronze. Seoul will be hosting the 1986 Asian Games two years before the Olympics. Korea's growing strength in the '86 Asian Games depends on its progress in swimming, track and field, long dominated by China and Japan.

Recently *taekwondo* has received world recognition as an international sport with the World Taekwondo Federation based in Seoul. Over one thousand instructors are teaching the sport in more than 80 countries. In the 1979 Championships held in Germany, Koreans won seven of the ten divisions with 64 nations participating. Discussion is now underway to make *taekwondo* one of the regular competitive events in the 1988 Seoul Olympics.

This indigenous sport is the oldest of martial arts as it is recorded to have been practiced as early as 37 BC. It is distinctly different from the Chinese *kungfu* and the Japanese *karate*. Koguryo royal tomb murals undeniably depict *taekwondo* scenes which prove that it must have been a popular national sport. An illustrated book was ordered to be compiled by Yongjo (21st Yi king) in 1706.

Westerners have come to see the potential and unquestionable force of human body and soul which are able to break bricks or piles of roof tiles with only bare hands or feet. In 1976 Rhee Jhoon, a Korean *taewondo* instructor, was named "Athlete of the Century" along with five other famous sportsmen.

Another Korean athletic activity which graduated from the martial arts of self defense to a sport is folk wrestling called *ssirum*. According to tomb mural paintings *ssirum* was practiced over 1500 years ago. Because of the simplicity of its rules the common people delight in this sport during festival times. In the old days a bull was awarded to the winner. *Ssirum* is quite different from *yudo* or wrestling.

Another of Korea's traditional sports is *paduk,* and at the moment Korea holds the championship. Cho Chi-hun won over Japan in 1976. Historically *paduk* came from China during the Silla period and moved from Korea to Japan shortly thereafter, where it is called *go.* A *paduk* board is made up of 361 intersections and played by placing white or black disk-shaped counters on the intersecting lines. Players are graded by rank and during any match the inferior player uses the black counters and plays first. He may play any portion of the board and establish his intent to try and control an area by placing his counter in the center of that area.

There are nine basic areas on the board: the four corners, the four sides and the center of the board. Roughly speaking, an area is controlled when it is surrounded by the counters of a player.

Usually the entire board is open for play and there are really few safe places as battle lines are not clearly defined. An attack may erupt unexpectedly from almost anywhere on the board.

Reflection on the strategy of *paduk* can provide rather interesting insight into the behavioral psychology of Asian nations, especially in time of war. Military superiority is looked upon differently by the Asian soldier who is willing to leave a difficult front and focus his energies through surprise attacks at a more vulnerable point. Each military victory along the route is not as important as the final control of territory. Let the Westerner know that

Korea's indigenous sport, taekwondo

photo, courtesy of Korea Taekwondo Association

Yang Chong-mo, Korea's first gold medal winner in 1976 Olympic Games △

Women alpinist conquer Lamjung Peak May 6, 1982, Himalayas   photo, courtesy of Sunkyong Group

310

the Asian's eyes are on the final tally, for to the winner goes the territory and laurels of victory. He has now the right to the white stones.

There is also a Korean chess game called *changgi* which involves kings, horses, elephants and soldiers, etc., that move in a manner similar to Western chess. It is not as popular as *paduk,* which emphasizes the fact that this Western-style game and its strategy do not have much appeal for the Asian.

The game of *hwat'u* is a popular card game indigenous to the Orient. It is played with forty-eight small cards brightly colored with flowers, hence the name "flower cards." Each suit consists of four cards with two as point counter and two with no value other than to be usable in obtaining a point bearing card. Each suit represents one month of the year from January through December, while the flowery design also is symbolic of that month. Koreans play *hwat'o* with great gusto and emotion, and often money is involved as this game is popular for gambling. If you are spending much time in Korea and enjoy playing cards then *hwat'u* is to be recommended as pleasurable way to get to know the people in a sociable setting.

Another popular game which is more frequently played during holiday seasons is *yut.* Four small sticks, round on one side and flat on the other are used.

These sticks are thrown like dice. Depending on how they land, round side up or flat side up, the number of moves the player can make over a given course is determined. A board can be used or the game can be played on the open ground. If played outside, usually crowds are attracted to watch the fun and excitement. All of these above games can be easily purchased in downtown stores or at tourist centers.

Other traditional games popular among the young people of Korea are seesawing and swinging. The most popular time for seesawing is during the lunar New Year with girls usually participants. The participants seesaw in a standing position on the board.

Swinging contests are popular during the *tano* season which is the fifth day of the fifth lunar month. Also like seesawing, swinging is primarily done by young women.

A dangerous traditional sport which is fortunately no longer practiced in Korea is "rock fighting." The boys and men from neighboring villages would compete until one team surrenders.

Kite flying is a sport still pursued by young and old. Usually in the spring contests between groups are held with kite strings coated with powdered glass. By clever manuvering kite strings are cut and the winner's kite soars higher in the sky.

hwat'o *game card*

The World of the Kisaeng

Many foreigners coming to Korea hear about the Korean "kisaeng" and may even have an opportunity to attend a "kisaeng" party where they are royally entertained by a bevy of attractive girls. For the average Westerner this sudden flood of feminine attention is almost overwhelming. The expense of an evening with "kisaeng" recreation can leave a heavy dent in one's pocketbook, so be prepared. However, most foreigners come and leave this country with very little knowledge of the "kisaeng" herself and her ancient traditions.

Though many differences exist, some foreigners try to compare the *kisaeng* to the Japanese entertainers called *geisha*. The literal meaning of the word *kisaeng* is "recreational creature." These recreational girls traditionally came from the lowest class of Korean society, yet were able to move freely between classes and were to become the most culturally educated of all women during the Yi Dynasty. The high class noblewomen usually received little formal education in strongly Confucian Korea and were restricted from leaving their own homes during daylight hours.

Though the origin of the *kisaeng* is not certain, it is generally believed that during the Three Kingdoms Period of the sixth century in the reign of Chinhung (24th Silla king) an organization called *wonhwa* (Original Flowers) was founded. Beautiful maidens throughout the kingdom were selected to serve as exemplary women for the nation. However, because of jealousy between two leaders which resulted in the murder of one, King Chinhung ordered the entire movement disbanded.

In its place the *hwarang* (Flower Youths) movement, for men who were to become the nation's leaders, was established. This elite military, religious and social group became the backbone for Silla unification. Though it is recognized that during this period the *kisaeng* institution did not die despite its tragic beginning it is, however, strange that in the historical records about Silla there is only one mention of a *kisaeng*. She was the young *kisaeng* Ch'on'gwan, the childhood sweetheart of Kim Yu-shin who was later to become Silla's most prominent general during the unification period. His mother worried about the seriousness of this love affair, and advised her son to give up Ch'on'gwan by admonishing him with a noted Confucian proverb, "If you hold black ink how can you expect your hands not to be dirty?" The dutiful son promised never to see Ch'on'gwan again.

One of Korea's best known folk tales relates how Kim Yu-shin was taken by his horse to Ch'on'gwan's home while he was sleeping soundly after a late drinking party with friends. The poor horse out of habit had many times taken his master to Ch'on'gwan's home and Kim Yu-shin was too drunk to realize fully the direction the horse was going. In anger Kim Yu-shin sprang from his horse and taking his great sword killed the poor animal because the beast had been instrumental in causing him to break his promise to his mother. Ch'on'gwan became a Buddhist nun while Kim Yu-shin married his niece after the age of forty. It is believed that he had one son by the *kisaeng* Ch'on'gwan.

Also during the Koryo Dynasty there is virtually no mention of the *kisaeng*, except one account where a group was sent as gifts to the Chinese court in the fourteenth century. But strangely enough during the Yi Dynasty the mention of *kisaeng* in historical records is conspicuously prevalent. During the Yi Dynasty a law was first made relative to the position of the *kisaeng,* indicating that they could only serve in the palace as dancing and singing entertainers or could pursue the skills of acupuncture.

During the Confucian Yi Dynasty formal education was reserved only for men of the *yangban* (gentry) class. Women normally had no opportunities for education of any type, with the exception of the *kisaeng,* who ranked with the lowest in Korea's class structure but often became secondary wives of the educated *yangban.*

It was at the beginning of the seventeenth century during the reign of Injo (16th Yi king) that the government permitted private *kisaeng.* Prior to Injo's reign the *kisaeng* were kept only in the palace and were not permitted to marry.

To fully understand the function of the *kisaeng* within Korean society one must understand fully the Confucian tradition established for all women. Following the Confucian principle, Oriental women must never exert themselves but always assist and follow men. A woman kept three basic obligations in life: to obey her father before marriage, to obey her husband after marriage, and to obey her son after her husband's death. The education of women was as impractical during the Yi Dynasty as sending the family cow to learn the Chinese classics. Yet in spite of this it was the *kisaeng* from the lowest class who rose above the mire of the educational stagnation to which Korean women were relegated.

The educational institution for the *kisaeng* was called *sojae* and operated on a continuous achievement program which averaged about three years, though brighter maidens could finish much sooner. The greatest emphasis at the *kisaeng* school was placed on poetry, because the most popular events at a

kisaeng function was the writing and reciting of poetry. A young girl would go far in the entertainment world if she showed real promise in creative poetry which was the Korean *sijo*. Consisting of three lines or verses, the *sijo* that remain in historical records reveal the Korean heart, passionate feelings, manners and attitudes. During these years of study the girl was called *tonggi* or young *kisaeng*. Usually at about age fifteen there was a ceremonial graduation when the *tonggi* becomes a "perfect woman." The older *kisaeng* took great care in finding a ranking nobleman to spend the first night with the newly graduated girl. Throughout her entire life the *kisaeng* was proud of her "first night man."

Unfortunately the working life of the *kisaeng* was short and they had to retire at the age of thirty. The retired *kisaeng* called *twegi* must then find another profession and often they open a saloon or become matchmakers. The *kisaeng* were permitted to marry and many became concubines of the gentry or government officials. However, their children could never be accepted into the nobility class called *yangban*. Exceptions occasionally occurred in the palace as several Yi Dynasty kings were actually the sons of royal concubines.

The *kisaeng* who came from different regions of Korea gained a reputation for particular talents. The Andong region of North Kyongsang Province was famous for the poetic *kisaeng,* while Kangnung on the east coast was better known for the singing talent of the *kisaeng*. The *kisaeng* of Cheju Island were renowned for their horse riding ability, while those from Hamhung and Pyongyang in northern Korea were celebrated for dancing ability. The *kisaeng* in the far north near Uiju had an illustrious reputation for the sword dance. The *kisaeng* of northern Korea were believed to possess more talent and beauty than the girls of the south. It is generally believed that women from the north and men from the south always make a perfect match.

In Chinju of southern Korea once lived the celebrated heroine called Non'gae. She was the *kisaeng* mistress of the garrison commander when attacking Japanese armies swept the countryside in 1592. After her patron's death in the capture of Chinju Fortress she willingly entertained the enemy officers during their victory celebration. As the evening wore late the ranking officers became quite drunk. Non'gae suggested to the amorous general that they stroll along the river's edge. Suddenly Non'gae, clasping the general, plunged into the river to her death, taking the Japanese general with her. Her patriotism is still recognized by ceremonies at her shrine in Chinju once every year.

Probably considered the most famous of all *kisaeng* is Hwang Chin-i who came from Kaesong, the ancient Koryo capital. Her notoriety as a *sijo* poetess overshadows all other Korean woman poets. Known as the most beautiful and talented *kisaeng* of the land, she could match wits with the most learned scholars of her time, while none could remain indifferent to her charms.

Unlike most *kisaeng* she was of noble birth. The legend is told that a youth living nearby fell desperately in love with Hwang Chin-i but because his love was unreturned pined away and died. As the funeral procession passed Hwang Chin-i's home the bier stopped and would not move, as if transfixed by a spell. Hwang Chin-i rushed out and untying her outer skirt flung it over the coffin, thus breaking the spell. After this incident the family found it difficult to give their daughter away in marriage as she was considered a widow.

Hwang Chin-i chose to become a *kisaeng* and quickly mastered all the feminine skills and arts expected of her profession. Outstanding was her literary and calligraphic talent which soon won her a widening circle of admirers. The gossip of her many love affairs among scholars and even Buddhist priests have become favorite legends to this day. However, it is said that although she was loved by many men, she gave herself in love to very few. Those she truly loved, she loved dearly and well.

Before her death she requested that

she not be buried among the lonely hills but that her body be left outside the east gate of Kaesong to serve as a dire warning to all women who passed to keep their life and body virtuous. Though her family did not comply with this request, she was buried in a field beside the road leading to the east gate and there a shrine was erected. Soon her grave instead of becoming an object of scorn became a pilgrimage shrine for poets to come to pay homage.

During her lifetime, many eminent scholars and renowned Buddhist priests would declare that Hwang Chin-i could never charm them. The expression of "ten years of study turns to emptiness," was coined by Hwang Chin-i as many men succumbed to her beauty and personal charm. One such scholar was Pyok Kye-sa for whom Hwang Chin-i composed this *sijo*.

Clear waters flow through purple valleys, but be not so proud of your swift flow.

Once you enter the limitless sea, it will not be easy to return.

The bright moon fills these quiet hills, so why do you not rest for a while?

"Clear Water" alludes to the scholar's penname while *myong-wol* (Bright Moon) was Hwang Chin-i penname. Pyok Kye-sa boasted to his friends that the bewitching Hwang Chin-i could never turn his head. Upon hearing this she wrote this *sijo* to the scholar who marveled first at her brilliance in poetry, and later upon meeting her found her irresistible, Hwang Chin-i flaunted his attentions for she only wished to prove the emptiness of his boast about her.

Another of the more famous *kisaeng* was So Ch'un-p'ung who came from Pyongyang, jokingly called the "kisaeng capital" of Korea. Her father was a Buddhist priest who while on a pilgrimage had been invited to stay in the home where her widowed mother lived. After the child's birth the widow in grief and shame killed herself . . . The baby was taken and raised by a

kisaeng house in Pyongyang City. She took the name of So which means "big laugh" while her first name implies "spring wind." Maybe the joke was on the priest.

She soon became a concubine of a ranking government official but her great beauty became a problem. He was reluctant to permit her to perform at civic functions for fear that a higher official might take her from him. Thus, So Ch'un-p'ung swore that she would always remain faithful to him. However, at one reception a visiting prime minister from Seoul upon seeing So Ch'un-pung immediately stated his desire to claim her. So Ch'un-p'ung's answer in poetry is remembered as a classic reply. She compared two big powers of China called Choe and Ch'o who were always fighting each other. She asked how could a small country in the middle follow both rulers?

The proud minister answered, "I have heard that the recreation girls would often eat in the east house but sleep in the west house. Is this not the accepted life of the *kisaeng?*"

But So Ch'un-p'ung answered, "Even though our life is like a fleeting cloud we never follow two husbands." The prime minister, realizing her insinuation, was ashamed, for he had been an official of the Koryo court who had changed his loyalty to the Yi Dynasty to save his life. He could see her wisdom and returned without her.

With the close of the Yi Dynasty the *kisaeng* tradition ceased to function in its true form, though the Japanese occupational authorities tried to perpetuate it for their own official use. The *kisaeng* mistress of Ito Hirobumi, the first Japanese Resident-General who forced Korea to sign a protectorate treaty, is controversial among historians. Possibly a true patriot, she may have given needed information to Ahn Chung-gun who assassinated Ito in 1909.

A century ago it was the *kisaeng* who maintained a higher level of cultural attainment and truly sophisticated education, beyond that of any other group of Yi Dynasty women. The true *kisaeng* has become a part of Korean history

316

and now only one historical chronicle
written in Chinese gives the account of
this particular Korean tradition. At the
turn of the century James Gale, a
Scottish missionary and prolific early
Western writer on Korea, gives a pro-
vocative account of his personal view
of these "dancing girls" in his *History
of the Korean People.* He notes that
"dancing-girls" and the laboring women
were the only groups seen during the
day.

"One of the noticeable features of
Korean life is the dancing girl. You
see her in the streets dressed in all her
fluff and feathers, coloured like a bird
in green, pink and yellow. She appears
thus in all the colours of the rainbow,
tipped with ermine edges; a picture for
the eye to see, not often pretty in
feature from the Western point of view,
but striking . . She rides about in the
best of rickshas . . . . and holds her
head up like a queen. It might seem
to a foreigner that a woman who not
only sells her gifts of song and her grace
of foot but her body as well ought to
hide her head . . . . . not so the *kisaeng*:
she is as blithe a bird as ever hopped,
with never a shadow across her easy-
sitting conscience; happy in the role
she is called upon to play, and feeling
that she is a very important part of what
the east calls society . . . . . Many noble
deeds are told of the dancing-girls. One,
specially known, comes from Chinju
. . . . . Non'gae, a dancing-girl . . . . .
One of Korea's commonest stories is
that of the dancing-girl, telling how by
dint of faithfulness she rises from a place
of obscurity, yes, of shame, to become
one of the first ladies of the land."

What Is Korean Food?

Korean food that is spicy and often hot includes red pepper . . . . and then one tries the "kimchi" which is really HOT, but a trip to Korea without a Korean meal is like going to Waikiki and not swimming.

Korean food consists of a wide variety of grains, subsidiary dishes, special foods and drinks. Cooking is usually done by broiling or frying. The traditional kitchen is simple and minimal in size and decor. It is usually located at the rear of the home and the fires from the kitchen enter the *ondol* floors circulating through the living and sleeping rooms. Even in modern homes the kitchen is not bright and cheerful; it has minimal windows and never is adjacent to gardens or the entertainment portion of the house.

Now modern urban homes and apartment buildings boast refrigerators, gas stoves and piped hot water. For this reason it is all the more remarkable that typical Korean food for invited guests tends to be quite elaborate and apparently difficult to prepare. The basic everyday meal is simple enough. It will include a bowl of white rice; a meat or fish soup and *kimchi,* considered to be Korea's unique dish.

Peppery hot fermented cabbage, radish and vegetable are pickled in salt brine and stored underground in earthen jars during the winter. This preparation of winter *kimchi* becomes a monumental family project during the late fall. In the warmer weather a summer *kimchi* is always present at every meal. Bright red peppers which are used in making *kimchi* and many other dishes are frequently seen drying on mats in the courtyard and occasionally on the thatched roofs of farmhouses in late fall.

Probably the most popular Korean dish among foreigners is *pulgogi* which consists of strips of beef charcoal-roasted

over a brazier at the table after it has been marinated in a complex mixture of soy sauce, sesame, and spices. *Kalbi* or short ribs are roasted in a marinade and are delectable. *Shinsollo,* a regal casserole of vegetables, eggs and strips of meat and fish mixed with pine and gingko nuts, tempts the most particular connoisseur of exotic foods. This dish was prepared only for royalty a century ago.

After walking into a Korean restaurant and being served an elaborate array of fish dishes, meats and vegetables, you will be surprised that after you eat all you can possibly manage the bill is reasonably small. Some of the restaurants are now blending Korean food with Western food. Especially in the larger cities Korea is now an eating paradise at reasonable cost.

For the traditional Korean meal, one small table is prepared for each person. Cooked rice, often mixed with barley, and soup are served in separate bowls and side dishes are put on the table in smaller bowls or dishes. Normally five or six different side dishes are served. When you ask for *jongshik* (Korean meal) in a small inn or restaurant this is what usually is served.

The side dishes might consist of bean sprouts, *toraji* (bellflower root), *kosari* (young fern frond) *meruchi* (small minnow-like fish), cabbage *kimchi,* turnip *kimchi* and maybe cucumber *kimchi* called *oi-kimchi.* To wrap around the rice, marinated sesame leaves or thin square wafers of seaweed are served. To use your chopsticks in wrapping the leaf or seaweed around the rice is a real demonstration of dexterity. A fried or broiled fish is also served.

A fancy meal could include 15 or more dishes. The possibilities then become endless and one begins to wonder if there is anything growing in Korea that the Koreans do not eat. Because the preparation of a first class Korean meal is truly tedious and time consuming it can generally be stated that contemporary trends in the Korean household are toward efficiency rather than sentiment and tradition.

If one really wants to sample the wide variety of Korean dishes available, call Korea House and make reservations for the buffet served six nights a week. The food is excellent and reasonable. If you ask the waiters they are willing to give a full explanation of the different dishes you are enjoying.

*(below) Sliced beef (*pulgogi*) is roasted on a charcoal burner right on the dinner table. (right page below) At home dinners are placed on a low table. Kimchi is seen in the dishes in front.*

① **Kalbi-chim** (beef rib stew)
Beef short ribs, turnips, chestnuts and mushrooms are marinated in seasoning and slowly cooked for a couple hours. Together with *pulgogi, kalbi* is the most popular dish among foreigners.

② **Pindaettok** (bean pancake)
Korean's favorite snack.... green onions and strips of pork are placed on bean pancake. *Pindaettok* is sold at the Korean drinking house.

③ **Ttokkuk** (rice cake soup)
New Year's food. Sliced rice cakes are boiled in beef soup stock. This one dish meal can be easily found in Korean restaurants during winter time.

④ **Chapchae** (mixed vegetables with soybean noodle)
Shredded beef, onion, cucumber, carrot, beansprouts, mushrooms and noodles are all seasoned then quickly stir fried. One needs a good ability with chopsticks or noodles will slip away.

Ginseng, the Panacea for Health

Ginseng in history, legend and common usage remains the most widely known, most firmly believed in and most interesting of the herb medicines of the Orient. This "elixir of life" is Korea's oldest export product.

Korean ginseng has been famous throughout the entire Orient from as early as the Three Kingdoms period. Records reveal that over 1,500 years ago ginseng root was being exported to both China and Japan. The ginseng root resembles a human figure; thus the first Chinese character *gin* means "man." Called ginseng in English and *insam* in Korean and *jensheng* in Chinese, it was formally given the Greek classification name of Panax Ginseng in 1843 (*pan*

meaning all and *axos* meaning medicine). So ginseng, worshipped by the ancient Orientals, continues to hold the status of king of herbs, among a wide variety of others in Korea.

Traditionally ginseng has been regarded as a magic "cure all" for a whole gallery of complaints ranging from insomnia and toothache to malaria and even epilepsy, not to mention the ability to prolong life. Though in some parts of Asia the use of ginseng has become more selective, in Korea its use has remained relatively unlimited, and it is still considered a general tonic to be used indiscriminately as a panacea. Even now in modern Korea ginseng is taken as a fatigue cure.

Korea is the prime source of the world's supply of the best ginseng as the climate is thought to be most suitable. Cultivated ginseng is tightly controlled by the government, with Kanghwa Island near Seoul having one of the largest concentrations of ginseng farming in the country. It is not a get-rich-quick product as the raising of ginseng is fraught with many difficulties despite the high value after the harvest. Five to six years are required to raise the plant to maturity, while great care and expertise are needed in its cultivation. Thatched straw-roof lean-tos are erected in long rows to protect the tender plants from too much rain, wind or direct sunlight. Proper drainage of the cultivated rows must be carefully planned. During harvest no rain must be allowed to touch the drying ginseng root.

The harvest period is a great occasion. The hopes and patient loving care that the plants have been given over the last six years are now coming to fruition. One by one the roots are carefully dug out with a two-pronged tool. Workers cut and scrape the small fine roots off, wash and peel the ginseng and sort them according to the size of the root at the top. The best are steamed while the rest are dried. This drying process is done on racks or wooden trays and baskets. The product is then packaged for sale. Many roots are also ground into various other extracts such as tea, wine or medicine.

In Korea there are two kinds of ginseng sold, white and red. Red ginseng is made from the best quality and often used for export. It has been cured by steaming over a fire until the root becomes pinkish in color. The roots sell for high prices as ginseng products are usually expensive; in ancient days people valued the ginseng as more precious than gold. Even today if a man is lucky enough to discover wild ginseng plants in the mountains he can make a fortune overnight. The location is often kept secret in the family circle for hundreds of years for fear of poaching. The wild ginseng brings the most exorbitant price, the sale of which is difficult to control by the government.

Claims for the ginseng root are remarkable, as advertised on various brochures enclosed with the root. The scope of these claims range as stated: "ginseng is reliable for the following symptoms; energy promotion, emaciation caused in or after illness, anemia, weakness after confinement, women's disease, weak constitution, neurasthenia, neurosis, hysteria, gastroenteritis, appetite stimulant, excessive fatigue, incipient growths, diabetes, etc." Other claims insist that ginseng is excellent for good blood circulation, generally rejuvenating but also particularly good for clearing up a "hangover" after a heavy drinking bout.

Occasionally the exact English words on the ginseng label will draw smiles of amusement from the tourist, such as: "Truly Korean ginseng deserves to be called: The Elixir of the Life and A Providential Gift. Korean ginseng is a proper product of Korea, it makes you surely prolong your youth and here in Korea ginseng is for you if you wish to live longer."

Recently in several countries scientific research is being done to determine the pharmaceutical properties of ginseng. Eventually when all of the elements of ginseng have been extracted and tested for medicinal and physiological effects on man and animals we may learn what claims are valid for this mysterious plant.

◁ *The ginseng root, resembling a person, is king of the herbs*

The Ancient Wisdom of Acupuncture

Acupuncture is synonymous with a whole Oriental philosophy. For the Korean, man is a small universe and the equilibrium of man's body, like the stars and planets, is controlled by the same mechanisms. Good health is the result of a balance between two opposing forces that confront society in all aspects of nature, and circulate in the human body in the form of energy flowing along precisely determined meridians. The physician's task is to maintain these forces in harmony within the body.

Oriental medicine or *hanyak* is basically preventive, and the superior practitioner treats to prevent illness while only the mediocre physician treats the sick. Even from ancient times the physician was paid by his client to keep him in good health. If the patient became ill it was the practitioner's responsibility to provide medicine at his own expense because he had failed his obligation. The use of acupuncture needles, moxas and an amazingly varied collection of herbs and natural medicine is far older than Western civilization, and by no means has been abolished by modern medicine.

The vogue of acupuncture has attracted greater attention over the last decade among a growing and convinced minority of Western doctors. However, there is still an element of mystery as the basic principles of acupuncture placed within the framework of modern science have no satisfying explanation for Western scientists. The vital energy flow along the meridians remains a mystery, but its effects have been verified scientifically. Hence again the difference between the East and West . . . . the Occidental needs to explain what he discovers, while the Oriental simply discovers and classifies. To obtain an explanation of every aspect of Oriental medicine would only lead to many unverifiable hypotheses.

Acupuncture was not the only means of controlling antagonistic forces. The *hanyak* doctors of Korea draw on an abundant stock of medicines made from plants, minerals and animal substances. The physician nearly always prescribes some of these medicines in addition to the acupuncture treatment. The great variety is demonstrated by the fact that the standard prescriptions now fill over fifty volumes. Massages, dieting, therapeutic baths and a form of gymnastics involving complex breathing exercises were also used for preserving health and speeding recovery. From the first contacts of the Koreans with the Chinese civilization, medicine was introduced to the peninsula, yet the West knew nothing of Oriental medicine until the 17th century.

China was the center of the would, and did not become aware of the existence of the Occident, "land of foreign devils," until the first contacts were made by the Portuguese in the early 16th century. China found the West to be a very complex and powerful civilization, as well as often barbarous and mercantile.

Jesuits were sent as missionaries to Peking and were amazed by what the court physicians revealed with supporting evidence. Upon returning to Europe they reported their discoveries and the word "acupuncture" was coined from the Latin words *acus,* "needle," and *punctura,* "pricking." However, acupuncture had to wait until the early 20th

◁ *Acupuncture doctor, Kyongju City*

century and George Soulié de Morant of France before it could truly make genuine progress in the Western world.

At the age of twenty Soulié de Morant was sent to China as a bank representative and because of his knowledge of Chinese became the French consul in Shanghai in 1900. When a cholera epidemic broke out he was amazed to find that treatment of patients by means of needles had better results than other medicines at the time.

He began a study which resulted in official recognition and title of "Master Physician" conferred by the Viceroy of Yunnan in 1908. After twenty years in China he returned to France and continued his study of acupuncture and did many translations. Published studies appeared in 1928, 1934 and 1939. Because of Soulié de Morant acupuncture and other Oriental medicines were being accepted by the West as a science rather than a fad.

The oldest of all known medical treatises is ascribed to Hwang-ti (Yellow Emperor of China, 1628 B.C.) who was a distinguished acupuncturist himself and with his court scribes recorded all knowledge acquired since time immemorial. The Nei-Cheing in its present form was actually rewritten about 200 B.C. and nearly all Oriental medicine is based on this record. During the unified Silla period when the T'ang Dynasty of China was in its "renaissance" medicine achieved full development and was divided into four specialties according to importance: physicians and pulse specialists who dealt in external and internal medicine, pediatrics, mouth, nose and throat; second, the acupuncturists; third, the masseurs and finally masters of incantations who practiced divinations.

With some influence from China, Korea has followed its own course of medical development. Especially noteworthy is the publication of the monumental twenty-five volume encyclopedic classic in 1610 called *Tong-I Pogam.* This "Treasury Book of Eastern Medicine" was compiled and written by Ho Chun. It is still an indispensible textbook for all Oriental physicians. At the time of publication it was requested by China, the cradle of Oriental herb medicine, because of the book's tremendous compilation of research which had been accomplished over a sixteen-year period by this court physician. Even today physicians are amazed at the correct information on human organs and methods of treatment.

Ho Chun was born to a concubine of a provincial governor near Kimpo town which automatically kept him from receiving any recognition and status. Though he became the personal physician for Sonjo (14th Yi king) and received a government position, he died a lonely and frustrated man in 1615 north of Seoul only five years after his book's publication.

All traditional Oriental medicine, which is basically free from foreign influence, rests solely on the application of certain philosophical principles. Man is a summary of the universe and all ancient knowledge can be summed up on the basis of *tao,* the single law that governs all Oriental philosophy. The dualistic force of *yang* and *um* (Yang and Yin) dictates the theory of the *tao.* The *yang* originally meant "light" while the *um* meant "absence of light."

Thirty centuries before the Christian era this cosmic theory was expounded. The sky and sun are *yang* while the earth and moon are *um.* All living things contain both principles. The *yang* is always masculine, active, splendid and hard while the *um* is feminine, passive, plain and soft. Odd numbers are *yang* and even numbers *um;* summer and south are *yang* while winter and north are *um,* denoting energy and growth for one and inactivity and hibernation for the other. Conformity with the *yang* and *um* are the precept of the *tao* and life itself.

The entire universe, with man included, is subject to slow and opposing pulsations. The *yang* and *um* wax and wane representing ebb and flow, the undulatory nature of two principles affecting all nature. Not only a person's health and character, but all events in the universe are determined by the preponderance of *yang* or *um*. The goal of all Oriental medicine is to maintain or restore balance between the *yang* and *um* principles.

The symbolic relations between *yang* and *um* are illustrated by trigrams as interpreted by the *Book of Changes,* and are said to have been invented by Emperor Fu Hsi (2953 B.C.). The 64 trigrams consist of three unbroken (*yang*) and broken (*um*) lines.

Another philosophy that influenced ancient medicine, originating twelve centuries before Christ, is the five primordial elements accounting for the structure and origin of the universe. At first these two philosophies were unrelated to each other but later were merged. These five elements are wood, fire, mineral, metal and water. The five planets which represent the five elements, five organs of the body, five directions (including center) and five colors, etc., all relate to this principle.

Human beings represent a harmonious combination of both celestial and earthly principles, and any change in balance is usually manifested by physiological disorders recognized by certain irregularities in the rhythmic pulsations of circulating energy. A distinction is made between "the pulse" and "the pulses," for there are 14 pulses of the radial arteries used by all acupuncturists.

Pulse examination therefore makes it possible to know whether an organic function is disturbed by either an excess of *um* or a deficiency of *yang*. To restore balance the physician must either dissipate or stimulate the deficient principle. The notion of individual energy is extremely important in traditional Oriental medicine and is identified with the *um-yang* cycle and natural balance.

The term "meridian" is used to refer to the circulatory paths of energy which are invisible. There are 12 double meridians. The six *yang* meridians are called: small-intestine, triple-warmer, large intestine (on the arms), urinary-bladder, gall-bladder, and stomach (on the legs). The six other *um* meridians located on the inside of the limbs are: lung, heart-governor, heart (on the arms), liver, spleen and kidney (on the legs).

As man is united with the cosmos there is a frontier at which the inner rhythms of the organism and the outer rhythms of the cosmos either clash or mingle. This frontier is the skin, through which one is able to restore a broken equilibrium. Along the meridians are specific points which are areas of special sensitivity, and action as these points has the effect of normalizing the disturbed balance. The total number of insertion points varies from 365 (number of days in the year) to 618 along the twelve double meridians. However, on each of the meridians some points are more important than others. From ancient times sixty-six control points are recognized on the twelve double meridians.

The area of an acupuncture point is scarcely larger than a pinhead and only by insertion at the precise spot can complete results be obtained. Some very powerful points such as point thirty-six of the stomach meridian still give results if needled a few millimeters away from the center of the point.

Forty-five centuries ago needles were made of jade or fish bone. Traditionally there were nine types of needles, usually made of iron, except the longest which were made of copper. Though gold and silver were never mentioned in early texts, class distinction required the use of gold and silver needles for the wealthy upper class. Today, as social distinction is not as important, needles are made from stainless steel, though some are still made of gold.

In a tradition such as acupuncture, which has filled hundreds of volumes over the centuries, what can be said in a few pages? For the West the gift of Oriental medicine is priceless, yet much remains to be done before the concepts of acupuncture can be fully intergrated into the Western world's intellectual tradition. The West cannot long afford to ignore such an effective means of relieving man's suffering and restoring energy which has been seriously impaired by the conditions of modern living.

Chapter VI.
Tourist Directory

◁ *Seoul National Museum, Kyongbok Palace*

Fly free like a bird with HAITAI!

General Tourist Information

HOW TO GET TO KOREA

There are over 200 flights weekly by international airlines connecting Korea with Japan, Taiwan, Philippines, Hong Kong, Thailand, Singapore and other world destinations. Only 1½ hours from Tokyo, Korea can be visited at no extra cost to your airfare enroute to other Asian countries.

ENTRY FORMALITIES

A tourist can easily enter Korea. Travelers are required to present a current passport and valid vaccination certificates when applying for a visa. Tourist visas may be granted for thirty days which can be renewed for an additional thirty days at the Ministry of Justice in Seoul. Tourists in transit may visit Korea for five days without visa, but must have proof of confirmed air reservation on to the next destination. Custom laws permit a visitor to bring in practically everything which is for personal use and not for resale. Upon leaving the country all imported effects must be taken from the country.

The main port of entry for Korea is Kimpo Airport located in the countryside about a thirty minute drive from downtown Seoul. Some international flights do arrive in Pusan, the southern port city of the Republic. Flight time between the two cities is approximately one hour. Passengers arriving in Korea must proceed through health, immigration and custom clearance. So long as documents and landing cards are in order, movement through the checkpoints is usually fast and efficient. Money can be changed at the airport. Porters are available for hand luggage and should be paid about 500 *won* (83 ¢) per bag. Airport taxis are all metered and the ride into downtown Seoul is approximately 4,000 *won* $6.00. However, if you take a gold colored *"call taxi"* sedan the price will be more than double as the metered rate is much higher. Often taxi drivers will speak a smattering of English from the airport to major hotels in Seoul.

BUSINESS HOURS

Government offices: Weekdays 9 a.m. — 6 p.m., Saturday 9 a.m. — 1 p.m.
Bank: Weekdays 10 a.m. — 4:30 p.m., Saturday 10 a.m. — 1:30 p.m.
Post office: Weekdays 9 a.m. — 5 p.m., Saturday 9 a.m. — 1 p.m.
Private businesses tend to open at 9 a.m. and close far later than 6 p.m. They all work on Saturday.
Major department stores are open at 10 a.m. and close 7 p.m. daily.
Major department stores close once a week as follow:
   Lotte Department Store: close on every Tuesday
   Shinsegae Department Store: close on every Monday
   Midopa Department Store: close on every Wednesday
Shops in the streets, markets and undergrounds tend to be open early morning to late in the evening, seven days week.

KOREAN CURRENCY

The unit of Korean currency is called *won* (₩) and coins are used for 1,5,10, 50, 100 and 500 *won*. (Some 500 *won* notes are still in circulation though they are no longer printed.) Notes come in 500, 1,000, 5,000 and 10,000 denominations. Bank drafts can be obtained for larger amounts which can serve the same as cash. The present exchange rate for one dollar is about ₩750, as of the date of this publication (there are small day to day variations).

TIPPING

Tipping is not really a common practice. Most waiters and waitresses do not expect tips. A major exception is seen in the nightclubs and entertainment houses where hostesses entertain customers. A fairly large tip is mandatory even though you may think very little service has been rendered. In hotel restaurants, tax and service charges are added on your bill thus it is not necessary to leave a tip.

CREDIT CARD

Major hotels, department stores, some specialty stores and restaurants will accept the following cards: American Express, VISA, Diners Club, Master Charge and Carte Blanche. Except for the several larger cities it will be difficult to use credit cards outside of Seoul.

MEDICARE

Medicines can be obtained at the drug stores without docter's perscription. Major hotels have house doctors. General hospitals listed below are recommended if the emergency arises.
SNU Hospital: Tel. 7601-1
Severance Hospital: 332-0171
St. Mary's Hospital, Myongdong: 771-76
St. Mary's Hospital, Kangnam: 593-5141
Paik Foundation Hospital: 266-1121
Sunchonhyang Hospital: 794-2681

ELECTRICITY

The current is mostly 100 volts but 220 volts current is supplied in the new developments. At most major hotels both 110 and 220 volts outlets are available.

POSTAL SERVICE

Stamps can be purchased in major hotels, certain shops along the streets or at the post office. Letters can be dropped at postal boxes while packages must be mailed at the post office. Local mail takes one day within Seoul and two-three days from Seoul to the provincial areas. International mail takes seven to ten days from Seoul to USA and even longer for Europe. There is DHL service available (Tel. 779-3241/9) for U$35.00 for one time delivery to any major city of the USA. (two day service)

TELEPHONE / TELEGRAM

Local calls can be made from red or green public phones by inserting two ten *won* coins. Connection will automatically breaks off after three minutes. Local long distance calls (any call to outside of Seoul) can be made through large yellow public pay phones available at major hotels. Have your coins ready. It takes only 100 *won* and ten *won* coins. Insert 100 *won* and dial area code and the telephone number. If you hear the "beeps" in the middle of your call, insert more coins to continue speaking or it will break off. Coin refund will be returned when you hang up.

International calls cannot be made through public phones. Dial 102 for USA, Canada, Italy, Hong Kong, France, Australia. Philippines, Taiwan, Singapore, Spain and Germany. Dial 117 for other areas and Dial 1030 for overseas information. These are all operator assisted calls. There is yet no direct dialing overseas from Korea.
Local and international telegrams can be sent by telephone dialing 115 or at the KIT (Korea International Telecommunication) office located near the capitol building.

Enjoy the Beautiful Mornings of Korea

HYUNDAI

THE LAND OF
THE MORNING CALM
— KOREA
ISES WITH THE SUN

Business Lines

- International Trading
- Engineering & Construction
- Shipbuilding & Shiprepair
- Automobiles & Rolling Stock
- Industrial & Chemical Plants
- Power Plants & Electrical Equipment
- Industrial Equipment & Machinery
- Containers
- Iron, Steel Products & Metal Pipes
- Building Materials
- General Merchandise
- Natural Resources Development in Abroad
- Shipping Services
- Financing

Daewoo
flower power.

Plant, sprout, grow and blossom
in a garden-full of industrial
and business activities – with us.

the "Let's" Corporation

TRADING	CONSTRUCTION
SHIPBUILDING	PLANT PROJECTS
MACHINERY	CHEMICALS
TEXTILES	FINANCE
ENERGY & RESOURCES DEVELOPMENT	
HEAVY CONSTRUCTION EQUIPMENT	

DAEWOO
DAEWOO CORPORATION

C.P.O.BOX 2810, 8269 SEOUL, KOREA
TLX.: DAEWOO K23341/5, DWDEV K24444, K22868

TRANSPORTATION INFORMATION

Taxis: Taxi fares are registered on meters. The basic fare is ₩600 for two kilometers and ₩40 for each additional 500 meters. It is not necessary to tip but it is often done when the taxi driver helps with additional baggage. Often it is hard to hail a taxi in downtown Seoul. There are regular taxi pickup points located throughout the city and many of them are covered to protect passengers waiting during inclement weather. Many taxi drivers speak some English.

Foreigners who are new to Korea must remember that there are two different metered taxi systems on the streets. The "call taxis" are large gold colored sedans which usually cruise about the major hotels looking for the "well-heeled" customers. Their meter begins at ₩1000 and the fare will be more than twice the price of regular smaller cabs.

Domestic Air Flights: Korean Air Lines (KAL) is the only airline that operates within the country. They provide flights to all the major cities. For information on schedules call Tel: 778-8221, 28-5223/4.

Railway Service: A well organized network of railroads connect the entire country. Fast express trains run between Seoul and Pusan as well as Seoul to Kwangju. For information on schedules and rates call:
Seoul Station Tel.: 28-7788/9 YS-3313
Chongnyangni, Tel: 966-7788

Highway Express Buses: The main trunk roads in Korea have been converted into several networks of well paved modern expressways. Comfortable high speed express buses busily transport passengers to and from major areas of the country including principal cities and resorts. Most of the bus lines come to the main bus terminal located in Yongdong directly on the south side of the Han River across the Chamsu Bridge. It is about a ten-fifteen minute ride from the downtown area. Usually no reservations are needed and departure times are frequent. Tourist agencies and hotel staff can assist you in travel plans.

Suburban Buses: Most of the population of Seoul ride buses. Since it is often difficult to find a seat be prepared to stand and don't look for comfort. Fare is now ₩120 for as long as you stay on the bus. There is a bus token system in operation which will save the rider ₩10; however, payment can also be made in cash. Fares will be collected by the bus girl as you get off. There is no transfer ticket system. All buses are numbered but to find a complete schedule of routes with corresponding bus numbers is impossible. For a tourist it will be at first a "trial and error" experience but expect to meet some of Seoul's nicest people.

Subway: An excellent subway system goes from Seoul's main Railway Station through the heart of the city to Chongnyangni. It passes the South Gate and Toksu Palace to turn right at Chong-ro. The subway stays under Chong-ro past East Gate to Seoul's second important railway station, Chongnyangni. In the southern direction the train surfaces near the Han River and continues on to Suwon or Inchon Port.

Car Rentals: Just beginning in Korea is a car rental system. Hotels and tourist agencies can provide further information. Tel: 795-0810/5

Ferries: An economical way to travel is by ferry. The Pukwan Ferry links Pusan with Japan's western port of Shimonoseki three times weekly. For reservations call Seoul 22-9716; Pusan 44-1471/5. (Tokyo office: (03) 567-0974; Osaka Office; (06) 345-2245; Shimonoseki Office; (0832) 66-8211. Car ferries connect Pusan with Cheju Island three times weekly. (Seoul: 23-5538; Pusan: 44-0606) Hydrofoils ply the scenic waters of the Hallyo Waterway linking Pusan with Yosu via the resorts of Chungmu and Namhae. (Pusan: 44-3851)

The Korean Turn of Mind–
Creativity where it counts.

The Rain Gauge, Made in the 15th Century Korea.

No one else in the whole world apparently had thought of when Koreans first made it in the 15th-century—a rain gauge for use in better managing agricultural resources. Coming up with this practical tool was a wonderful creative feat for its time.

The rain gauges made in Korea on August 16, 1441, the reign of the Great King Sejong in the early Yi-Dynasty were not much different in size and appearance from those in use now at weather stations around the world.

As heirs to the wisdom of their forefathers, Koreans of today are doing their utmost to create new technology.

Especially noteworthy is Sunkyong's continuous concentrated investment in the development of precision technology from early on.

Photo: ruler-like depth gauge.
It was used to measure the depth of the water gathered in the rain gauge.

The result is that now Sunkyong is using its very own techniques to produce and export polyester film and color video tape.

The quality and price of Sunkyong's video tape offers you some profitable advantages over tape produced in other countries now dominating the world market.

Sunkyong promises to go right on devoting must of its attention to quiet investment in further technological development.

The S.K. video cassette, developed with independently manufacturing technology by Sunkyong Chemical Limited.

Photo: This rain guage, the only official one extant from old Korea, was made in 1837, the third year of the reign of King Hyeonjong of the Yi Dynasty, the stone stand shown holding the rain gauge was made in 1770, the 46th year of the reign of King Yeongjo. It is now on display at the Central Meteorological Observatory in Seoul (Tangible National Treasure No. 561)

⟨SK⟩ Sunkyong Group

The Sunkyong Group is playing an important part in Kroean business today in such fields as general trading, textiles, chemicals, construction and oil refining.

Head Office: Sunkyong Bldg. 5-3 Namdaemun-ro 2-ga, Chung-gu, Seoul, Korea/Tel: 771-88
Cable: SUNKYONG SEOUL/Telex: SNKYONG K24851-5 SKFIBRE K28445/C.P.O. BOX: 1780 SEOUL

MASS MEDIA

In Korea there are two English language newspapers, the *Korea Herald* and the *Korea Times.* Both are under private ownership. They are both dailies except on Monday and legal holidays. Sponsored by the International Cultural Society of Korea through the *Korea Herald* is an excellent weekly news-magazine called *Korea Newsreview*. Also the US military newspaper *Stars and Stripes* is available for home delivery near military installations.

The Republic of Korea has three television channels and an educational channel. AFKN-TV is a US military broadcasting station which offers a variety of programs in English.

DEPARTURE FROM KOREA

Departing passengers should arrive at the airport two hours before scheduled flight time. An airport tax of 3,000 *won* ($4.00) must be paid and it is best to use the local currency as other currencies will have to be converted. All bags and parcels as well as hand luggage will be searched by custom officials. After you pass through customs, duty free shops are found in the waiting lounge prior to boarding. Foreign currency is acceptable at the duty free shops.

No Korean cultural properties should be carried out of Korea that date back to 1910 or earlier without permits which can be obtained from the Ministry of Culture and Information in advance. For further information call Tel: 725 3053. In regard to ginseng, up to three kilograms of both the white and red can be taken from Korea without permits; however, sale slips must be shown. Up to 20 boxes of powdered ginseng are allowed to be taken from Korea. Remember if you take a taxi to the airport the rate for the "call taxi" which is also metered will be considerably more expensive than Seoul's regular metered cabs.

If you are a resident in Korea you must take your residency permit with you to give to authorities. A receipt is given if you are returning to Korea. These permits must be picked up within two weeks after arrival at Kimpo.

The Walker Hill Travel Service at the Sheraton operates the airport shuttle and stops at all major hotels on its way to the airport. For further information call, Tel: 444-8211 or 720-8571. The fee is ₩500 per person.

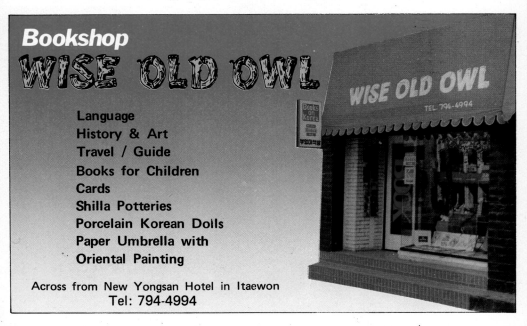

YUHAN KIMBERLY LTD.

*REGD. TRADEMARKS KIMBERLY-CLARK CORP., U.S.A.

Clean Spirit
Gentle Life

"We can trust Yuhan-Kimberly"
We at Yuhan-Kimberly always appreciate your constant supports.
Our products will be great gift with your honest wishes to your friends.
In return for your supports, we will continue to work harder.
We hope, all the people and whole society are filled with clean spirit and gentle life.

Night Life

NIGHT CLUBS:

Night clubs are usually restricted to hotels and most major hotels in the larger cities, including Kyongju, have their own hotel clubs. Only one casino is available in Seoul (located at the Sheraton Walker Hill Hotel). At Pomun Lake in Kyongju a casino and game rooms are operating under the management of the Kyongju Chosun Hotel. Also casinos have been established in the Korean Air Lines Hotel on Cheju Island and the Olympos Hotel at the port of Inchon, a 45 minute drive from Seoul.

Because of taxation night clubs can be rather expensive. Table charge usually starts at ₩3,000 per table. The cost of beer is usually ₩2,000.- per bottle and cocktails are out of sight. Most of the night clubs have live bands which perform continuously for your dancing and listening pleasure.

COCKTAIL HOUSES AND BEERHALLS:

Cocktail houses are a recent phenomena in Korea and run the full range from pleasant to "rip off" so the word to the wise is be careful and have plenty of cash with you. Often it is best to go with someone who knows his way around. Most establishments have bars and "private rooms" in which patrons may want the services of hostesses and be willing to spend money. A tip for a hostess could very well be ₩10,000 or more for just an evening of chatter. Prestige labels on drinks are unbelievably expensive. Highball prices vary from ₩1500.- to ₩2000.- a drink with brand name scotch and bourbon selling for even more. Always ask for a menu or price list before ordering if you are unfamiliar with the place.

Beer halls are cheaper and also can offer a lively entertaining evening. There are two types of Korean beer — OB and Crown. They can be ordered draft or by the bottle. You will usually be expected to order some form of side-dish

snack which might consist of mixed nuts, dried fish, vegetables or fresh fruit. If it is not crowded you are under no pressure to order immediately. Usually one waitress will serve you and it is customary to tip though not mandatory. Depending on the beer hall you may be required to pay when served or a tab may be kept until the end of the evening. Many beer halls present continuous stage shows featuring well-known talent. The cost is about ₩1500.- per bottle for beer.

MAKKOLLI HOUSES:

If you wish to indulge in an evening with less elegance but more adventure then an evening in a MAKKOLLI HOUSE (막걸리집) is recommended. This traditional common man's drinking house is located every where in Korea. The drink is a native rice brew which is milky white in color and has a not too unpleasant taste. It appears to be mild but in fact is quite potent. The side dishes served with the makkolli are even more interesting. Usually the popular houses are crowded and noisy especially as the evening wears on. At the Makkolli Houses one can order *pindaeduk* (빈대떡) a pancake paddy with vegetables. The entire evening can be fun and not too hard on your wallet.

KISAENG HOUSES:

If you should have the good fortune to be invited to a *Kisaeng* House by all means do not pass up this opportunity. It is sure to be a thoroughly entertaining night, which you will not soon forget. Many foreigners coming to Korea hear about the Korean *kisaeng* (기생) and many have been royally entertained by these very attractive girls. For the average foreigner this sudden flood of feminine attention is almost overwhelming.

The expense of an evening with *kisaeng* recreation can leave a heavy dent in one's pocketbook, so be prepared. Most foreigners come and leave this country with very little knowledge of the *kisaeng* herself and her ancient tradition. The true *kisaeng* disappeared from the Korean scene at the turn of the century but the

lure and excitement still lingers on in Korea's 20th century *kisaeng* houses. This form of evening recreation is still by far the most expensive. (For more detailed information on the *kisaeng* tradition refer to p. 311).

Tearoom Business

In the Orient the *tabang* or *tashil* of Korea is unique. Aside from offering light beverages and snacks, they serve as an invaluable social function and inexpensive place to meet . . . the young at heart . . . . . or a businessman's meeting.

The standard cost for tea or coffee will be ₩300, while a few of the elite and fashionable coffee houses (such as in hotels) will charge ₩500 or more. With more than 5,000 teahouses in Seoul it will not be difficult to find one. Look for this sign (찻집) or (다실). Each coffee shop has its own personality, decor and clientele. Many cater to the young but others draw the older set. Music varies from classical to hard rock. During the summer months cool drinks such as strawberry juice (딸기쥬스), watermelon or peach may be served. Apple drink or pineapple can be requested during some periods. A ginger tea or ginseng tea might be requested. Even a poached egg served in a dish is available upon request at most tea rooms.

In the winter for those who wish to try the more exotic ask for *hodocha* (호도차) which is a walnut tea. It is a thick soupy syrup sprinkled with pinenuts. Served hot in a covered cup, a raw egg is dropped in at the last minute. All this is mixed before drinking. If you can pass the hurdle of the raw egg you will find *hodocha* a most filling and satisfying repast.

Barley tea is always served and refills will keep coming. Upon entering a *tabang* something must be ordered initially but you may stay as long as you like, waiting for an appointment or discussing business. The girls are always pleasant and sociable. Foreigners are welcomed and will usually be escorted to the better seats if the place is not overcrowded.

Tong Yang

What do confectionery and cement have in common.

The Tong Yang Cement Manufacturing Co., Ltd., has been involved in the manufacture of cement in Korea for the past 40 years.

It has exported these products to many countries all over the world.

In 1956, Tong Yang established the Tong Yang Confectionery Co., Ltd, to meet another demand in Korea.

Since then, Tong Yang has been producing quality sweets for the children of this country.

Whatever the business. Tong Yang aims to provide the best in quality.

TONGYANG CEMENT MFG. CO., LTD.
1, EUIJU-RO, 1GA, CHUNG-GU, SEOUL, KOREA TEL.: 720/8791
TEX.: TYCEMEN K27541 CABLE: JEILCO SEOUL

TONGYANG CONF. CO., LTD.
30, MUNBAI-DONG, YONGSAN-GU, SEOUL, KOREA TEL.: 713/5011-21
TEX.: TYCOMF K25795 CABLE: CONF TONGYANG SEOUL

Korea House

Korea House, located near Taegye-ro at the foot of South Mountain, is a place that should be visited. Korea House first began under the Ministry of Culture and Information in 1956. It was renovated and reopened in February 1981. Korea House is presently managed by the Foundation for the Preservation of Cultural Properties. It is the largest single traditional Korean house in Korea today. The architectural design is in strict accordance with traditional Korean palace design patterned after Chagyong-jon in Kyongbok Palace which was used as a residence for Yi Dynasty queens.

Korean buffet lunch and dinner are offered as well as formal multicourse Korean meals. Tea and rice cakes are served in the afternoon. The selection of different types of Korean food from the various provinces is the best to be found in the Seoul area for the price. The dinnerware used in the dining areas are reproductions of ancient Korean ceramics created by noted potters.

Exhibition and sale of traditional art and handicraft include woodwork, lacquerware, metal work, pottery, rush and bamboo ware and woven items. Also traditional Korean folk music and dance performances are given at 8:30 PM every night (except Sunday) in the Korea House Theater. This theater is one of the few places in Korea where genuine Korean music and dance are presented on a regular basis. The quality is excellent and varied.

Occasionally· traditional wedding ceremonies take place at Korea House. If a tourist sees this ceremony they are indeed fortunate. From ancient times Koreans have developed a wide range of traditional musical instruments made from a variety of materials. In the lobby of Korea House over one hundred musical instruments are on display.

It is recommended that reservations be made for lunch, dinner or folk performance as early as possible as often when large groups come the facility is filled. (Tel: 267-8752)

We're the leader in the Korean foodstuff industry, fully equipped with integrated food producing facilities.

Cheil Sugar has become a multi-product foodstuff producing company by extensive investment in facilities and successful development of highly skilled manpower.

We're doing our best today to create a healthier tomorrow.

Products

Sugar	•5‍IMP, 5‍GMP, Mixed Salt	Ham, Sausage, Bacon
•Refined Granulated Sugar	Dashida	Premix
•Soft Brown Sugar	•Instant Beef Soup Stock	•Doughnut Powder Mix
•Washed Sugar	•Instant Anchovy	•Hot Cake Powder Mix
•Coffee Sugar	Soup Stock	Frying Powder Mix
•Tea Sugar		Soup
Seasoning	Flour	•Beef Soup
•Mono Sodium Glutamate	•High Protein Flour	•Mushroom Soup
•MSG Coated Salt	•Medium Protein Flour	Formulated Feed
•5‍IMP, 5‍GMP	Soybean Oil	Organic Fertilizer
Mixed MSG (AIMI)		

CHEIL SUGAR COMPANY LIMITED.

C.P.O. Box: 1155 Seoul Tel: 771-33 Telex: CHESUCO K23762
Cable Add: CHESUCO SEOUL

WHITE SNOW

Korean Names

As Koreans are a strong homogenous group the total number of family names is very few with Kim, Pak and Lee falling into the larger groups. Most Koreans have three Chinese character names with the family name placed first. For boys only one character of the given name is decided, usually by the family's ancestral charts, while the other character of the given name can be selected by the parents. For girls there is more flexibility.

Changing Korean names to Western spelling has caused diversity of spelling styles. For example the one name of (이) can be written as Lee, Yi, Rii, Rhee, I, Ee, Ree, Li, etc. This problem is common with many Korean names. Also this confusion about Korean names is further complicated by the fact that Korean women retain their maiden name even after marriage.

Usually in business Koreans really do not remember or even know the full names of individuals and refer to them by the rank of their position in the organization. This is important for it is a fact that there could be more than a dozen "Mr. Kims" in the same office area and to ask simply for a Mr. Kim is meaningless.

When one calls on the home and wishes to speak to the wife of Vice President Chung, you would not refer to her by name but would ask for the mother of the son of Vice President Chung. Hence the importance of having a son in the family because now the wife has a position.

The family trees of most Koreans have been accurately kept for many centuries with some traced to over 1500 years. Koreans have a pride in their ancestry and the origin of their family name.

Foreigners in Korea soon learn to have a card ready when meeting someone for the first time. For the Korean this is an essential way of not making a mistake in the relationship to a person's position and importance.

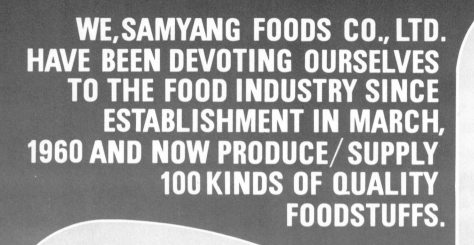

WE, SAMYANG FOODS CO., LTD. HAVE BEEN DEVOTING OURSELVES TO THE FOOD INDUSTRY SINCE ESTABLISHMENT IN MARCH, 1960 AND NOW PRODUCE/SUPPLY 100 KINDS OF QUALITY FOODSTUFFS.

INSTANT NOODLES (20 KINDS)　　　　　SAMYANG LIVESTOCK CO.

Taste plus nutrition makes
SAMYANG FOODS CO., LTD.

- INSTANT NOODLES (20 KINDS)
- SNACKS (15 KINDS)
- EDIBLE OILS (5 KINDS)
- DAIRY PRODUCTS (45 KINDS)
- SOYSAUCES (15 KINDS)
- OTHER AGRI-MARINE PRODUCTS
  :EXPORT

DAEGUANRYONG RANCH

DAIRY PRODUCTS (45 KINDS)

**Relax, even in the city—
at the Hyatt Regency Seoul.**

Indulge in the luxury of a resort hotel only seven minutes from down town. Take in a game of tennis or a refreshing swim in one of our two pools. There's also a sauna and health club.

Dine in an atmosphere of elegance and graciousness at Hugo's or discover authentic cuisine at any of the other four restaurants.

Revive your spirits at the Hyatt Regency Seoul—the hotel on the hill with the magnificent view of the city.

relax

HYATT REGENCY ⊞ SEOUL

CAPTURE THE HYATT SPIRIT WORLDWIDE

Hotels

Most of Seoul's hotels are in the center of the city. Though all of the hotels listed are adequate for foreign tourists some can be ranked in a class better than average. Reservations should be made in advance especially in the spring and fall. Most of the hotels have brochures which can be requested through travel agencies.

Followings are the list of the first class hotels in Seoul. Room prices will range from U$50.00 to U$80.00.

Deluxe ☆☆☆☆☆

Seoul

CHOSUN HOTEL (Deluxe)
87, Sokong-dong, Chung-ku, Seoul
Telex: K24256 CHOSUN
Cable: "WESTCHOSUN"
Tel: 771-05
Rooms: 470

HOTEL AMBASSADOR (Deluxe)
186-54, 2-ka, Changchung-dong, Chung-ku

Telex: K23269 AMHOSK
Cable: AMBASSADOR HOTEL SEOUL
Tel: 261-1101
Rooms: 449

HOTEL LOTTE (Deluxe)
1, Sokong-dong, Chung-ku, Seoul
Telex: LOTTEHO K28313, K23533
Cable: HOTELOTTE
Tel: 771-10
Rooms: 965

HOTEL SHILLA (Deluxe)
202, 2-ka, Changchung-dong, Chung-ku, Seoul
Telex: SHILLA K24160
Cable: HOTEL SHILLA
Tel: 255-3111
Rooms: 672

HYATT REGENCY SEOUL (Deluxe)
747-7, Hannam-dong, Yongsan-ku, Seoul
Telex: HYATT K24136
Cable: HYATT SEOUL
Tel: 795-0061/9
Rooms: 655
(see p. 344 for advertisement)

What
a refreshing way
to do business in Seoul

Sheraton Walker Hill
The Orient's most spectacular resort hotel

With 806 handsomely furnished rooms and suites, including 26 separate villa units, the impressive complex occupies an exquisitely landscaped 139 acre park.

For entertainment, there's the Kayagum Theater Restaurant with its spectacular Korean entertainment, or our 7 superb restaurants and cocktail lounges—many of which also feature entertainment.

For leisure, there are three tennis courts and golf driving range, indoor and outdoor swimming pools, Health Center, and zogging toils.

Our separate Convention Center, features the largest Banquet and Convention facilities in Korea.

The Crystal Room, Asia's most lavish casino, solely operated by the Casino Walker Hill, is located at the hotel's lower lobby and features Blackjack, Roulette, Craps, Baccarat, Tai-Sai, and more, 24 hours a day.

For reservations, call the Sheraton Hotel in your city or have your Travel Agent call Sheraton.

Sheraton Walker Hill
SHERATON HOTELS & INNS, WORLDWIDE
C.P.O. BOX 714 SEOUL, KOREA PHONE 444-8211/9
TELEX WALKHTL K28517

KING SEJONG HOTEL (Deluxe)
61-3, 2-ka, Chungmu-ro, Chung-ku, Seoul
Telex: SEJONTE K27265
Cable: HOTESEJONG
Tel: 776-4011
Rooms: 322

KOREANA HOTEL (Deluxe)
61-1, 1-ka, Taepyong-ro, Chung-ku, Seoul
Telex: KOTEL K26241
Cable: HOTELKOREANA SEOUL
Tel: 720-9911/20
Rooms: 277

OLYMPIA HOTEL (Deluxe)
108-2, Pyungchang-dong, Chongro-ku,
Seoul, Korea
Telex: K23171 SELOLYM
Cable: SELOLYM
Tel: 725-0151/5, 725-5121/5

PRESIDENT HOTEL (Deluxe)
188-3, 1-ka, Ulchi-ro, Chung-ku, Seoul
Telex: PRETEL K27521
Cable: HOTEL PRESIDENT
Tel: 753-3131/9
Rooms: 303

SEOUL GARDEN HOTEL (Deluxe)
169-1, Dohwa-dong, Mapo-ku, Seoul
Telex: SGARDEN K24742
CABLE: SGARDEN
Tel: 713-9731/9
Rooms: 410
(For military ID card holders only)

SEOUL PALACE HOTEL (Deluxe)
528, Banpo-dong, Kangnam-ku, Seoul
Telex: PALACHL K22657
Cable: SELPALCEHTL
Tel: 532-0101, 1818, 4100, 5000
Rooms: 320

SEOUL PLAZA HOTEL (Deluxe)
23, 2-ka, Taepyong-ro, Chung-ku, Seoul
Telex: K26215
Cable: PLAZA HL SEOUL
Tel: 771-22
Rooms: 540

SEOUL ROYAL HOTEL (Deluxe)
6, 1-ka, Myong-dong, Chung-ku, Seoul
Telex: SLROYAL K27239
Cable: ROYALHOTEL
Tel: 771-45
Rooms: 319

SHERATON WALKER HILL (Deluxe)
San 21, Kwangjang-dong, Songdong-ku, Seoul
Telex: WALKHTL K28517
Cable: WAKLERHILL SEOUL
Tel: 444-8211/9
Rooms: 806
(see p. 352 for advertisement)

HILTON INTERNATIONAL (Deluxe)
395, 5-ka, Namdaemun-ro, Chung-ku, Seoul
Telex: K26695 K HILTON
Cable: HILTELS SEOUL
Tel: 753-4514
Rooms: 712
(To open fall 1983)

☆☆☆☆ **or** ☆☆☆

Followings are the list of the second class hotels in Seoul. Room prices will range from $30.00 to U$45.00

ACADEMY HOUSE
San 76, Suyu-dong, Tobong-ku, Seoul
Tel: 989-1181/5

ASTORIA HOTEL
13-2, Namhak-dong, Chung-ku, Seoul
Tel: 267-7111/8
Rooms: 80

BANDO YOUTH HOSTEL
San 60-13, Yuksam-dong, Kangnam-ku, Seoul
Tel: 567-2141/5

BUKAK PARK HOTEL
113-1, Pyongchang-dong, Chongro-ku,
Cable: SEL PARK
Tel: 724-7101/8
Rooms: 134

CROWN HOTEL
34-69, Itaewon-dong, Yongsan-ku, Seoul
Telex: CROWNTH K25951
Cable: HOTEL CROWN
Tel: 792-8224
Rooms: 127

EMPIRE HOTEL
63, Mukyo-dong, Chung-ku, Seoul
Telex: K23480 EMPIRE
Cable: EMPIREHOTEL
Tel: 777-5511
Rooms: 120

GREEN PARK HOTEL
San 14, Ui-dong, Tobong-ku, Seoul
Telex: METROHO K26486
Cable: METROHO
Tel: 993-2171/9
Room: 92

HAMILTON HOTEL
119-25, Itaewon-dong, Yongsan-ku, Seoul
Telex: KSHAMIL K24491
Cable: HOTEL HAMILTON
Tel: 794-0171/7
Rooms: 139

MAMMOTH HOTEL
620-69, Chonnong-dong, Tongdaemun-ku
Seoul
Telex: K27241
Cable: MAMMOTH HOTEL
Tel: 435-3131/9
Rooms 219

METRO HOTEL
199-33, 2-ka, Ulchi-ro, Chung-ku, Seoul
Telex: METROHO K26486
Cable: METROHOTEL SEOUL
Tel: 776-8221/7
Rooms: 83

NAM SEOUL HOTEL
San 78-23, Nonhyun-dong, Kangnam-ku,
Seoul
Telex: NASOTEL K25019
Cable: NASOTEL
Tel: 562-7111/9
Rooms: 179

NEW KUKJE HOTEL
29-2, 1-ka, Taepyong-ro, Chung-ku, Seoul
Telex: K24760
Cable: NEW KUKJE HOTEL
Tel: 722-0161/9
Rooms: 149

NEW NAIJA HOTEL
201-9, Naija-dong, Chongro-ku, Seoul
Cable: NEW NAIJA HOTEL
Tel: 723-9011/5
Room: 80

NEW SEOUL HOTEL
29-1, 1-ka, Taepyong-ro, Chung-ku, Seoul
Telex: K27220
Cable: SELOTEL
Tel: 725-9071/9
Rooms: 151

NEW SKY HOTEL
108-2, Pyongchang-dong, Chongro-ku,
Seoul
Telex: K23171
Cable: NEWSKY
Tel: 725-5121/5

NEW YONGSAN HOTEL
737-32, Hannam-dong, Yongsan-ku,
Seoul
Telex: SJINE K26358
Tel: 795-0051/8
Room: 56

PACIFIC HOTEL
31-1, 2-ka, Namsan-dong, Chung-ku, Seoul
Telex: K26249 PACITEL
Cable: HOTEL PACIFIC
Tel: 752-5101/9
Rooms: 103

PALACE TOURIST HOTEL
92-6, 1-ka, Hoihyun-dong, Chung-ku,
Seoul
Tel: 777-7731/9

POONG JUN HOTEL
73-1, 2-ka, Inhyun-dong, Chung-ku,
Seoul
Cable: HOTEL POONGJUN
Tel: 266-2151/9
Room: 227

PRINCE HOTEL
1, 2-ka, Namsan-dong, Chung-ku, Seoul
Telex: PRINCE K25918
Cable: HOTEL PRINCE
Tel: 752-7111/5
Room: 87

RIVERSIDE HOTEL
342, Sinsa-dong, Kangnam-ku, Seoul
Tel: 556-1001
Rooms: 230

SAMCHUNG HOTEL
604-11, Yueksam-dong, Kangnam-ku,
Seoul, Korea
Tel: 557-1221, 556-8374, 8376, 8431
Rooms: 170

SAVOY HOTEL
23-1, 1-ka, Chungmu-ro, Chung-ku, Seoul
Telex: SAVOY K23222
Cable: SAVOY HOTEL
Tel: 776-2641/9
Room: 107

SEOUL BANDO HOTEL
1-75, Yoido-dong, Yongdeungpo-ku,
Seoul
Telex: BANDO K24767
Cable: SELBANDO
Tel: 782-8001/11
Rooms: 272

SEOULIN HOTEL
149, Seoulin-dong, Chongro-ku, Seoul
Telex: SEOULIN K28510
Cable: HOTEL SEOULIN
Tel: 722-0181/8
Rooms: 216

SEOUL HOTEL
92, Chongjin-dong, Chongro-ku,
Seoul
Cable: OYANG TEL
Tel: 725-9001/5
Rooms: 102

TOWER HOTEL
San 5-5, 2-ka, Changchung-dong, Chung-ku,
Seoul
Telex: TOWER K28246
Cable: TOWERTEL
Tel: 253-9181/9
Rooms: 245

YONGDONG HOTEL
238-3, Sinsa-dong, Kangnam-ku, Seoul
Tel: 556-7883/5
Rooms: 160

YOIDO HOTEL
1-496, Yoido-dong, Yongdeungpo-ku,
Seoul
Cable: YOIDHOTEL
Tel: 782-0121/5
Rooms: 120

Pusan

CHOSUN BEACH HOTEL (Deluxe)
73-7, Wooil-dong, Haeundae-ku, Pusan
Telex: CHOSUN B K3718
Cable: WESTCHOSUN BUSAN
Tel: 72-7411/20
Rooms: 333

COMMODORE DYNASTY HOTEL (Deluxe)
743-80, Yongju-dong, Chung-ku, Pusan
Telex: COMOTEL K3717
Cable: COMMODORE BUSAN
Tel: 44-9101/7
Rooms: 325

CROWN HOTEL (Deluxe)
830-30, Pomil-dong, Tong-ku, Pusan
Telex: CROWN B. K3422
Tel: 69-1241/7
Rooms: 135

BANDO HOTEL
36, 4-ka, Chungang-dong, Chung-ku,
Pusan
Tel: 44-0561
Rooms: 146

BUSAN HOTEL
12, 2-ka, Tongkwang-dong, Chung-ku,
Pusan
Telex: BSHOTEL K3657
Cable: BUSANHOTEL
Tel: 23-4301/9
Rooms: 289

BUSAN PLAZA HOTEL
90-15, 3-ka, Taechang-dong, Tong-ku,
Pusan
Cable: PLAZA BUSAN
Tel: 45-5011/9
Rooms: 123

BUSAN ROYAL HOTEL
2-72, 2-ka, Kwangbok-dong, Chung-ku,
Pusan
Telex: BROYAL K3824
Cable: ELEPHANTEL
Tel: 23-1051/9
Rooms: 121

The house of Ssangyong stands secure.

When we built Ssangyong we made sure that we stood on solid foundation.
Cement, oil refining, machinery, chemical manufacturing . . . .
These are the building blocks of a modern industrial society.
Through our dependability and the quality of our products, we have contributed to Korea's progress. But we haven't stopped there. Now you find us in more than a dozen enterprises. . . . marine shipping and transport, insurance construction, paper, engineering, electronics, and university, while sponsoring academic and cultural foundations. We export cement, fertilizers, iron and steel products, rolling stock, diesel engines, cars, motorcycles. . . . and much more. Customers from six continents have come to rely on us. Try us. You will agree.

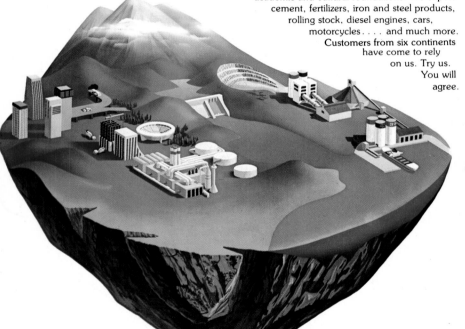

SSANGYONG

BUSAN TOWER HOTEL
20, 3-ka, Tongkwang-dong, Chung-ku,
Pusan, Korea
Tel: 23-5151/9
Rooms: 108

FERRY HOTEL
37-16, 4-ka, Chungang-dong, Chung-ku,
Pusan
Tel: 45-0881/90
Rooms: 122

HOTEL BUSAN ARIRANG
86-1, 3-ka, Taechang-dong, Tong-ku,
Pusan
Telex: HOTEL AR K3707
Cable: HOTEL BUSAN ARIRANG
Tel: 45-5001/8
Rooms: 121

HOTEL PHOENIX
8-1, 2-ka, Chungmu-dong, Chung-ku,
Pusan
Telex: PNIXTEL K3704
Tel: 22-8061/9
Rooms: 120

HOTEL TONGYANG
27, 1-ka, Kwangbok-dong, Chung-ku,
Pusan
Tel: 22-1205

KUKDONG HOTEL
1124, Chung-dong, Tongnae-ku, Pusan
Telex: KUKDONG K3758
Cable: HOTEL KUKDONG BUSAN
Tel: 72-0081/90
Rooms: 108

MOONHWA TOURIST HOTEL
517-65, Pujon-dong, Pusanjin-ku, Pusan
Cable: MOONHWA HOTEL
Tel: 66-8001/7
Rooms: 93

NEW PORT HOTEL
31-18, 3-ka, Taech'ang-dong, Tong-ku,
Pusan
Cable: HOTEL NEWPORT
Tel: 43-8001/6
Rooms: 92

PARADISE BEACH HOTEL
1408-5, Chung-dong, Haeundae-ku,
Pusan
Cable: HOTEL HAEUNDAE
Tel: 72-1461/8
Rooms: 38

TONGNAE HOTEL
212, Onchon-dong, Tongnae-ku, Pusan
Tel: 52-1121/7
Rooms: 80

Kyongju

KYONGJU CHOSUN HOTEL (Deluxe)
410, Sinpyong-dong, Kyongju-si,
Kyongsangpuk-do
Telex: CHOSUN K4467
Cable: WESTCHOSUN KYO
Tel: 2-9600/19
Rooms: 304

KOLON HOTEL (Deluxe)
111-1, Ma-dong, Kyongju-si,
Kyongsangpuk-do
Telex: K4469
Cable: KOLHTL
Tel: 2-9001/14
Rooms: 240

KYONGJU TOKYU HOTEL (Deluxe)
410, Shinpyong-dong, Kyongju-si,
Kyongsanpuk-do
Telex: KJ TOKYU K4328
Cable: KYONGJU TOKYU
Tel: 2-9901/16
Rooms: 303

KYONGJU TOURIST HOTEL
406-2, Songdong-dong, Kyongju-si,
Kyongsangpuk-do
Tel: 2-3821/8
Rooms: 107

DABO YOUTH HOTEL
145-1, Kujong-dong, Kyongsangpuk-do
Tel: Kyongju 2-3882
     Seoul 778-9906

SALES IN SIGHT- A BRIGHT PROSPECT

Our production begins with raw cotton to the finished products, including spinning, knitting, dyeing, cutting and sewing.

We are ready to serve our buyers at competitive prices with the following goods.

*Ladies' and men's wear
*Sportswear
*Ladies' and men's underwear
*Pajamas
*Knitted fabric
*Cotton & cotton blended yarns from 10's to 120's
*Cotton & polyester/cotton blended sewing thread

SSANG BANG WOOL LTD.

C.P.O. Box 6672, Seoul, Korea
Cable: "SSANGBANGWOOL" SEOUL
Telex: GOODWIL K26262
Tel.: 254-2101/2, 253-9885/7

Cheju

CHEJU KAL HOTEL (Deluxe)
1691-9, 2-do 1-dong, Cheju-si, Cheju-do
Cable: CHEJUKALHTEL
Tel: 2-6151
Rooms: 310

CHEJU GRAND HOTEL (Deluxe)
263, Youn-dong, Cheju-si, Cheju-do
Telex: GRANHTL K712
Cable: CHEJUGRANHTL
Tel: 7-2131/41
Rooms: 522

HOTEL CHEJU ROYAL
272-34, Youn-dong, Cheju-si, Cheju-do
Tel: 7-4161/80

HOTEL PARADISE CHEJU
1315, 2-do 1-dong, Cheju-si, Cheju-do
Telex: PARAHTL K-728
Cable: PARADISE JEJU HTL
Tel: 3-0171/5, 2-3114
Rooms: 57

HOTEL PARADISE SOGWIPO
674-1, Sokwi 3-ri, Sokwi-up, Namcheju-kun, Cheju-do
Telex: PARAHTL K728
Cable: PARADISE JEJU HTL
Tel: 2-2161/7
Rooms: 90

SEOGWIPO LIONS HOTEL
803, Sokwi 2-ri, Sokwi-up, Namcheju-kun, Cheju-do
Tel: 2-4141/4

YOGWAN BRIEFS (Korean Inns)

There are hundreds of Korean Inns or *yogwan* (여관) throughout the country. Though some luxurious comforts admittedly may be absent there are many aspects to recommend that the tourist should stay at a typical Korean inn. Even in Seoul a comfortable *yogwan* can easily be found with prices ranging under $20.00. In the countryside prices for a *ondol* room will range from $10.00 to $15.00 per night. Usually the room is rented with minimal charge for additional people. Your shoes must be taken off before entering the room.

Clean bedding is brought and spread out on the floor. The smaller mattress called a *yo* is used beneath while the quilt called a *ibul* is used for covering. The pillow is usually filled with rice husks and is quite hard and thick. In the summer a mosquito repellent is often handy though some *yogwan* do provide nets.

In winter the *ondol* floor is heated. This system of heating was first used two thousand years ago. In rooms which are used night after night there is little danger from noxious fumes yet it is always wise to leave some outside ventilation. Some Korean inns now have bathing facilities in the rooms or down the hall. In most towns there will be a public bath house within easy walking distance. Bathing is segregated. There is no mixed bathing in Korea.

Food can be ordered at the *yogwan* though it will be typically Korean in style. The meal price will range from $2.00 — $3.00. Most foreigners take their own snacks and even some minor cooking can be done at the *yogwan* with little camp burners. Plan to rough it more when you stay at a *yogwan* and if you remember to be patient you will find that *yogwan* traveling about Korea can provide some of your most pleasant memories.

This writer has found many of the tourist hotels lacking in courtesy and technical knowledge or Western hotel management, especially outside the capital city. Korean inns are usually managed by a family and the friendly atmosphere frequently prevalent in most *yogwan* will quickly convince you of the genuine service the Korean inn offers to the traveling tourist both Korean and foreign. If you would like to stay in a better class *yogwan* request your tourist agency to make the arrangements.

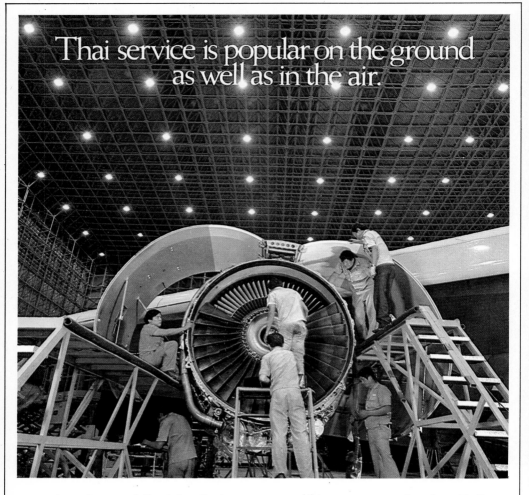

Thai service is popular on the ground as well as in the air.

More and more airlines that fly into Bangkok are entrusting their aircraft to Thai for servicing. And that makes us very proud. Because it shows just how highly regarded our maintenance crews are.

To help them we've installed some of the most advance equipment in the world in our new engine shop. Built a giant hangar for our 747 Jumbos. And instigated advanced training courses.

That's why other airlines appreciate our ground services, almost as much as we do.

Thai
Smooth as silk.

Proud to be Thai

Airline Agencies

Air France
2nd Floor of Chosun Hotel
Tel: 752-1027

Air India
Rm. 225 Chosun Hotel
Tel: 28-0069, 771-05 (Ext. 277)

Air Siam Company
1st Floor, Chosun Hotel
Tel: 752-0824, 753-0824

Alitalia Airlines
Rm. 111, Chosun Hotel
Tel: 779-1676/8

American Airlines
Rm. 1st Fl. Chosun Hotel
Tel: 28-3314

Canadian Pacific Airlines
Rm. 150 Chosun Hotel
Tel: 753-8271/5

Cargolux Airlines International
202-3, 1-ka, Haehyun-dong,
C.P.O. Box 7222, Seoul
Tel: 752-2700

Cathay Pacific Airways Ltd.
1st & 7th Floors, Kolon Bldg.
Tel: 779-0321/9

China Airlines
2nd Floor, Chosun Hotel
Tel: 28-3678

Delta Airlines
1st Floor New Korea Bldg.
Tel: 753-8087

Eastern Airlines
Rm. 1st. Floor, Chosun Hotel
Tel: 777-9786

Flying Tiger Line, Inc.
91-1, Sokong-dong, Chung-ku, Seoul
Tel: 776-5491/4

Japan Air Lines
1st Floor, Baiknam Bldg.
Tel: 777-8081/4

KLM Royal Dutch Airlines
2nd Floor, Chosun Hotel
87, Sokong-dong, Chung-ku, Seoul
Tel: 777-2495

Korean Air Lines
KAL Building
C.P.O. Box 864, Seoul
Tel: 28-5223/4
(see p. 364 for advertisement)

Lufthansa German Airlines
1st Floor, Chosun Hotel
Tel: 777-9655/6
(see p. 363 for advertisement)

Malaysian Airline System
1st Floor, Lotte Hotel
Tel: 777-7761/2

Northwest Orient Airlines Inc.
2nd Floor, Chosun Hotel
Tel: 753-6106

Pakistan Int'l Airlines
Rm. 110, Chosun Hotel
Tel: 28-6994

Pan America World Airways (PAA)
Rm. 312, New Korea Bldg.
Tel: 777-7701/3

Scandinavian Airlines System
2nd Floor, Chosun Hotel
Tel: 779-2621/5

Singapore Airlines
2nd Floor, Chosun Hotel
Tel: 753-2244
(see p. 362 for advertisement)

Swiss Air Transport Co., Ltd.
Tel: 753-8271/5

Thai Airways International Ltd.
2nd Floor, Chosun Hotel
C.P.O. Box 1330, Seoul
Tel: 779-2624/6
(see p. 360 for advertisement)

Trans Mediterranean Airways
Rm. 702, Samil Bldg.
Tel: 777-5764/5

Trans World Airlines
Rm. 150, Chosun Hotel

United Airlines
Rm. 312, New Korea Bldg.
Tel: 753-5107

Varig Brazilian Airlines
2nd Floor, New Korea Bldg.
Tel: 28-4305

The airline with the most modern fleet in the world,
still believes in the romance of travel.

We care enough not to have your wife wait late for you at the airport.

When you're late, a waiting wife can become anxious or even worried. We at Lufthansa take special care in assuring that our flights from Frankfurt and 57 other destinations in Europe, depart . . . and arrive on time. Punctuality . . . one of many qualities for which Lufthansa is famous.

Lufthansa
German Airlines

We show our honored guests

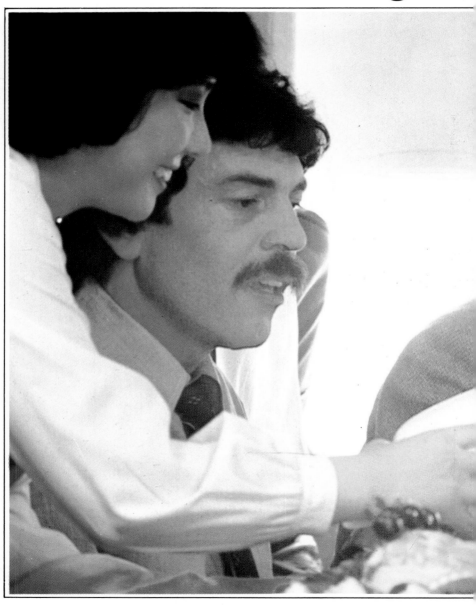

As an honored guest on Korean, you'll experience all the warm hospitality and service that is part of Korea's heritage. Hospitality and service, that is measured by the smile on your face.

all the comforts of home.

![KAL] **KOREAN AIR LINES**
We treat you as an honored guest.

AIRPORT DUTY FREE SHOPS

A Pleasure for Seasoned travellers!

Savings up to 50%

Enjoy shopping with the most reasonable prices at Airpot Duty Free Shops before leaving Korea. Various goods from all over the world await your wide selection.

 KOREA NATIONAL TOURISM CORPORATION

Kimpo (Seoul), Kimhae (Pusan), Cheju Int'l Airport & Pukwan (Pusan) Ferry Terminal.

Travel Agencies

Aju Tourist Service
Tel: 753-5051
Rm. 606, Kyongseo Bldg.
26, Seosomun-dong, Chung-ku, Seoul

American Express Representative
Tel: 28-9260
87, Sogong-dong, Chung-ku,
C.P.O. Box 1330, Seoul

Asia Travel Service Co., Ltd.
Tel: 776-5501/3
72-2, Eulzi-ro, Chung-ku, Seoul

Dong You Travel Service
Tel: 752-2700, 752-7324
C.P.O. Box 7222, Seoul

Global Tour, Ltd.
Tel: 752-4431
C.P.O. Box 2944, Seoul

Hanjin Travel Service Co.
Tel: 778-0331/9
3Fl., KAL Bldg.
C.P.O. Box 389, Seoul

Hannam Travel Service
Tel: 713-5507/8
61-1, Taepyungro-1ka, Seoul
Tel: 724-5507/8

Kodco Travel Agency
Tel: 793-1355
14-20, 1-ka, Hangang-ro, Yo ngsan-ku,
Seoul

Korea Tourist Bureau Ltd. (KTB)
Tel: 722-1191/5
198-1, Kwanhoon-dong, Chongro-ku,
C.P.O. Box 3533, Seoul

Korea Travel Service, Inc.
Tel: 777-7151/5
17-12, 4-ka, Namdaemun-ro, Chung-ku,
C.P.O. Box 7903, Seoul

Korean National Tourism Corp. (KNTC)
Tel: 261-7001/6
60-1, Chungmu-ro 3-ka, Chung-ku, Seoul
C.P.O. Box 1493, Seoul

Kyung Choon Tourist Co., Ltd.
Tel: 777-6681/4
24-2, Mugyo-dong, Chung-ku, Seoul

Kyung Nam Tourist Co., Ltd.
Tel: 777-8711/6
112-9, Sogong-dong, Chung-ku, Seoul

Lotte Travel Service, Ltd.
Tel: 723-0201/3
228, Kwanchul-dong, Chongro-ku, Seoul

New World Tourist Service Co.
Tel: 265-0041/3
17-8, Cho-dong, 2-ka, Chung-ku, Seoul

Orient Express Corporation
Tel: 752-4071/4
69-23, 2-ka, Taepyung-ro, Chung-ku, Seoul

Pana Travel Service
Tel: 777-7961
C.P.O. Box 2662, Seoul

Universal Travel Service Co., Ltd.
Tel: 725-0001
C.P.O. Box 2196, Seoul

Department Stores

Lotte Shopping Center
1, Sokong-dong, Chung-ku, Seoul
Tel: 771-25

Mammoth Dept. Store
620-69, Chunnong-dong, Tongdaemun-ku
Tel: 435-3131

Midopa Department Store
123, Namdaemun-ro, Chung-ku
Tel: 754-2222
(see p. 369 for advertisement)

Sarona Department Store
1-2, Namchang-dong, Chung-ku
Tel: 778-8170/9

Shinsegae Department Store
52-5, 1-ka, Chungmu-ro, Chung-ku
(C.P.O. Box 200, Seoul)
Tel: 753-2181/9
(see p. 368 for advertisement)

AS THE WHOLE HEARTEDNESS
TO RAISE A LOVELY ROSE.

Having a good stock of a wide variety
of quality articles, we always give our
whole mind to make our Department store,
the best place of pleasant shopping.

- MIDOPA MYONG DONG STORE ☎ 754-2222
- MIDOPA CHONGRYANGRI STORE ☎ 213-2301

MIDOPA

■Business hours 10:30A.M. − 7:30P.M.

Global Education in a Progressive Climate

New Campus soon to be opened

PRE-SCHOOL THROUGH HIGH SCHOOL

- * Fully Certified Teachers
- * U.S. Curriculum
- * Advanced Placement Courses Offered
- * Low Teacher-Pupil Ratio

Accreditied by Western Association of Schools and Colleges
Member of the East Asia Regional Council of Overseas Schools

SEOUL INTERNATIONAL SCHOOL

4-1 Hwayang-dong, Songdong-ku, Seoul, Korea Tel. 445-2119, 445-6091, YS7883

Foreign Schools

Department of Defense Dependent Schools, DODD Schools, APO 96301
Tel: YS-4378, 7904-4905, 7904-5922
(grades 1-12)
Schools are located on the Yongsan Military Compound and open only to dependents of command sponsored US military personnel. (DODD Schools are also located in Osan, Taegu, Pusan and Chinhae.)

Korea Christian Academy (KCA)
210-3, Ojung-dong, Taejon
Tel: (Taejon) 2-2662 (grades K-12)
KCA is located on the outskirts of Taejon City in central Korea and is operated primarily for children of missionary families. A dormitory is available for the older students. US curriculum is used. Religious instruction is required.

Seoul Foreign School (SFS)
55, Yunhi-dong, Sodaemun-ku, Seoul
Tel: 322-3660, YS-6301 (grades K-12)
Initially opened as a school for children of Protestant missionaries, SFS now caters to the entire foreign community. Religious instruction is still required. A standard US curriculum is maintained. SFS is located near the Yonsei University campus in Western Seoul.

Seoul International School (SIS)
4-1, Hwayang-dong, Songdong-ku, Seoul (see p. 370 for advertisement)
Tel: 445-2119, 445-6091, YS-7883
(grades K-12)
SIS is the only private international school in Korea that is not affiliated with a company or religious group, kindergarten through grade twelve. In 1973 SIS became the first foreign school to be officially licensed by the ROK Ministry of Education. Located in southeastern Seoul, SIS has been the fastest growing multinational school over the past ten years and in 1983 moved to its new campus south of the Han River. The curriculum is consistent with the philosophy set forth by most US schools with cross cultural adjustments unique in overseas schools. SIS, as well as SFS and KCA, are fully accredited by the Western Association of Schools and Colleges (WASC) in California.

KorAm Bank:
A Joint Venture Bank with Bank of America and The Seventh Nationwide City Bank in Korea Offers Advanced Banking Know-How.

KorAm Opens March 16

KorAm Bank conveys its greetings on the occasion of its grand opening. The seventh nationwide city bank in Korea, KorAm is a joint venture between Bank of America, one of the world's largest banks and major business groups in Korea. Drawing on the strong points of both Korean and American banks, KorAm will offer new banking methods and abundant financial information to you in an expedient manner. KorAm is concerned with only service to their customers and wants to become your partner in planning for the next 10 to 20 years of your tomorrows.

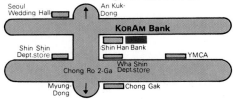

KORAM BANK

Head Office: Hanmie Building. #1, Gongpyung-dong, Chongro-gu, Seoul 110, Korea Telephone: 744-8800 K.P.O. Box: 1084
Telex No.: K27814, K27815, K27816, Cable Address; KORAMBANK, SEOUL, KOREA

Foreign Embassies

Embassy of the Argentine Republic
135-53, Itaewon-dong, Yongsan-ku,
C.P.O. Box 3889, Seoul
Tel: 793-4062

Embassy of Australian Commonwealth
5th Floor, Kuktong Shell House
58-1, 1-ka, Sinmun-ro, Chongro-ku, Seoul
K.P.O. Box 562
Tel: 720-6491/5

Embassy of Austria
10, Kwanchul-dong, Chongro-ku,
25 Floor, Samil Bldg.
C.P.O. Box 6417 Seoul
Tel: 722-6649

Embassy of the Kingdom of Belgium
1-65, Dongbinggo-dong, Yongsan-ku,
Seoul
Tel: 720-4565

Embassy of the Federative Republic of Brazil
3rd Floor, New Korea Bldg.
192-11, 1-ka, Ulchi-ro, Chung-ku,
C.P.O. Box 2164, Seoul
Tel: 720-4769

Embassy of Canada
10Fl. Kolon Bldg.
45, Mugyo-dong, Chongro-ku,
Seoul, C.P.O. Box 6299
Tel: 776-4062

Embassy of Chile
142-5, Itaewon-dong, Yongsan-ku
C.P.O. Box 7398, Seoul
Tel: 792-9519

Embassy of the Republic of China
83, 2-ka, Myong-dong, Chung-ku, Seoul
Tel: 776-2721/5

Embassy of Denmark
260-199, Itaewon-dong, Yongsan-ku,
C.P.O. Box 3364 Seoul
Tel: 792-4187/9

Embassy of Finland
1-1, Chongro-1ka, Chongro-ku, Seoul
Tel: 722-6223

Embassy of the French Republic
30, Hap-dong, Sodaemun-ku, Seoul
Tel: 362-5547

Embassy of the Gabonese Republic
43-2, Nonhyun-dong, Kangnam-ku, Seoul
Tel: 562-9912

Embassy of the Federal Republic of Germany
51-1, Namchang-dong, Chung-ku, Seoul
Tel: 779-3271/3

Holy See (Office of the Apostolic Nuncio)
2, Kungjung-dong, Chongro-ku, Seoul
Tel: 722-5725

Embassy of the Republic of Guatemala
A-206, Namsan Village Apt.
Itaewon-dong, Yongsan-ku, Seoul
Tel: 793-3721

Embassy of India
7-48, Dongbinggo-dong, Yongsan-ku,
Seoul
Tel: 793-4142

Embassy of the Republic of Indonesia
1-887, Yoido-dong, Yongdungpo-ku,
Seoul
Tel: 782-5116/8

Embassy of Iran
726-126, Hannam-dong, Yongsan-ku,
Seoul
Tel: 793-7751/3

Embassy of the Italian Republic
1-169, 2-ka, Shinmun-ro Chongro-ku,
Seoul
Tel: 724-7405

Embassy of Japan
18-11, Chunghak-dong, Chongro-ku,
Seoul
Tel: 723-5626/9

Embassy of Malaysia
726-115, Hannam-dong, Yongsan-ku,
Seoul
Tel: 792-9203

Embassy of the United Mexican States
House 142, Namsan Village
New Itaewon-dong, Yongsan-ku,
Seoul
Tel: 795-0380

Royal Netherlands Embassy
1-48, Dongbinggo-dong, Yongsan-ku,
Seoul
Tel: 793-0651/2

Royal Norwegian Embassy
124-12, Itaewon-dong, Yongsan-ku, Seoul
Tel: 792-6850, 792-6851

Embassy of New Zealand
105-2, Sagan-dong, Chongro-ku, Seoul
Tel: 720-4255

Embassy of the Republic of Panama
98-78, Wooni-dong, Chongro-ku, Seoul
Tel: 720-4164

Embassy of the Republic of Peru
House 129, Namsan-Village,
Itaewon-dong, Yongsan-ku, Seoul
Tel: 792-2235, 792-3669

Embassy of the Republic of the Philippines
559-510, Yuksam-dong, Kangnam-ku,
Seoul
Tel: 569-9434

Embassy of Saudi Arabia
1-112, 2-ka, Sinmun-ro, Chongro-ku, Seoul
Tel: 725-9263

Embassy of the Kingdom of Sweden
108-2, Pyung-dong, Chongro-ku, Seoul
724-0864

Embassy of the Swiss Confederation
32-10, Songwol-dong, Sodaemun-ku,
Seoul
Tel: 723-7876, 720-4861

Royal Thai Embassy
House 133, Namsan Village, Itaewon-
dong, Yongsan-ku, Seoul
Tel: 792-3098, 793-1301/5

Embassy of the Republic of Turkey
339-294, Songbuk-dong, Songbuk-ku,
Seoul
Tel: 762-1571

Embassy of the United Kingdom
4, Chung-dong, Chongro-ku, Seoul
Tel: 725-7341/3, YS-6942

Embassy of the United States of America
82, Sejong-ro, Chongro-ku, Seoul
Tel: 722-2601/19

Embassy of Uruguay
60-27, Hannam-dong, Yongsan-ku, Seoul
Tel: 795-0561

HONORARY CONSULAR MISSIONS:

Consulate of Central African Republic
302-61 Ichon-dong, Yongsan-ku
C.P.O. Box 3232, Seoul
Tel: 793-4475

Consulate of Costa Rica
258-59, Itaewon-dong, Yongsan-ku, Seoul
Tel: 792-9847

Consulate of El Salvador
1-16, Eulzi-ro, Chung-ku, Seoul
Tel: 720-4179, 777-2790

Consulate of Greece
34, Susomun-dong, Chung-ku, Seoul
Tel: 752-9662

Consulate of Jordan
58-12, Susomun-dong, Chung-ku, Seoul
Tel. 771-21, 753-9785

Consulate of Liberia
1-866, Yeuido-dong, Yongdungpo-ku,
Seoul
Tel: 720-4256, 782-1820

Consulate of Nicaragua
57-9, Susomun-dong, Chung-ku, Seoul
Tel: 752-0165

Civic Organizations

American Chamber of Commerce	753-6471
American Cultural Center	722-2601
American Legion Int'l Club	51-1046
American Red Cross	YS-3888
Boy Scouts of America	YS-4890
Boy Scouts of Korea	782-1867
Christian Literature Society of Korea	724-1792
Christian Servicemen Center	YS-6445
Clark Hatch's Physical Fitness Center	752-5269
Cultural & Social Center for the Asian and Pacific Region (ASPAC)	633-7822
Eighth Army Golf Club	7904-4340
Eighth Army Officers Club	YS-5988
Family Sports Club	793-5653
Fulbright House	752-0273
Girls Scouts of America	YS-4890
Girl Scouts of Korea	723-4347
Hankang Bowling Center	794-7041
Harvard Business Club of Korea	753-7750
Hillside House (Servicemen's Center)	794-6951
International Cultural Society of Korea (ICSK)	753-6461
Int'l Human Assistance Program	723-0231
International Pen Club (Korea Chapter)	725-9854
International Press Institute	724-6055
Int'l Society for Oriental Medicine	724-7388
Journalists Association of Korea (JAK)	725-6851
Korea Amateur Sports Assoc.	777-6081
Korea America Friendship Assoc.	783-6137
Korea Art & Culture Promotion	762-5230
Korea Assoc. of Registered Architects q	723-9491
Korea Assoc. of Voluntary Agencies	269-6973

Korea Chamber of Commerce	777-8031
Korea Foreigners Counselling Service	32-4647
Korea Golf Association	266-0487
Korea Ho use	266-9101
Korea National Tourism Corp.	261-7001
Korea Social Communication Research Institute ("Korea Friend" Newsletter)	722-2853
Korea Tourist Association	724-2702
Korea Trade Promotion Corp. (KOTRA)	753-4181
Korea Trade Service Center	778-2151
Korea Trading Agencies Assoc.	782-2205
Korean American Assoc.	753-1876
Korean American Business Institute	725-4181
Korean Classical Music Association	724-7908
Korean National Red Cross	777-9301
Korean Scuba Diving Club	92-9065
Korean Traders' Association	268-8251
Korean Veterans Association	269-5171
Lions International (Dist. 309-Korea)	266-8566
Lutheran Servicemen's Center	794-6274
Moyer Service Club (8th Army)	7904-3921
Naija R & R Center	753-5580
Namsan Athletic Club	792-0131
Red Cross of Korea	777-9301
Royal Asiatic Society (RAS)	763-9483
Sae Seoul Lions Club	462-9093
Scandinavian Club	265-9279
Seoul Club	362-3129
Seoul Jaycees	244-6023
Seoul Union Club (inter-church)	752-2871
UNESCO	776-3950
UNICEF	725-2315
UNDP	633-9451
Union Church (Interdenominational)	724-4772
USO Club	YS-7301 793-3478
YWCA	777-5725
YMCA	722-8291
Yongsan Library	YS-3380
YWCA	777-5725

Useful Telephone Numbers

Ambulance		
National Medical Center		265-9130
Sacred Heart		776-1002
Severance		322-0161
US Army		YS-4581
Antique Clearance		
Certificate Office		725-3053
Arirang Taxi Service	YS-5113	792-7348
Emergency (US Embassy)		YS-110
Fire		119
Florist (Telegram)		752-5643
Information (Local)		114
(Yongsan)		113

KIT Overseas Telephones & Telegraph		720-4424
Lost & Found Center		752-8639
Overseas Operator		117
Police (Local)		112
Police (US Military)		29-1110
Power Failure		777-3111
Seoul Immigration Office		724-4178
SOFA	YS-6771	792-0460
Telegram by phone (local)		115
Telegram by phone (int'l)		115
Telephone Trouble		prefix. 1166
Towing	YS-5572	792-8132
Weather		723-0011
Commercial Line to Yongsan Line		prefix. 0011
Yongsan Line to Commercial Line		prefix. 9

The Royal Asiatic Society (RAS)

The RAS is Korea's most active cultural society for those interested in tours, publications and outstanding lectures. The Korea Branch of the Royal Asiatic Society (RAS) was founded in 1900 by a group of foreigners living in Seoul who were interested in learning about the history and culture of Korea. Affiliated with the prestigious RAS of London it has continued its productive activities for over 75 years with some interruption during the war period. Today it offers a great variety of privileges and opportunities while visitors are always welcomed.

For a place to buy books on Korea in English the RAS offers the largest complete selection of books for sale. The office has normal hours Monday through Friday. Semi-monthly meetings are usually held on Wednesday evening throughout the year, presenting highly diversified programs. There is no admission charge. During the spring and fall RAS tours highlight most weekends and are conducted by knowledgeable leaders. Members are given discount on tours and publications.

Members are placed on a mailing list and will receive all information concerning tour and lecture schedules. Also members may retain their membership after departing Korea at reduced rates.

Yearly *Transactions* of the RAS are given to members without charge.

Tel. 763-9483

International Cultural Society of Korea (ICSK)

The International Cultural Society of Korea, a non-profit, private organization, offers cultural programs and services to all foreign friends in order to promote mutual understanding and friendship among different peoples, which ISCK believes will contribute to international peace.

ICSK organizes and sponsors extensive exchange programs for scholars, journalists, artists and other leading personalities in diverse cultural fields. ICSK seeks to develop closer ties with other organizations around the world which are also striving for the same goal of a better international community through deeper understanding among nations. ICSK organizes seminars and symposiums on a wide range of cultural topics in conjuction with foreign institutions. These many culturally oriented programs are designed to assist foreign visitors and residents in Korea to deeper understanding of things that are Korean in general as well as in specific areas of interest. An Informational Material Center is available at Korea House. For further information you may call Tel. 723-6466

KYUNG IN ENERGY CO.

Highest Quality Petroleum Products
for Industry and
for Transportation;
also
Electricity for Seoul City

Service
to
International Business

Korean - American   KA📖BI   Business Institute

International
   Management Training
   Business Consulting
   Conference Services

Rm. 808, President Hotel
Seoul, Korea
CPO Box: 4158
Tel.: 753-7750, 752-6921,
       778-7916

Recommended Books on Korea

GENERAL HISTORY:

History of Korea. Vols. I and II by Homer Hulbert, published: 1905. (ed. by Clarence Weems in 1962) Though written prior to Japanese occupation the books are still a leading authority on Korean history up to 1900.

History of Korea, by Han Woo-keun, published: 1970. (translated by Lee Kyong-si, and edited by Grafton K. Mintz) Of the several histories of Korea published during the last decade this particular history is one of the best.

James S. Gale's History of the Korean People by Richard Rutt, published: 1972. Gale was most romantic of Korea's early missionaries and a prolific writer. His history published in 1972 with Bishop Rutt's new biography of this Scottish Canadian are commentaries upon each other.

HISTORICAL PERIODS (prior to 1900):

Dutch Come to Korea by Gari Ledyard, published: 1971. The absorbing story of the shipwreck of a Dutch vessel in the mid-seventeenth century is recreated by the author who tells of the adventures of the crew during 13 years of captivity in the "Hermit Kingdom."

Korea's 1884 Incident by Harold F. Cook, published: 1972. The historical background of Kim Ok-kyun's elusive dream is evaluated in a period of controversial reforms and struggles for modernization.

Modern Transformation of Korea by Yi Kyu-tae, published: 1970. Glimpses of traditional Korea, as the country came in contact with Western ideas and institutions, are presented by a veteran journalist.

Samguk Yusa: Legends of the Three Kingdoms by Priest Ilyon, published: 1972. (translated by Ha Tae-hung and Grafton K. Mintz) First written during the 13th century Koryo period the *Samguk Yusa* is one of two oldest histories of Korea in existence. For an in-depth study into the Silla period this book is recommended. Deletions were made from the original.

HISTORICAL PERIODS (20th century):

First Encounters by (edited) Peter Underwood, Samuel Moffett, and Norman Sibley, published: 1982. A fascinating collection of old photographs taken at the turn of the century. The subject areas are history, the Westerners, architecture and Korean society of that period.

Korea's Fight for Freedom by F.A. McKenzie, published: 1920. (reprint by Yonsei Press in 1967) This fascinating account vividly depicts Korea's struggle during the early days of the annexation period in Japanese-occupied Korea.

Korea's Tragic Hour by George A McGrane, published: 1973 (edited by Harold F. Cook and Alan M. MacDougall) This small paperback book gives an absorbing account of the closing years of the Yi Dynasty. The author tragically died in Korea as the book was nearing completion.

Passing of Korea by Homer Hulbert, Published: 1906. (reprint by Yonsei Press in 1967) The tragic account of gradual domination of Korea by the Japanese during the late 19th century until final annexation is vividly described by one of Korea's prolific early writers.

Tragedy of Korea by F.A. McKenzie, published: 1908. (reprint by Yonsei Press in 1967.) This is an absorbing account of Korea's loss of freedom in the early years of the 20th century when the 500 years of the Yi Dynasty were dramatically coming to a close in 1910.

World Is One, by Yi Pangja (Masako), published: 1973. The wife of the last Crown Prince of Korea who was born a Japanese tells the tragedy of her life as a Princess of Sorrow but portrays her simple quiet strength and personal conviction that her position could bridge the chasm between Korea and Japan.

HISTORICAL GUIDEBOOKS:

Kyongju Guide by Edward B. Adams, published: 1979 (Both English and Japanese Editions) To serve as a companion book to **Korea Guide** this exciting pictorial and historical guide portrays Korea's fascinating legacy of one thousand years when Silla's capital was the fourth largest city of the ancient world. Rich in tradition, the Kyongju Valley rightly deserves the title of an "Open Air Museum." (360 color and 300 B & W photos) **Note:** Special Edition used for PATA conference 1979.

Old Hanyang, New Seoul by John K. Kim, published: 1978. Small paperback which gives useful information for the casual tourist. Historical information is given in brief summaries.

Palaces of Seoul by Edward B. Adams published: 1982. This small paperback book is a convenient guide to the many palaces of Seoul with maps and many color plates.

Seoul Past and Present by Allen D. Clark and Donald N. Clark published: 1969. This is a very useful and compact book that gives information on almost anyplace one might care to see in Seoul and vicinity.

Some Korean Journeys by William and Dorothy Middleton. published: 1976. This paperback book with numerous color plates as well as B & W will be an indispensable companion to the many scenic regions in a picturesque Korea.

Through Gates of Seoul, Vols. I and II by Edward B. Adams published: 1971-72. This two-volume set of books is the ultimate in a complete tourist guide to places of interest such as palaces, temples and tombs within Seoul and vicinity. The many B & W and colored plates with detailed ancestry charts of the Yi kings make these books a collector's item.

GEOGRAPHY OF THE COUNTRY:

Korea's Heritage by Shannon McCune published: 1956. This regional and social geographic book on Korea gives detailed accounts of the varied regions within this mountainous peninsula including climate, geology and topography.

South Korea by Patricia M. Bartz published: 1972. This recent detailed geography is a treasure of information set in an attractive format with numerous photographs.

CULTURAL HERITAGE:

A Handbook of Korea by KOIS, Ministry of Culture and Information, 1980 Edition: An encyclopedic volume of over 800 pages with over 1000 photos this book produced by the ROK government is one of the best. All aspects of Korea's life and culture are presented. A 3rd edition is now in print.

In This Earth and in That Wind by Lee O-Young published: 1967. Korean attitudes, customs and thought patterns are presented by a Korean looking at his own people. Concepts are thought provoking and well described.

Korea and Her Neighbours by Isabella Bishop published: 1898. (reprint by Yonsei Press in 1967). This is an intriguing account of an English lady who traveled extensively through Korea and China during the closing period of the dynasty. With great literary skill she has provided for the reader a remarkable account of the customs of this period.

Koreans and Their Culture, The by Cornelius Osgood. published: 1951. Korean village life is depicted in an interesting account based on the author's study while living in a rural village on Kanghwa Island.

Korea's Cultural Roots by Jon Carter Covell, Published: 1982. An excellent book to begin in the understanding of Korean culture. Covell is a recognized expert in Asian art and comparative art from Korea and Japan..

Korea, Beyond The Hills by Edward Kim, Published: 1980. The author is a staff writer for National Geographic.

The color photographs illustrating this book are some the finest seen in any publication. Though expensive this book is well worth the price.

Korean Patterns by Paul Crane
Published: 1967. Most foreigners find this a most useful book about Korean attitudes, customs and Korean values placed in general and specific situations. The author grew up in this country, and it is written with humor and affection for the Korean people.

Korean Sketches by James S. Gale
published: 1898. (reprint by RAS Korea in 1975) A collection of essays written by a Scotch Canadian missionary designed to give an idea of Korean life and character.

Korean Traditions by Joo, Myong-dok,
published: 1981, 1982. Black and White prints nicely illustrate Korea's tradition which is fast fading from the landscape. An unusual art pictorial as "seen through paper windows."

Korean Works and Days by Richard Rutt
published: 1964. Written as notes from the diary of a country priest a great many aspects of Korean life and customs are presented by the author's experiences while living in a rural Korean village.

Things Korean by Horace N. Allen
published: 1908. (reprint by RAS Korea in 1975) A collection of essays on a wide variety of cultural subjects. The author came to Korea as a missionary but served for 15 years as an American diplomat.

West Meets East by James Wade
published: 1976. As a journalist, critic and long-time resident in Korea the author of this book provides an entertaining collection of short articles touching on a wide variety of subjects in the Korea of the 1960s. The life and culture with special emphasis on arts, dance and music, both traditional and modern, are presented.

RELIGIOUS ASPECTS:

History of the Protestant Mission in Korea by George Paik
Published: 1927. (reprint by Yonsei Press in 1976) This book is still considered the foremost historic authority concerning the introduction of the Protestant missionaries to Korea at the turn of the century.

Korean Temple Paintings, Depicting the Life of Buddha by Zo Zayong
Published: 1975. Many full page color reproductions depict ancient painting still to be found on temple walls throughout Korea which have never previously been photographed.

Kut, Korean Shamanist Rituals by Halla Pai Huhm,
Published: 1980. This book is excellent in the presentation of the shamanistic tradition both historically and present in Korea today. Author lives in Hawaii.

Lotus and I by Erna Moen.
Published: 1974. In this small paperback book the author recounts the week she spent living in a nunnery and sharing her life with the nuns of Haein-sa.

Pine Tree by Michael Daniels
published: 1975. This small paperback book deals with Confucianism and contains a biographical sketch of the life of Confucius.

Religions of Old Korea by Charles Allen Clark
published: 1961 (reprint). Originally delivered as a series of lectures in 1921 this book is still one of the best resources for Korean Buddhism, Confucianism, Shamanism and various other cults. Also the first contact of Christianity with these religions is outlined.

Spirit of Korean Tiger and Humour of Korean Tiger by Zo Zayong
published: 1972. With large color plates the folk customs which relate closely to shaman beliefs are interestingly presented in two paperback books by the curator of the Emileh Folk Art Museum, Seoul.

POLITICS PAST AND PRESENT:

Korean Politics in Transition by Edward Wright (editor)
published: 1975. Providing a comprehensive survey this book introduces the reader to contemporary South Korean politics by a group of specialists in their fields.

Modern Korea by Andrew Grajdanzev
published: 1944. (reprint by RAS Korea in 1975). This book was first written during the Second World War as an analysis of the political and economic circumstances of Korea under Japanese colonial rule.

Undiplomatic Memories by William F. Sands
published: 1930. (reprint by RAS Korea in 1975) This intriguing book relates the Korean political affairs and foreign policy in Seoul at the turn of the century as seen by a young American foreign service officer.

THE ARTS:

Art Treasures of Seoul by Edward B. Adams published: 1980 A pictorial art survey of the capital city of Seoul is beautifully portrayed with over 360 color photographs taken mostly by the author. All aspects of sculpturing, painting, ceramics and architecture in both classic as well as folk art are well illustrated. 5000 Years of Korean Art in the City of Seoul is portrayed masterfully within 180 pages.

Arts of Korea by Kim Che-won and Lena Kim Lee published: 1974. This large comprehensive book compiled by father and daughter is a masterpiece in the field of Korean art treasures. Because of the many excellent color plates the cost is high.

Arts of Korea by Evelyn McCune
published: 1962. This authoritative book though written several years ago is highly recommended for the study and understanding of Korean art through the different periods.

Art of The Korean Potter by Asia Society published: 1968. This delightful book is an Asia House Gallery publication and distributed by New York Graphic Society, Ltd. It is a compilation of an exhibition shown at the Asia House Gallery in 1968 under the direction of Robert Griffing, Jr., Curatorial Consultant, Honolulu Academy of Arts.

Ancient Arts of Korea by Ministry of Culture and Information,
published: 1970. This concise pictorial paperback guide to art treasures of Korea is an excellent summary but is now difficult to obtain as it is out of print.

Guardians of Happiness by Zo Zayong,
published: 1982. Produced by the Emileh Museum which moved to Soknisan this recent publication was produced by Dr. Zo in honor of the USA-Korea Centennial. The shamanistic tradition of Korean folk painting is presented as a forgotten art.

Korean Art Seen Through Museum by John K. Kim,
published: 1979. An excellent survey book on the many museums located not only in Seoul but throughout the entire country. Well known Korean art authorities have contributed articles to this excellent guidebook.

Korean Chests by Michael Wickman
published: 1978. Books on Korean chests are rare in English. Written by a longtime resident of Seoul, this book has met a real need in the foreign community. Numerous illustrations of the different types of chests are shown.

Korean Dance by Alan Heyman
published: 1960. This small booklet is a thorough survey of the development of Korean dance and its future in Korean society.

Pictorial Encyclopedia of The Oriental Arts, Korea
published: 1968. produced by Crown Publishers, Inc. N.Y. and edited by a Japanese scholar, the book includes Korean art objects to be found in both Korea and Japan.

Traditional Performing Arts of Korea by UNESCO
published: 1975. The tradition of music and dance is thoroughly researched by a group of prominent authors in their fields.

CHILDREN'S BOOKS

Korean Folkstories for Children by Edward B. Adams and illustrated by Choi Dong-ho.
Published: 1982-83. This series of five books are beautifully illustrated on every page. Reading level is about 3rd grade. At the end of each book is an editorial comment for parents. Each book has a Korean translation in *han'gul* (Korean script). The titles include: *Blindman's Daughter, Two Brothers and Their Magic Gourds, Herdboy and Weaver, Korean Cinderella and Woodcutter and Nymph.*

Sun and Moon (Fairy Tales from Korea) by Kathleen Seros,
Published: 1982. This is a collection of seven well-known folktales is illustrated with rather modernistic art, bright and colorful.

POETRY OF KOREA:

Bamboo Grove by Richard Rutt
published: 1971. Written by one of Korea's outstanding foreign scholars, this small book is a collection of *sijo* poetry translations with introduction and background description of each contributing author.

The Everwhite Mountain by Pai Inez Kong
published: 1965. This is the first major publication of Korean *sijo* translations in English. Background descriptions are given of each author.

MISCELLANEOUS SUBJECTS:

The Family of Dolls by H. Edward Kim, published: Korean dolls created by Kim Young-hee are photographically depicted by a National Geographic staff photographer.

Far Reaching Fragrance by Michael O'Brien,
published: 1981. This book is a collection of over 100 color photos taken with an eye for design in a photogenic land.

A Guide to Korean Characters by Bruce K. Grant,
Published: 1979. This is a very complete book of Chinese characters used in Korean and is a handy reference for those who are studying Korean.

Korean With Chinese Characters by Richard B. Rucci,
Published: 1981. This small paperback spiral book is illustrated by Choi Dong-ho. Many of the Chinese character illustrations have appeared in the Korea Times. Good book for beginners.

Lee Wade's Korean Cookbook by Lee Wade published: 1974. (Edited by Joan Rutt) Compiled by a longtime resident of Korea this book is the best for those interested in learning about Korean cooking. Names are given in both languages.

Living in Korea by Richard B. Rucci published: 1982. (Third Edition) Sponsored by the American Chamber of Commerce, this guide is an indispensable book for newcomers arriving to live in Korea.

Index

388

Z

ADVERTISER'S INDEX

BAIK YANG KNIT WEAR
IT'S A FANTASTIC.

MAIN PRODUCTS

- Cotton under wear
- Warm-up suits
- T-shirt & Polo shirt
- Tennis wear
- Casual wear

MANUFACTURERS & EXPORTERS
BAIK YANG CO., LTD.

1002, DAELIM-DONG, YOUNGDEUNG-POKU, SEOUL, KOREA
CABLE ADD : KNITHAN SEOUL TELEX : K 28416
C.P.O. BOX : 1942   PHONE : 832-0090~8, 833-0091~7